I SHOULDN'T BE TELLING YOU THIS

(BUT I'M GOING TO ANYWAY)

CHELSEA DEVANTEZ

I SHOULDN'T BE TELLING YOU THIS

(BUT I'M GOING)
TO ANYWAY

HANOVER
SQUARE
PRESS

HANOVER
SQUARE
PRESS™

Recycling programs
for this product may
not exist in your area.

Hanover Square Press
22 Adelaide St. West, 41st Floor
Toronto, Ontario M5H 4E3, Canada
HanoverSqPress.com

Printed in U.S.A.

"One day I'll catch them, the memories.
And I'll begin to tell stories."
—Me to my teenage journal, poetic as fuck

"My darling girl, when are you going to realize
that being normal is not necessarily a virtue?
It rather denotes a lack of courage!"
—Aunt Frances, *Practical Magic*

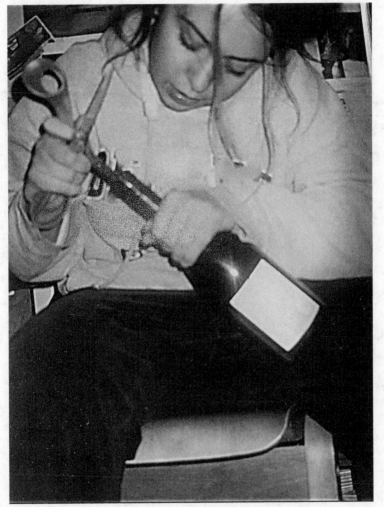

Teenage me, trying to open a bottle of wine with scissors,
unaware that this is a metaphor for my life.

TABLE OF CONTENTS

YOUNG ME

This book is going to start off very sad, and then it's going to get a lot happier. But before you get to the good stuff, you're gonna have to make it through some tragic shit. Just like I had to.

CHELSEA, UNIDENTIFIED TIME AND PLACE

The year ███ *in the town of* ████████

I didn't want to have an ugly story, and for a long time I thought I wouldn't have to if I simply never told it.

Over the years I've tried many different things to leave the worst of my tragedies behind, but nothing has ever eased their grip on me: not cutting off contact with old friends, not joining an improv cult—hell, not even when I got bangs. In fact, the tragedies in these pages probably delayed my journey to even getting bangs in the first place, which is unfortunate because they've always been my hair's true destiny. I might have even called this book *Behind the Bangs*, except it would give you the false idea that these chapters are filled with glib reckonings like "Girlie, it's called self-care!" And while, yes, more fun stuff is going to come later, I simply cannot begin my story anywhere but here, with what's actually behind my bangs: a sorrow-filled, ravenously pained anger.

Where might all of this anger and sorrow have originated? Well, when I was ████████ boyfriend ████████ shot at ███

███
██ .

Um, excuse me? What the hell are those black bars doing here!? I was only trying to say that ████████████████████████
███
████████████████████████ .

WELL FUCK. HOW AM I SUPPOSED TO TELL YOU MY GODDAMN ORIGIN STORY IF IT'S GONNA BE FUCKING BLACKED OUT?!?

Okay, okay. Sorry for shouting. Like I said, ravenously pained!

Hmm. How about this: at a time and place that will both remain unspecified, I fell in love for the first time. With that came a very disturbing event in my timeline, one that changed the course of my life for the far worse. Going forward in these pages, I'm going to call what happened The Big Scary Domestic Violence Thing. Not because I want to, but because ██████
████████████████████████ . We'll come back to these cute literary blackouts at the end of the book, where I can hopefully explain them a little better after I've calmed down. It takes me a solid hour before a Xanax reaches peak effect, so we should be good by then.

The irony of all this is pretty infuriating: I used to hate that anyone could know this part of me, and now I hate that you don't. Long before there were black bars in these pages forcing me to keep The Big Scary Domestic Violence Thing a secret, I happily kept it hidden, of my own volition! I had thought surviving something so disgusting and awful meant that I, too, was disgusting and awful. Shame's a tricky little bitch like that. I didn't want to court misery forever, so I trudged along pretending to have a normal past, hoping that maybe then I could somehow have a normal future.

Well, we love the effort.

After a lifetime of bursting into tears at the bottom of the mi-

mosa's carafe, I eventually needed to accept that all those ways
I'd chosen to funnel my anguish had only made things worse.
Burying my shame did not bring me closer to feeling normal.
Keeping my humiliation cowering in the corners of my heart
did not make everyone like me. I'd stacked up a life of punchy
pleasantries, fake smiles, and a handful of unfortunate years spent
in boleros and ballet flats—to hide my arms, hide my height,
hide, hide, hide—only to one day realize that my sadness had
evolved into its own new monstrosity.

Without another option available, I finally tried courage. Out
came the details that ████████████████████████████████
██
██████████████████████████████, and now my comedy
gal memoir is more redacted than the fucking Watergate files.

So now what?

Now that the most important part of my story, the part I
worked my entire life to have the stamina to share, ██████████
██
██
██?

Sadly, this is probably a more important story than the one I
was going to tell anyway—the story of how our systems silence
victims, women, and anyone who is considered an "other," while
the offender has a Vegas buffet of legal protections to choose
from. But for the victim, there always seems to be a catch. Their
"tools for protection" conveniently double as weapons to en-
force silence. Meanwhile, justice at the highest levels still offers
nothing for those who actually suffered the crime. For perpetrators, we offer consequences, punishment, a little jail time. But
what justice is there for victims? Let's see…an online fundraiser
with a catchy headline? Sympathy carnations? A legal ruling on
a piece of paper? That all sounds nice in theory, but when that
offender shows up again, a legal ruling on a piece of paper is not

the ideal defense for the victim, as if she can just wave around a court-sealed 8½ by 11, like, *Not this time, boys!*

Well, I'll just continue on, head held high, shoulders back, tits en garde, and cursing everyone to hell, as the women who raised me taught me to do. Before I go forward here, I just need you to know that at one point, my life almost ended. The Big Scary Domestic Violence Thing brought with it a destruction that went far beyond just the actual attack. It disrupted every cell of my body. The process of getting back up with the scrambled brain it left me with is the mountain I've been climbing every day. It is not who I am, but it is the obstacle I've wrestled with for years, and it has shaped me into the wobbly woman with a bold lip who stands before you now.

So come, take a walk with me, let me show you the scraps of what formed my personhood, and then we'll scurry along to the happier parts where I became a comedian and wore gowns and sipped free luxury-branded martinis.

When I was ███████████████████████████████
██
███.

Statistically, if you grow up in a home that has abuse in it, you are way more likely to get into an abusive relationship yourself. Ever the rule-follower, I leaped right into my probability.

███
███
███
███
███
███
███
███
███
███████████████████████████. I'm going to call

him Earl, because writing "Piece of Fucking Dog Shit" over
and over again would get old pretty fast.

██

██

██████████████████ I want to tell you what it was like,
falling in love ███████████████████████████████████.

██

████████████████████████████████████

He was adored, reaping the kind of respect that only appears
for ██.

██

██████████████████████████ then I heard from friends ████

████ boasted to everyone about how ████████████████
██████████████████████████████████████.

██

████ . "He said ████████████████ that you were a slut,"████

██

██

██████████████████████████████████████.

██

████████████████████████ but he always found a new, grander
romantic stunt to make up for whatever he'd done. █████████

██

██

████████████ romantic gestures became more menacing.

███

██

██

███████████████████████████████████ no one else was allowed
near me, and would threaten anyone who tried. ███████████

██

██

██

██

███████ had terrorized me so much at that point, that even the
sound of his voice made me physically sick. ██████████████

██

████████████████████████████████████.

Then he upped the ante.

██

███████████████████ the gun. █████████████████████

███████ shooting ████████████████████████████████

██

██

██

██

███.

The second █████████████████████████████████████

██████████████████████████████████████ shooting ██████

██

████████████████████████████ trying to get me back.

██

███████████.

The third ██████████████████████████████████████
██
████ the shots came through █████████████████████
███████████████████████████████ got down on the floor ███.
██
████
████████████████████████████████████. As I cleaned up
the glass, I told myself I just had to endure it a little bit longer,
and then it would go away.

██████████████████████ the police station ██████████████████.
██
████████████████████████████████
████████████████

At one point the other cop asked me if we'd ever had sex,
and I began crying, feeling humiliated. ██████████ asked why that
question was necessary. Apparently, it was to find out if they
should classify it as domestic violence or something they should
take more seriously, you know, like regular violence.
    I told them █████████████████████████████████████
████████████████████████████.

That's how I thought of it back then, just "sex I didn't want
to have."
██
███████████████████████████. The judge ████████████████
██
████████. I didn't know this until much, much later, but ████
████████ incredibly rare. ███████████████████████████████
██

And even though the abuse was bad enough in the judge's
eyes to warrant this ruling, I was only beginning to accept that
it had been abusive at all.

██
██

▆▆▆▆▆▆▆▆▆▆▆▆▆▆▆▆▆▆▆▆▆▆▆▆▆▆▆▆▆▆▆▆▆▆▆▆▆
▆▆▆▆▆▆▆▆▆▆▆▆▆▆▆▆▆▆▆▆▆▆▆▆▆▆▆▆▆▆▆▆▆▆▆▆▆

Abuse occurs in the mundane: it happens as you're grabbing a
Slurpee from 7-Eleven, or when he's telling you how beautiful
you look that day. While you're living the low stakes of wor-
rying if it's going to rain or thinking about the king-size candy
bar you stored in the fridge for later, you're also witnessing the
high stakes of the emotional blows of his temper. The banalities
in life exist hand in hand with the terror in the same moment,
and the duality softens the edges of your fears.

If abuse was foreshadowed like it was in a movie, we'd all run
fleeing, but there's no piercing soundtrack with a shrill violin
string to alert you to something bad ahead. Abuse feels mostly
like another bad day, up until the very moment it gets so bad
that you don't even need a violin to sound the call because you
yourself are already screaming. In the middle of the worst of it
I was not a shattered woman hiding in a dark room, I was still
wondering if I left my flat iron plugged in or if my butt looked
okay in my jeans.

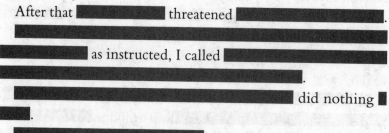

It was not just the violence that was scary, it was the reaction
to it: who sides with the salaried bros, and who sides with the
household of bitches drinking margaritas in the front yard while
blasting a Martina McBride CD. It is here where I first learned
that you must be likable so that if something violent ever happens to you, others will feel you deserve help. Domestic-violence
victims cannot just be victims, they must be beloved if they are
going to stand a chance at justice. Those who've suffered the

crime must be sweet enough and flawless enough for people to be willing to stand up and say something.

███████████████████████████████████████
██████ and so I quit █████████████████████████.
███████████████████████████████████
███████████████████████████████████████
███████████████████████████████████████
███████████████████████████████████████
██████████████████████████ I spent every day hiding at home, but this did not protect me. It was like I was living in a cage and █████████████ had the address.

███████████████████████████████████████
███████████████████████████████████████
████████████████████████████ watching █████
███████████████████████████████████████
███████████████████████████████████████
█████████████████████ once, █████████████ climbed up in the tree outside my bedroom at night, shined a laser pointer through my window. I lay in bed, terrified to move, wondering if he was trying to get my attention, or practicing his aim.

███████████████████████████████████████
███████████████████████████████████████
██████████████████████████
██████████████████████████ nothing but a piece of paper at the end of the day.

███████████████████████████████████████
███████████████████████████
██████████████████████ never going to stop as long as he knew where I was. ██████████████████████████
██████████████████████████.

███████████████████████████████████████
███████████████████████████████████████
███████████████████████████████████████

██████████████████████████████████

██████████████████████████████████

███████████████, finally I found a way out of the state. My exit made me feel like maybe I'd get a chance to become the type of girl that men didn't hit. As if it were up to me.

My mom, my godmother, and I drove ████████████ ████████████████████████████████ ████████████████████████████████ ████████████████████████████████ ████████████████████████████████ ████████████████████████████████ ████████████████████████████████ ████████████████████████████████ ████████████████████████████████ ████████████████████████████████ █████████████████████████ and I began to relax into my new life.

████████████████████████ ████████████████████████████ the phone rang, ████████████████████████████████ ███████ knew where I was. ████████████ ████████████████████████.

████████████████████████ my mom had already suggested we change my last name again, and now it felt doing so was the only way I'd ever be free of him.

Oh yes, that's right, I said change my last name *again*.

I'd already had a few different last names throughout my life, and they were attached to terrible memories and the kinds of father figures who ate ribs without a napkin and wore cowboy boots for the height boost. Names were not the only thing that changed. When I was growing up, we lived in six different states all across the Southwest, and at a few points I lived only with my single mom and my godmother Grace, a two-best-friends household springing forth where their husbands had failed.

The husband failings also showed up in my signature: after my parents divorced when I was four, I took my new stepdad's last name. Several years later when *they* divorced, I got rid of my stepdad's name and took on my mom's maiden name. Then I reverted back to my dad's last name as a teenager. Each of my yearbooks as a kid had a different name listed underneath the same strained, eager school-photo smiles. If you were to put all my dinky spelling-bee awards and track-race ribbons up on a shelf, it would look like three completely different girls had competed in all those things. And all three of them were mediocre at sports, but they sure excelled in drama!

Changing my last name again wasn't a difficult decision, it was a happy one. Everyone in my family all went by different last names—me, my mom, and my brothers, who at a few points didn't live with us, so growing up I'd never had a single name to hang onto for the sake of a family unit anyway. In fact, without The Big Scary Domestic Violence Thing, I wouldn't have thought there was a reason to change your last name outside of flagging which dad is currently in the picture.

But here I was, going to court, borrowing my mom's sweater and wrap skirt that I wore on my past court visits, since my own closet of rhinestone velour sweatpants didn't seem to be a fit for the occasion. I now lived a life that included a go-to-court outfit. Feeling a new sense of empowerment, I met with the judge, who changed my last name, and I happily released the signage of shitty men, and in doing so escaped the shittiest one of them all—the one I had found all by myself. ██████████████████ I moved to ████████ ██████████████████████████████████ ██████████████████████████████████ ██████████████████████████████████ ██████████████████████, hoping he wouldn't be able to find me there. And then it was finally over.

★ ★ ★

██████████████████████████ may not have killed me, but
he killed the woman I was going to become, and I'll never get
her back or know what she would have been like. And who
knows, maybe she would've been a huge bitch! Maybe she'd
order tequila with Splenda, tip 10 percent, and join a sorority
where you Magic-Marker each other's cellulite.

But maybe she also would have been lovely, lighter, able to
go on vacation, and relax, unburdened by the thought of what
horrible thing could happen next.

I see this other version of me every now and then. I'll be at the
opening of a show, looking like the life of the party as I clutch
someone's face, exuberantly declaring that we simply must get
dinner! And that's when I catch a glimpse of Other Chelsea,
not scream-laughing or yelling jokes or flailing around mani-
cally as a distraction from all the angst inside. She's just having
a conversation.

I see Other Chelsea at bachelorette parties when everyone is
dancing and collectively singing the lyrics to a late '90s throw-
back like Train's "Meet Virginia"—as if a girl who was described
in the lyrics as not owning a dress and having shitty hair would
have even been accepted back then. Other Chelsea is singing
along. I'll watch her from the corner where I actually sit, clutching my millionth drink, trying to bop along to the music so
that I seem like a Fun and Good Friend. But the truth is that
I'm an impostor in a sundress, studying what it must be like to
feel this way, and coming up with nothing but hateful comments about it, because the other option—carefree, fun Other
Chelsea—doesn't seem available to me.

I see Other Chelsea when I'm in the morning traffic in Los
Angeles and she passes me on the road, upset, but it's just about
how her landlord won't fix the washing machine. She's not like
me, a woman clutching a steering wheel, trying to control a
panic attack over decades-old memories before it's even 8:00 a.m.

When ████████████████████████████, I lost the person I was going to become. It's like the hand of God came down and shattered that girl into a thousand tiny pieces, and then I stumbled along and figured out how to move all the pieces through the world, creating a mirage of a Chelsea-like human. Over time I've been able to move those pieces into a person I feel proud of, and other times I still feel the pain of breaking. If I didn't have the help of the wild, incredible (and honestly, sometimes terrible!) women you'll meet in each of the coming chapters, the option to keep going wouldn't have felt possible.

But no matter how far I've run and how many jokes I've told, stages I've stepped onto, and goals I've achieved, there are times, just brief moments late at night when I'm out enjoying myself enough to loosen my grasp on reality, when those haunted years will lurch up out of my psyche and pull me back down into the crack in the desert where I attempted to leave the past.

It took him ████ years before he found me again.

So here we are…and still waiting for that Xanax to hit. I'll have to come back to finish this piece of the story later in the book.

Until then, let's have some fun.

AMAZING GRACE

My fairy godmother in a leopard-print leotard

It was three in the morning, and my godmother Grace tore across US 93 chugging an extra-large vanilla latte from 7-Eleven. I sat beside her as the navigator, holding a road map in one hand and my ten-year-old version of a latte, a giant chocolate Yoo-hoo, in the other. We flew through the night, her little red Camry speeding along the road with ease, likely because there was zero tread left on those tires. The latte, Grace told me, was not helping her stay awake, so to help distract herself, she decided to teach me how to sing her favorite song.

I belted out the notes for her. "A-ma-zing Grace! How sweet the sound!"

"No!" she maestroed. "From your stomach, from the bottom of your stomach, really belt it!"

I tried my best to harness the bottom of my stomach—which is scientifically not the part of your body that produces sound—and bellowed even louder, "A-ma-zing Grace! How sweet the sound!"

This continued throughout the night until I proudly achieved what she told me was the most important quality of a good singer: volume.

Shortly after that road trip, Grace would officially become my godmother. The title "godmother" was, of course, never ordained in a formal church ceremony, but she did teach me how to use a tampon, which I believe is a stronger religious experience. Besides, what else could I call my mom's best friend who sat through all my school choir concerts, throwing Mardi Gras beads at the kids onstage? What other label would fit the woman who taught me how to kiss by handing me a book called *The Seven Laws of Seduction*; spiked the cider at every holiday party; smashed her face into a plate of risotto if dinner was feeling boring; and owned more feather boas than pairs of jeans? Grace was fabulous, over-the-top, and relentless. She was my fairy godmother in a leopard-print leotard.

Grace and my mom first met in their thirties on a river-rafting trip down the Grand Canyon. They quickly bonded over a few common interests: their Tevas, the healing properties of jade amulets, and the fact that both of their second husbands were charismatic, violent assholes. Both of those assholes were, unfortunately, also on the rafting trip—Grace's husband was a passenger, and my mom's husband, who everyone called Bubba, was the river guide, which was his full-time job for most of my early childhood when we lived in Utah. Bubba would captain these week-long charters, manning the engine, cooking all the food, and trying his very best not to let the passengers drown in the class 5 rapids. It was typically a job for younger men, but my stepdad was a raging alcoholic, so he was young at heart.

When they first became friends, Grace had a decade-long career as an osteopathic physician (and prior to that, a career as a convent nun, because her résumé is its own one-woman show). But after their rafting excursion, she decided she needed a break, so she quit her practice and left her asshole husband at home while she pursued her real dream: a cross-country road trip to visit the nation's best nude hot springs.

Grace became a deity to me on our Valley of Fire camping trip when I was ten. Grace was not expected to join this camping trip—it was just for my family. The way she tells it, she was driving through Nevada. She knew our family was camping somewhere in the Valley of Fire—a state park that's over forty-six thousand acres. Grace didn't have any more information than that, and while cell phones existed, they weren't common enough for us to have them yet. But Grace didn't need a cell signal to track us down! As she hit the Nevada state line, she got a strong intuitive ping that we were in trouble and that she should take a sharp right. She let her intuition guide her through the desert, right, left, right…until she was at our campsite.

My mom, Bubba, my two brothers Jesse and Lucas, and I were milling around the campground when her red Camry ripped through the dirt and came to a halt in a cloud of golden dust. The door opened and out stepped Grace, smiling from ear to ear, her red mane of hair blowing in the wind. Everyone was shocked into silence as we all, Grace included, tried to understand how she was standing before us.

Like most of our family camping trips, this one had not been going well. Bubba claimed to love the wilderness, but once we got out there, he was always mad at something—the grill, the tent, the rock in his shoe, his old college-baseball career, and of course, us kids. I remember one particularly notorious trip: Bubba had come into the kids' tent, picked up the bottom of Lucas's sleeping bag—with him still inside—and held it high so that my brother fell out of it onto the ground. Bubba then stormed off into the forest with the sleeping bag and a case of beer, leaving Lucas bedless in our tent and our mother faintly crying in hers.

Somehow it was decided among the adults that I'd leave our trip and join Grace's adventure. Whatever way this trip was careening, my mom must've felt it was doomed to fall into familiar patterns and she might as well at least get one of her kids away from it all. So, into Grace's Camry I went.

By the end of the night, I had learned every verse of "Amazing Grace" from start to finish, even though my godmother herself did not know how to sing. In fact, the only thing she might've been even worse at than singing was, unfortunately, driving. When Grace was at the wheel, rarely were more than two tires ever touching the ground.

Somewhere along the way she had stopped paying attention to the road, and with a dusty screech we were off the highway and spinning our tires in the dirt. In the distance we saw a couple of trailers and folding tables covered in stacks of old books, pottery, and random knickknacks, which is how we ended up at a highway yard sale halfway across Nevada.

She gasped with glee. Ever the fiend for hidden treasure and bedazzled junk, my godmother giddily pulled up and we jumped out of the car to check it out. After walking around for a bit, we eventually sat down in some dirt-crusted, half-broken lawn chairs and struck up a conversation with a weathered gentleman perched on an old barrel across from us.

The man was holding a fedora with several bullet holes in it, spinning it around on his pointer finger to show off the goods. The hat had belonged to his grandpa, he said, a brave man who'd successfully robbed several banks and even survived getting shot, as you could see from the holes. He came close to dying several times but always managed to escape, until one day he got caught robbing the largest bank in town and spent the rest of his life in jail. The police never recovered the money and the bank couldn't survive the loss, so they had to shut down. Serendipitously, though, someone swooped in to purchase the bank and brought the town back from ruin. Who were the new owners? The bank robber's family, of course!

The man gave a little wink and smacked the dust off the hat. I had just learned my first lesson in upward mobility.

My godmother grandly declared, "She needs that hat." Grace gave him a wad of cash and said to me, "This hat will be a reminder to always follow your dreams, no matter how scary it gets."

The man agreed. His grandpa was shot at all the time, but he never stopped robbing banks! The two of them were getting really riled up now, swapping details of their favorite Vegas casinos and the best nearby road stops for Frito pie.

The bullet-holed fedora still hangs on my wall today. It ended up being a pretty apt metaphor for pursuing a career in Hollywood.

We had just moved into a new house in Utah the next time Grace's red Camry sped into the driveway for a visit when I was twelve. She burst through the back door and joined me outside, where I sat on the patio. My stepdad used to play Jeff Foxworthy's tape "You might be a redneck if..." and count how many jokes described our family. *"If your patio furniture used to be your living room furniture...you might be a redneck."* That's us! Everyone would laugh as we sat on the old living room couch that was now on the patio.

On the outside couch, Grace and I caught up on the past two years since our Camry escape. I excitedly told her that I was going to move to Georgia for high school because I'd just heard on Channel One News that Georgia's lottery program would fund scholarships to state colleges for all seniors who had Bs or above. Grace had told me on our road trip that going to college was really important if I wanted to be successful in life, and now with Georgia's lottery, I felt excited that I'd finally found a way to go. But Grace shook her head, and instead she took out a sheet of paper to make a different plan for me.

I didn't have to move to Georgia, she said, because I could get accepted to whatever school I wanted and get financial aid and a scholarship. She had once told me I reminded her of a younger version of herself, a "uniquely unbridled genius with the potential to change the world." All I had to do was make straight As, always get extra credit, participate in every extra-curricular, try out for all the plays, and win as many awards as possible. Always run for student council, always join leadership boards, always get on the dean's list—anything for an accolade. A wonderful, *very* likable personality trait was born.

Grace remained steady in our lives while my mom's marriage to Bubba finally hurtled into the abyss. Or perhaps it was always in the abyss and had just become impossible to ignore. As I had watched my mom wilt under Bubba's grasp over the years, I wanted so badly for us to escape, but as a child I didn't realize what an almost impossible task this was, given the million unfair obstacles that face a woman when she's trying to leave an abusive marriage. One often needs a miracle to pull it off. And when no miracles are in sight, the next best thing is an enterprising and relentless female friend who is down to fuck some shit up with you.

It was messier and more complicated than this, but when I was thirteen, my mom and my godmother essentially clasped hands and held on for dear life and divorced their alcoholic second husbands. Together they agreed to start over somewhere new and finally create the beautiful lives they had both dreamed of in a small provincial town in Colorado.

My godmother arrived there first. How did she even decide on such a location, you ask? It was right in the middle of two fabulous, nudity-optional mineral hot springs! Grace purchased a small cabin in the mountains with no running water or electricity, dreaming of a new life where she would read books all day and live off the grid.

My older brother Lucas had gone to live with his and my dad a few years earlier, and so it was just me, my mom, and my little brother Jesse now leaving Utah together.

The first year there we struggled to find somewhere to live.

Bubba had decimated my mom's finances in the divorce. We squatted in an office building for a summer and bounced around a couple places after that, until my mom eventually met a nice older woman at the coffee shop in town who was a Jehovah's Witness. After hearing about my mom's struggle to find somewhere nice to raise her kids, she offered up her extra property and cut my mom a great deal on rent. We moved into her adorable second house, which had a charming backyard and a picturesque giant Hackberry tree perched right outside my window. It wasn't long before Grace began spending so much time at our place that she eventually became our pseudo-roommate. After all, we had running water and her cabin did not.

Just as the rest of the world was recovering from the paranoia of Y2K, my mom and Grace were officially beginning their fresh start, and I was just entering high school—which meant my "not a girl, not yet a woman" years were ensconced in some peak early-aughts fuckery. To refresh all those fond old memories you've probably tried to black out, this was the era of trucker hats, Playboy Bunny belly-button rings, and little butterfly gems sparkling on the back of the thong that peeked out of your low-rise jeans. Atkins ruled the diet world, and *American Idol* had only just begun. Girls were pulling out two single strands of hair from their ponytails and flat-ironing them into dehydrated wisps; boys were bleaching the tips of their spiky, gelled haircuts, creating stiff blond lawns atop their heads. Julia Roberts and Sandra Bullock were considered our quirkiest, funniest leading ladies, because having curly hair and being brunette was cRaZy in the early 2000s, y'all!

With George Bush's presidential campaign flourishing (and Bath & Body Works's Cucumber Melon lotion doing the actual work of leaving no child behind), it wasn't exactly the best time for two wild, gorgeous, newly single women to storm into a conservative town that was so small the neighboring state penitentiary had a higher population. Bored out of their minds, my mom and godmother would often put on cocktail dresses and wigs just to go pick up milk. On lazier days they would accessorize their nightgowns with loud jackets, weird furry boots, and colorful knitted hats and traipse around town, laughing their asses off.

During my freshman year, my classmates tapped into that early-aughts homophobia and theorized that she and my mom were lesbians while I'd shout in protest, "They're just really good friends!" The adults were even worse: Grace once overheard someone in the grocery store calling them drunks and sluts, and she marched right over in her cheetah-print leggings and said, "Thank you for noticing."

Just as Grace had taught me, I had enrolled in my new school and quickly became a 4.0 student. Class vice president. The lead in school plays. An Academic Decathlon state champion. Editor-in-chief of the school newspaper. I know, I know, a very cool list of things that make a person very cool! My try-hard résumé might lead you to believe I was crushing it, but my gregarious outgoing nature had only made me a louder target among my classmates.

Early on I was beaten up by four popular boys as payback for telling a guy named Dirk that I didn't want to go out with him because I thought he had a unibrow. He did, but I guess I shouldn't have said so out loud! The whole thing lasted less than ten seconds. In that time, they'd managed to throw me to the floor, spit on me, kick me in the face, and call me a whore, which I wrote in my journal as *hoar*. Fun! It's a fun story!

Those same four boys had also attacked me at a school event that had included an egg toss, a traditionally fun activity that they managed to flip right into what would become several years' worth of therapy sessions. They had fantastic aim, and I remember the stinging humiliation as yolk dripped down my face and clothes in front of my classmates. But it didn't stop there. In the months that followed, the guys in our grade would maneuver themselves in the hallway so that one would trip me and another would be poised to catch my boobs as I fell into their outstretched hands. A few times when I turned my back to open my locker, actual rocks were thrown at my head.

By the end of the year, it became too much to handle. I begged my mom to move us away. This town was not the sanctuary we had expected, and I was never going to survive here. My mom later said she wished she had listened to me, but she didn't have the money to move us again after we left Bubba, and she didn't even know where we could go. We'd already retreated alongside the one person my mom knew she could count on—my godmother Grace—and there was no one else to turn to now. I was stuck in a new reality at my school, and it was one I could not understand. Most of my classmates in Utah had liked me. At my old school, a kid named Brandon had collected superlatives for the eighth-grade class, a prestigious self-esteem bloodbath for the yearbook, and I had been voted Best Personality. *That* is the confidence I had enrolled in this new school with, a gal with several different colors of Old Navy flip-flops and the best fucking personality!

I couldn't bring myself to talk about the full depth of the horrors I was experiencing at school, but I would soon find a small reprieve that summer. When ninth grade ended, my godmother's little red Camry sped us across the state toward a small neighboring town that she knew was home to a flourishing little stock theater. Since I had expressed an interest in plays and musicals, Grace and my mom had decided to drop me off here for the summer to "get an internship" at the theater. I was fifteen at the time and spent those couple months living by myself in a small camper that Grace had parked there with her then husband a few years back.

Living alone in a camper at fifteen might have been a shock to my system, but I wasn't really a stranger to spending chunks of time by myself during those years. At this point, my little brother Jesse had gone back to live with his dad, Bubba, in Utah. My mom and Grace would occasionally take off on little trips or adventures together—sometimes just for a weekend, occasionally for longer. I was headstrong and (seemingly) responsible, so perhaps it was easy to believe me when I said that I wanted to spend the summer there and would be just fine on my own. I'd been called an *old soul* enough times to understand that this was just a cute way for adults to say that you'd had to grow up too fast.

That summer, Grace gave me $40 for each week I would be there, along with two PSAT books to get cooking on during my downtime. I spent all the money at the bead store on my first day in town and had nothing left for food. Not only did that bead store take all my money, but for the next decade every bead store I ever entered would continue to take every dollar in my pocket. Who needs food when you have the ravenous joys of beading!

Getting an internship at the local theater was a truly ridiculous idea—small-town summer repertory theaters don't hire interns, especially ones who are fifteen and show up halfway through the season. But just as Grace instructed, I marched right up to the ticket counter and asked to be their intern. I think they were too freaked out to say no, so they assigned me the esteemed task of ushering and passing out programs with local retirees. But hey, if there was room in the balcony, at least I could stay and see the show.

Since I had spent all my food money on the beads for necklaces, I fed myself on snack bags at the theater gift shop, dipping into Grace's emergency stock of canned tomato soup buried in the back of the camper, and one time I even stole a loaf of banana bread from the trailer next door. I spent my weeks mostly hate-reading my PSAT books. The absolute worst highlight of the summer was when I made out with a 21-year-old at the wrap party, using one of Grace's seduction tips—purr in a low voice, "You're so smart!" while giving him puppy-dog eyes—which, sadly, worked.

At the end of the summer, Grace's red Camry pulled back up. I couldn't be happier to see my ride home. I was fucking starving.

My godmother's life decisions were just as wild as her outfit choices. Grace's aesthetic went one of two ways: an unkempt, unshowered mountain woman or a dressed-to-the-nines Vegas showgirl. When she was in her off mode, she was fully off. In Old Navy once, I heard some of my classmates giggling and pointing at the apparently homeless woman shopping a few aisles over and turned to see that they were talking about my godmother. But when she was on, she was Heidi Klum's stand-in—strutting around in gorgeous makeup, beautiful out-fits, and throwing on a luxurious wig if she felt the man she had her eye on would prefer a blonde over a redhead.

Grace adored beauty, and she wanted to be in full control of hers. One day, she was at our house when I invited a choir friend named Tanya to come over after school. We were sitting on our couch as I tried to impress Tanya with how chill we all were, and how I bet my mom would be super awesome and chaper-one us if we wanted to smoke pot.

In the middle of our timorous hangout, my godmother came sashaying out of the bathroom with a completely shaved head. She was grinning ear to ear and silently showing it off, waiting for our applause. Behind her, my mom was giggling from the bathroom holding the clippers.

I sprang off the couch and shoved Grace back into the bath-room as fast as I could. "What are you doing? Why did you shave your head!?"

Grace looked back at me with a steely, cryptic calm. "I wanted to see if I was truly beautiful."

Later, she had photographs taken with her newly shaved head

and made them into laminated bookmarks, which she handed out to strangers everywhere we went.

The thing about Grace was that, in her mind, beauty was inseparable from power. She was brought up in a world where you couldn't have power as a woman unless you were beautiful, and you couldn't be beautiful unless you were also thin, like she and my mom were. And I, too, wanted to be thin! Only, my desire to be thin was always at odds with my constant bingeing, which was brought on by the unrelenting panic I felt at school. One night, I remember walking over to the sink where a strainer of leftover spaghetti was sitting. The noodles were cold. They had been sitting there for hours. I picked up a spaghetti string and dangled it into my mouth as I heard Grace behind me. "One more pound and you'll be really fat," she said. "Right now you're just chubby."

The next week, Grace came home from shopping and dumped a grocery bag of The Zone diet bars on the counter for my school lunches. Then she brought out a measuring tape and pulled it across each part of my body as she wrote down the numbers in The Zone workbook. You see, in this particular diet, you want more protein than carbs for all of your meals: 30 percent fat, 30 percent protein, 40 percent carbs—that's The Zone, baby!!! For years after that, whenever I ate a dessert, I would also eat a piece of chicken or protein bar alongside it to get in The Zone.

At school that year, a girl in my grade had lined up a bunch of us in the hallway to prove to everyone that *she* didn't have the biggest butt in our class, I did! This was the year of "no butts are the best butts." Size double zero had hit the malls, and every clothing advertisement broadcasted pants that hung by the jut of your hip bones. I'd never seen those bones on me in my life, but I was sure they were there...if I just got in The Zone!!! I fantasized about the day I would announce another butt contest at school and waltz down the hallway, twirl around to show my backside, and in place of my bubble butt I'd now dazzle every-one with two saggy denim pockets.

I never fully lost the weight. I'd go up on the scale and I'd go down, but there wasn't a day I could have shared my mom's jeans or Grace's—and the pockets on the back of mine would remain full. The only zone I could get into was my comfort zone, and my comfort zone always seemed to need a sugar fix.

Road trips with Grace defined my womanhood. A trip in the Camry had come to mean that the season was changing, and life was altering its course. When I was sixteen, that red Camry sped down the highway yet again, my godmother at the wheel, my mom in the passenger seat, and me in the back. Grace was driving me to New Mexico where I would attend a new high school, the United World College, a scholarship boarding school that offered International Baccalaureate degrees for high schoolers with a history of service work. And how had she dis-covered this beacon of opportunity? Well, right outside of the school grounds sat one of New Mexico's best nude mineral hot springs, of course!

On this road trip, I was feeling miles away from the person my godmother had told me years ago that I could be, when we sat on the inside-outside couch. Grace didn't sugarcoat anything, and as we drove, she launched into a firm, foreboding mono-logue about how I couldn't blow it at the UWC and how this was my last chance at that good ol' upward mobility. The bul-lying at my previous school had escalated, taking new twists and turns that not even a Lifetime movie would dare to attempt. Fi-nally, in one twist no one saw coming, I had dropped out half-way through my junior year.

My mom peppered in softer advice, saying that we would always figure something out and not to be too hard on myself—but my godmother blew right past her, insisting I had to get perfect grades, join activity groups, and beware a long-term relationship. I gazed out the window to see New Mexico greet us with a large yellow sign that read *Welcome to the Land of Enchantment.*

These hours in the car were *the escape*, and the escape had become my favorite part—the moment before the arrival, when I felt safest, whisked away from whatever nightmare was behind us and on the way toward a new life. The escape was the moment in time when hope was at its highest.

My godmother and mom dropped me off at my new school and moved in all my precious belongings, including a trunk full of costumes, a craft box full of magazine clippings to paste in my journals, and two books gifted from Grace: one an exposé on teenage abuse titled *Saving Beauty from the Beast*, and then in a brutal contrast, that trusty *The Seven Laws of Seduction* book. Grace then took out three Costco-size boxes of condoms and put them under my extra-long twin bed. She told me to fuck as much as I could while I was still young. If I didn't, I would regret it. My new roommate smiled weakly at me.

That high school in New Mexico was wonderful, but I wasted almost every second of the experience. My brain was scrambled with the trauma of my last school, yet I went along pretending nothing was wrong with me as I organized talent shows and started a Beatles-themed zine, *8 Days a Week*, which I put out... once a month. I wasn't even a Beatles fan. I spent my time bingeing on ice cream from the cafeteria, acting in student shows, and writing zine articles called things like "Strawberry Fields, Whatever."

Two years later, my godmother was in the audience of my high-school graduation, waving noisemakers and tossing—you guessed it—Mardi Gras beads. After the ceremony, she walked up to my room to help me gather my things and pack up the car. When we went to move the costume trunk, it revealed three Costco-size boxes of condoms under my bed, untouched, unopened, and covered in dust. I had not been fucking. The look of disappointment on her face still haunts me.

I did all the things Grace had taught me in order to get into good colleges. My grades were top of the class, and I had extremely high SAT scores—you know, from all that beading I did on top of those PSAT books during my "theater internship." I had devoted my life to charity work and collecting accolades for my résumé, I handwrote my essays, made magazines from scratch about my life, and even sent a 3D diorama to one of the school's admissions officers. Grace's grooming paid off: I was accepted into every school I applied to. But at the last second, I had secretly auditioned for an arts conservatory—NYU's Tisch School of the Arts. I told myself I was "just checking" to see if I was maybe a talented actor, and if they rejected me, I could throw away my dream of being an artist and move on in peace.

When I was accepted, I went into an adrenaline-fueled shock. Unfortunately, NYU was the only one of my options that didn't offer me full financial aid or a full scholarship. The countdown for choosing a school began, and I spiraled for weeks until the day before decisions were due. Grace called me up and told me I'd likely ruin my life if I turned down the Ivy League and other prestigious universities, that I'd probably never make good money, and that I might struggle forever. Was losing all that worth the dream of being an artist? I cried and said yes, it was. I heard her take in a sharp breath, then she told me that was all she needed to hear. Since my mom's credit wouldn't qualify her as my guarantor, Grace agreed to cosign thousands of dollars of loans so that I could attend classes where you roll around on the floor like a worm.

My dream began, and what a dream it was—I hated every second of acting college. I had gone from New Mexico to New York City, and I was woefully unprepared. I remember asking a friend what kind of coats people wore in the city. She looked at me, perplexed. "Just normal coats, I guess." I knew from movies they had chic city folk jackets and just didn't know the word for *peacoat*. I showed up to college wearing a T-shirt I got for free at a marathon I hadn't run and overalls from a thrift store, about a decade before that look became acceptable.

Throughout college, I wasn't cast in even one of the big drama department productions. Every semester I stood in front of my acting teachers to get feedback like "We get it, you like to make jokes," "You need to look more presentable," and "Try using a curling iron." I had become the first person in my family to graduate from college, but having gone to acting school, it was kind of a wash. I'll never know if I really had to take out all those loans and face off with New York City just so that I could find my life's calling, but what I do know is that one lonely night, wearing my not-a-peacoat windbreaker, I walked up to Twenty-Sixth Street and Ninth Avenue, and I found comedy.

I remember waiting three hours in line to see an Upright Citizens Brigade improv show called *Assssscat* in a basement black-box theater, because it was a free event I'd read about in *Time Out* magazine. I'd been one of the first in line and sat in the center middle row. That night, I watched Amy Poehler and a dozen incredibly talented performers improvise the greatest comedy I'd ever seen in my life. The show before me was so different than all the theater I'd seen that year—long-winded, meandering plays usually starring the untalented child of some-one famous. But here in this dingy basement that sold $5 bot-tles of beer out of a cooler in the back, I had found art that felt alive and impactful, even though the art at that particular mo-ment included a comedian pretending to be the Italian Santa of "the North-ah Pole-ah" and would later mime jacking off all the naughty elves.

Soaking in all the women before me who were tearing through scenes with abandon, delivering just the right quip off the top of their head, I had finally found the path in life I had been looking for: comedy. But it was too late to join the improv groups at school or become a part of the college sketch team. The kids in those clubs had arrived already knowing comedy was their dream and auditioned early in their first year. I had just seen my first improv show at twenty years old. I believed I was decades behind my peers. We didn't have TV for most of my life, so I never had a favorite sitcom or stand-up comedian, and I hadn't grown up watching all the men named Jimmy who hosted late-night shows. I knew about them just as references, but I hadn't sat there and studied the form, familiarizing myself with their comedy rhythms. There were hundreds of hours of TV I felt I'd missed out on and needed to watch immediately in order to have a chance at a career of making people laugh.

I became obsessed with catching up, and I found an advertisement in a theater magazine for a semester-long program called Comedy Studies in Chicago run by Anne Libera. I gathered all the paperwork and pled my case to the NYU officials that it should count as my study-abroad credits, and they said yes.

Or so I thought. I must not have understood exactly what I finagled, because that semester I spent in Chicago would later mean the six-month grace period I had to pay off my loans after graduating was already used up. I freaked out. I had sort of assumed paying off thousands of dollars in school debt would be, like, twenty-five bucks every month until I died, not five hundred on the reg.

Every day an unknown number called my cell phone: it was Sallie Mae Loans demanding that I pay them those thousands of dollars. When the first call came through, I remembered a piece of wisdom that Grace often mentioned when she found herself in a sticky situation: "Honey, honesty is the best policy, but insanity is a better defense." So I held the phone close to my mouth, took a big breath, and meowed like a cat.

One day the loan officer let that cat know they would be calling my guarantor, the person who had cosigned all my fancy-ass college loans, Grace. A week later the phone rang again. It was my godmother. She told me I had ruined her credit. I promised to make it right, though I was unsure it was a promise I could keep. I didn't know where I was ever going to get that kind of money.

"Well," she said, "I guess you're going to have to make it in show business, aren't you?"

The next time I saw that little red Camry, Grace was picking me up at home in New Mexico to drive me to Chicago to start my post-college career as a comedian. After spending that semester there for my comedy studies course, I knew I needed to get back there as soon as possible. New York had ground me up like the beans they used for their $8 cups of coffee, but Chicago had offered me community, endless comedy classes, and rent I could actually afford, even if that rent was for a windowless room with no furniture. Grace helped me load up her trunk, no longer bothering with the condoms, and we set off for our three-day journey. We were back in my favorite part: the escape and the hope.

On our way to Chicago, Grace almost crashed several times, we stopped at every giant Midwestern thrift store, and she spent the entire journey dishing advice on how to make it in entertainment, despite never having worked in the biz herself. She was adamant that I get business cards and a real silver business-card holder to stash them in, so people would know those business cards really meant business. When she dropped me off at my windowless craigslist apartment, she left me with something of far greater value: a $100 Subway gift card for my meals. The footlong daily special was $5, and I split that thing into quarters and feasted for days at a time. I had made it: I was finally in...THE ZONE!!!

When I was twenty-five and had signed with my first acting agent, Grace sped into the city, picked me up from my apartment and drove me to a plastic surgeon's office in downtown Chicago that she'd had a "strong intuitive hit" about. We sat down for the appointment, and Grace explained that I needed a breast reduction if I was ever going to make it in show business. She felt I could be a star, an ingenue even! But ingenues weren't curvy like me, and they had round perky breasts, not the gelatinous pumpkins that overtook my frame.

The surgeon asked me questions like, *Do they droop? Is one bigger than the other?* I said, Nope! Besides giving me crushing back problems and spinal deformities, they were great! I then undressed, and he measured and marked me, calling out things to the nurse nearby: "The right one is way lower than the left... Wow, hmm, very droopy."

Grace and I walked into a little room where they instructed me to take off my shirt again for a Before photo, after which I could contact my insurance and see if they would pay for my surgery. I began to sob uncontrollably.

The nurse tried to tell me not to worry, that my face wouldn't be in it, but I still couldn't let her take the picture. She left the room to give us space and I turned to Grace, choked up. I didn't want to go through with the surgery, I told her, but how was I ever supposed to let a man see my medically imperfect boobs again? She hugged me and offered what she genuinely thought was a word of comfort: "Don't worry, men will fuck anything."

By the time I found myself standing in the reception hall for Grace's third wedding, I was making my living solely from comedy and finally paying those monthly student loan bills on time. Unsteady and slightly drunk, I walked toward the stage of the wedding venue and looked out at the crowd, focusing my vision on Grace. She was radiant in her flowy white wedding dress and flower crown, beaming next to her lovely new husband. The backing track began to play, and the DJ handed me the mic. I was not nervous. I could sing this song in my sleep. I began. *Ah-ma-zing Grace, how sweet the sound, that saved a wretch like meee!*

When I was a child, I really needed someone to believe in me, to promise me that I could have a life I was proud of. My mom had always supported me, but at times I lost sight of the wisdom and care she was offering because we were too entangled in the daily oppression from my stepdad. My mom gave me everything she had, but sometimes the only way you'll believe you are great is if it comes from someone who doesn't feel obligated to say it, because they are not your blood.

It was an utterly fateful day when a fiery redhead arrived at our house in her matching red Camry, stepped outside and pointed at me like, *You, kid, you're gonna make it.*

My godmother showed me the way out and gave me the tools I needed to get there, from cosigning my loans to buying me that wildly expensive TI-89 calculator in high school. She handed down every piece of advice she ever came across, even when that advice was wrong. She created a fire inside me that night on our first road trip and stoked it through the years. She helped me continue putting one foot forward, even when it felt too hard. What a gift to be a child who learned to navigate the world from a woman who considers cheetah print a neutral.

How precious did that Grace appear, the hour I first believed.

REBECCA

The best friend breakup

I was racing down the sidewalk in downtown Chicago: I had an audition in a little over an hour, followed by an improv show later, but most importantly, in three minutes I was scheduled for an appointment with a phone psychic. I ran into the Starbucks on the corner and put in headphones, wondering if the psychic would know I was taking refuge here without buying a coffee—*and* with the audacity to ask for a cup of water. The psychic's name was Fred, which was very hard to get past. I just wasn't sure the spirit guides show up for you if your name is Fred, you know? But my mom said he was incredible, the best she'd ever spoken to, and so I grabbed a seat by the corner window and waited for his call to come in.

"You're up for something big at work this week," Fred said a few minutes into the session. That was true: it was the whole reason I had asked my mom to set up this psychic appointment in the first place. I was twenty-seven years old and finally being considered for a position where I'd be writing and performing on The Second City Mainstage, a sketch and improv theater in Chicago that had been home to dozens of our most famous and beloved contemporary comedians. The Mainstage was considered the biggest and best stage in the theater. Rebecca, my best friend, was a ridiculously talented comedy powerhouse and had already been cast in the one other open spot on the stage, but I was still waiting to hear back. Was I as good as her? Did I deserve to be up there? Had we performed together for years, only for her to succeed and for me to be the loser sidekick who got left behind?

It was between me and one other girl for the last open spot. As the stage manager clicked on that video camera each night of our "auditions" (which were essentially hour-long improv sets), it was as if a king had thrown two swords to the ground and said it was time to fucking duel. One peasant would die, and the other would get to perform eight comedy shows a week for $100 a night and a discount on the chicken fingers they sold during the show.

"You're going to get it," psychic Fred began saying on the phone. "You're gonna get this thing you're up for—"

"*What?!*" I whispered excitedly.

"You're getting the thing you're up for, but you're not going to like it. It's not what you think it is," he continued. I told him I really didn't care, I needed that job, it was the one thing I knew that helped you get a career in comedy, the thing I wanted most. Who was this future me that didn't like her goddamn dream job? Fuck that bitch!

"Let's move on," Fred said, intensely bored. We talked about my career, my family, and just before our hour was up and as the barista gave me their last *get the fuck out of here* glance, Fred added one more prediction.

"Oh, and your best friend, Rebecca...she's going to stab you in the back, and it will end your friendship. You two are not in a good partnership. It's toxic. Years from now, you'll just be people who wave in passing."

A shock traveled through my body, which instantly morphed into defiance. Then, I really let Fred have it. I no longer cared that I was loudly shouting at a psychic in Starbucks, now with only ten minutes before I was supposed to be auditioning for the commercial role of Woman Who Eats Cereal and Likes It. I was so happy when he said I would get the job, but now I was sure this psychic was full of shit. I should have known not to trust some channeler with the name of a refrigerator repairman! Reeling with anxiety, I ended the call and ran to my audition, where I smiled and pantomimed eating cereal as the casting director asked if I could look like I was "enjoying it more."

Sure enough, Fred's first prediction came true: a week later I was called in to Second City, where they told me I had the job. I was joining the Mainstage cast. This cereal-eating peasant was a champion! Ecstatic, I immediately called Rebecca, and we screamed at the top of our lungs in celebration. I was so elated by my career dreams coming true that I didn't even think about Fred's other prediction until later. In a panic that night in my apartment, I called Rebecca again and told her everything. "Fred said you would backstab me, and that we won't be friends! He said we are bad for each other. He said we're not supposed to be partners!"

Rebecca, ever the grounded skeptic, laughed her ass off. The only thing more ridiculous to her than Fred's prophecy was the fact that I had paid $90 to hear it. Still, I worried about what he'd said. A few times that year when I got drunk, I left Rebecca voicemails about how we just couldn't let Fred be right, and we needed to fix every single issue that ever came between us…as soon as we were sober again.

Eventually, I pushed Fred's prediction out of my mind and tried to focus on rehearsals for the Mainstage. Whatever I would write and create over the next three months—if it was good enough—would be included in the final show that we'd perform every night for the next year. These three grueling months were going to determine the show that every fellow comedian, every reporter, and every agent and manager would come see. This was the show that *SNL* recruiters attended once a year to watch the performers and ask themselves, *Did anyone here have "it"?*

Joining the Mainstage was the victorious culmination of years of sacrifice, starting with the three-day drive my godmother and I had suffered through to get me to Chicago. It meant that buying one saucepan from the thrift store for $2 and using it for every single thing—from scrambling an egg, to stirring cookie dough, to using it as a bowl for yogurt—was worth it. Every shitty gig that paid for every shitty class, every embarrassing bar improv set where a male castmate had made me play their Mom/Secretary/Mistress (yes, all one character), everything had led to being cast on the Mainstage.

Not only had I gotten my dream job but I would face this notoriously difficult profession with my best friend, venturing forth to conquer the stage hand in hand, with years of performing experience under our very chunky 2013 fashion belts.

Rebecca first entered my life six years prior to the Mainstage casting, back when I was at my mom's house in New Mexico and getting ready to move to Chicago to pursue comedy. I had spent hours scouring the internet for blogs, videos, tweets— anyone dropping details about life in my new mecca. On Facebook one night, I saw a video taken at a bar after a show where a bunch of young comedians were singing and dancing around. Behind a few of the students, a tall, striking beauty with a curly bob of hair was stealing the show. She was barely in frame, but I couldn't look away from her little throwaway gestures—mini neck swivels and wrist-flips, as if she had just shot a tiny three-pointer. If I were a casting director I would've stood up right then and shouted, "You back there, you're a STAH!"

On the first day of my level-one improv class at a theater called iO in Chicago, I walked into the room and my breath escaped my chest. THE STAH herself was sitting right there in a folding chair, in *my* intro class.

I don't know what came over me—an anxiety disorder, fate, or just pure unbridled insanity, but I sat down next to her and, like I was five years old, said, "Hi, I'm Chelsea. I think we should be best friends." Rebecca looked at me as if I had just tried to return a sopping-wet bathing suit: amused that I would try it but with absolutely no desire to engage further. I'd have to think of a new approach.

All the same, I was in love with Rebecca from the moment I saw her. The type of love where your guard is never up because your souls recognize each other from a dance orgy in another multiverse or making hats out of rocks in a cave during your past life together. At that point, I knew that men could hurt you, and that wasn't just a possibility, but a guarantee. Women, though, were saviors to me. I'd been raised by strong women like my mom and godmother and felt safest in the presence of feminine strength. Women like Rebecca made life better and stable. I was a heat-seeking missile for their friendship, homing in on the strongest, most confident woman in the room and pledging her my allegiance.

What drew me to Rebecca the most was that she possessed two contradictory qualities that somehow defined her in equal part: she was just as laid-back as she was forceful. The calm inside her was almost aggressive. Her inner peace was contagious and thrust upon anyone who came near.

While my opening line in class had flopped, after a month or two of improv classes I worked up the courage to invite Rebecca to my twenty-second birthday party. She replied breezily, "I'll see what I have going on that night."

I felt elated when Rebecca glided through the door of my miniature fourth-floor walk-up and entered the party, a small, girls-only gathering consisting of my current roommate and my college roommate visiting from out of town. My attire for the evening was a beige cotton tutu from H&M with a black vest on top. I was really feeling myself, and had declared at the start of the night that I was only drinking brown liquors so that I wouldn't get sick.

The last thing I remember is Rebecca handing me a shot of Jägermeister at a drag bar called Hydrate, which was completely empty because we'd shown up way too early. Well, that's my last full memory. After that I have a glimpse of Rebecca putting me in a cab and the wind hitting my ass as I thought—is my ass just like, *fully out*? It was. For someone trying to get this person to be her best friend, I wasn't doing a great job of selling myself.

At that point, I had spent some of my first months in Chicago doing a solo comedy competition, and after that I continued to perform alone, begging for slots in little sketch shows at bars where I would bring GarageBand tracks I had made and sing comedy songs to them. I didn't yet have the confidence to just talk to the audience and do stand-up, and I didn't know how to write a joke unless I was using a song as a crutch to create comedic rhythm. But something was clearly working, because the smattering of fellow struggling comedians in the audience began to grumble a *Hello* or sometimes even a *Good job* at the bar afterward. After one particularly smashing night where Rebecca's improv team also performed on the lineup, I received a one-sentence email from her that said: *We should perform stuff together*

Her unpunctuated prose offered a cool handshake, and I responded with a voracious blowjob. *Ohmygodyes I would love that! When are you free? Woop Woop YAYYYYY!!!!!!*

When we started working together, I gave Rebecca half the lyrics in my songs, and then we began to write new ones together. We sang about horrible dates, incredible dates, and really just a lot about dating. We sang about the time we both waitressed at diners and dated felons. The lyrics to the chorus were, unsurprisingly, "I dated a felon."

It often felt like Rebecca and I shared the same brain but made entirely different choices with it. Onstage, we'd think of the same joke at the exact same time, but we'd deliver it in completely different styles. Where my comedy had a sense of panic swarming around each punch line, Rebecca had grit and surety, dropping jokes swiftly to their knees. We were as different as we were similar, but in a way that still made each other wildly better, like two prints in the same color palette that clash so intensely it's suddenly fashion.

Rebecca and I were twin flames in many ways, and we held similar tragedies buried underneath a mountain of tragic decisions. Even when it took her years to open up her deepest pains to me, I felt as if I had already known them. I spent much of our early relationship holding a small blowtorch to the icy walls she'd built up, and when they finally melted, I cherished the hard-won intimacy as if it was proof that yes, I was special to her...this friendship was different.

Where we perhaps diverged the most was in our approaches to dating and men. When I first met Rebecca, I was trying to date again after a long hiatus from any sort of love life at all. It was the 2010s, and just as I was getting ready to put these tits back on the market, I found myself right in the misogynist epicenter of the nine-men-to-one-woman ratio on every improv team. In other words, I had found the dick jackpot.

To many people's standards I was probably still a prude, but in my eyes, I was balling the fuck out. One summer I made out with five different guys, and it was mind-blowing. I was finally the slut of my dreams! Boys were paying attention to me, and even though most of them blew through me like a BOGO deal at Chili's and I was the free baked potato, I felt ravishing. I jumped from one failed crush to another, then circled back to the worst ones for extra punishment. Rebecca rolled her eyes at my escapades, and the more attention I received, the more her annoyance with my wealth of gentleman callers in musty plaid shirts and Converses began to grow.

On the other end of the spectrum, Rebecca seemed to get all the professional attention and comedic respect. We took all our improv classes together at iO and became a little lady clique with our two other friends, Mallory and Jo. When we got to level five, my dreams came true: our teacher decided that I was the star of the whole class. Not Rebecca, but me—*I* had the comedic prowess he had always been looking for! Our teacher, a fifty-five-year-old bald-in-the-bad-way kind of man, started emailing me after hours, so taken with my talent that he wanted to do a two-person show with me. How lucky was I? Twenty-two years old, new to the city, and this veteran of improv wanted to create a show together? Rebecca was skeptical of his motives, but I didn't listen to her because I was too obsessed with his obsession with MY TALENT! He emailed me to schedule some private rehearsals. Then he told me he loved me and had started dreaming about me.

Rebecca, Mallory, and Jo sat around my laptop as we carefully typed back my reply. "Tell him that you're drunk," they suggested. "That way he forgives how honest you're being, and write *haha* to soften it." I emailed him that I knew he loved his wife haha so surely he didn't mean it when he said he loved me hahaha, and I just wanted to clarify that this was about...my... *talent*?

He never wrote back. I skipped our last two classes and our student show so I wouldn't have to see him. We confessed it all to a female teacher who did nothing, then we enrolled in level six like it had never happened. Years later, the theater would get its first HR rep, and I would report it all to her and hand over the emails. She flatly replied to not worry, he'd been reported by dozens of other women already, so they now had him teaching only the out-of-town workshops!

A few years into our friendship, Rebecca needed a new place to live and moved in with me and my roommate, and I loved every second of having her around more. I never stopped thinking about work and projects, so by 8:00 a.m. I was already pitching jokes for sketches as she poured her coffee. I'd tell Rebecca my idea, and then she'd act it out at the kitchen table as I watched, getting a feel for it and tweaking the wording if something wasn't working. I adored these collaborative moments between us, and after seeing her perform my ideas, I was able to walk into rehearsals and pitch my jokes with a confidence I'd never had before.

When we were twenty-four, Second City held auditions for comedians to perform on their cruise-ship shows. The theater had recently started sending casts out on ships for months at a time, and if you were willing to live in what was essentially a floating 1980s shopping mall, this was your shot to become a professional. Every cast on a ship had spots for three men and two women, and they hired Rebecca and me to go out on the same boat. Our comedy dreams were dashed early on when we discovered that all the cruise-ship sketches had been written for old-school audiences, where the women would be in smaller supporting roles and divided into two types: the wifey one and the funny one. I was cast in all the wifey roles, and Rebecca was cast in all the funny roles. We were livid. All we wanted was the reverse.

Performing on that cruise ship was the most amazing thing I'd never, ever, ever do again. Out on the open sea, maritime law reigned supreme, which meant HR was a teenager in a magnetic badge and bottles of wine were $1 for the crew. The quality of the wine was so terrible that we had to cut the red with a bottle of white. This became our cocktail of choice on the cruise, which we astutely named *wine drink*.

But the big upset of the high seas was the small handful of available single dudes. It was crushing to come aboard this dazzling piña colada paradise only to be met with the bargain bin of available ass. I scoured the prospects, finding seventy-year-old casino kings and very-married crew members who were still throwing their hat in the ring. The only worthy candidate left was the flute player in the ship's band. Was he cute? Enough/ no. Early on in our tepid affair, I walked up behind him and saw that he was using the ship internet, which cost a dollar a minute, to swipe through OkCupid girls from back home in Tallahassee, despite the fact that he would be living on a cruise ship for the next six months.

One night into our rendezvous, he asked if I wanted to hang out, and I said yes, but I didn't want to hook up again. We ate pizza in my cabin and watched *Die Hard 2*, and I eventually fell asleep. Now, beds on a ship are barely the width of your own body, and with two people you're practically stacked. There are no windows in the crew bedrooms because you are living so far below deck, and when the door closes and the lights are off, you might as well be sleeping in a pitch-black sensory-deprivation tank. So I had fallen asleep, and in the middle of the night I woke up to an intense rubbing sound. It was *rubbing rubbing rubbing*, and in my sleep state it hit me: he was masturbating.

I shifted a little and it stopped. I waited for a few seconds that felt like an eternity. Then it started again and then stopped. I shifted my elbow and felt wetness. I took a deep breath and told myself I would count to 100, slowly get up, grab my key card off my desk, and very elegantly sneak out of the cabin. I made it to 2 before I violently leaped out of bed, swung my arms wildly for my card, and ran out the door.

For a while I lay on a patio chair on the deck up top, trying to figure out if that had just happened. I heard it, I felt it, but also I had been sleeping. Was it a weird dream? Was it punishment for not fellating the flautist? As the sun rose, a few passengers spotted me from the show and waved hello, then witnessed the look of a woman haunted by the sounds of night jizz and quickly walked away. I crept back down below and knocked quietly but urgently on Rebecca's door.

Her ship cabin was directly across from mine, so I needed her to open up that door right fucking now before the flautist heard us, should he still be there. When she let me in, I rushed inside and crawled into bed with her.

"What is it?" she whispered, scared. I shook my head and buried my face in her pillow and started laughing uncontrollably.

"Bitch, what happened!" Rebecca pressed. She cycled through different ways of nudging me to talk, coaxing, demanding, then finally gave up. I turned my face to the wall so I could get out the words that the flute player had just played his tune...to completion.

She shrieked with horror and then buried into the bed with me as we laughed until we cried. When we ran out of jokes to make about his dick being like a flute, she turned on the Cruise TV in her room that was always playing the same shows on repeat, usually the Jonestown massacre documentary series. A few hours later, the kitchen was open, and Rebecca raced up to the buffet and got us breakfast and ran it back down to her cabin. At around three o'clock, we both decided it was probably safe to go back to my room.

Rebecca opened her door and then hid behind it, watching through the crack as I crept toward mine and nervously swiped my key card. The door clicked open, and I stepped in. The flautist eagerly called out, "Hey, where ya been?"

Behind me, I heard Rebecca choke on a gasp of laughter as I took in the sight of this man *still fucking there.* In the trash can were several attempts at notes he'd written me: *Where did you go? What happened? Okay I ordered a pizza on your account?*

I turned back to look at Rebecca who was vigorously shaking her head *No, no, don't go in there!* The look on her face willed me to be strong, to do what she would do, and tell him off with such a fury that his dick would violently detach itself from his body and flee to shore in a dinghy. I took a step inside my room, gathered all my courage, and squeaked, "Heyyy, how's it going?"

As Rebecca and I continued doing improv together at Second City, I decided that we needed to make one of these web-series things that all the newly successful comedians kept talking about in their interviews after it catapulted them to success. My first pitch for a video series was *Sex and the City* but for poor, ugly people. Quite frankly, I have never stopped pitching different versions of that show. I made our first web series by holding a $300 Canon camera in one hand and the manual in the other and taught myself to edit by watching YouTube tutorials. Every single year we made another web series, short film, or pilot on a budget of $3 and a prayer, till finally something we'd made took off—a web series we'd (regrettably) called *Dumb Bitch Village*.

I sent our brilliant new series to every agent and every manager I could get an email address for. One of them wrote back and said she was blown away by the originality of our videos. I eagerly awaited her next reply, which I just knew would include an offer to sign us. Over breakfast the next day, Rebecca casually mentioned that the manager had reached out to sign her. My call never came. I fished for sympathy or outrage from Rebecca, but she had simply accepted that she was the one worthy of being signed. For Rebecca, this was a peaceful retribution that the wifey one didn't always win. I tried to swallow my pride and move on.

One of our videos eventually went to the New York Television Festival, and Rebecca and I treated it like the Met Gala. We were the next Tina Fey and Amy Poehler, destined to one day host the Emmys just as soon as our pilot screened. Then, we actually did start getting attention from some network executives, who booked meetings with us in their big-time network offices in the city. One morning during the festival, I woke up next to Rebecca on an air mattress in our Airbnb and took a photo of her looking a giggling, hungover mess. As I held my phone out, showing her the photo, that fancy manager from Chicago lit up my phone. I picked up immediately.

"Hey, Chelsea. So I actually meant to do this earlier, sorry, ha ha, but um, we loved your web series and are so excited for you both, and we would like to sign you as well. Sorry, I meant to call you a while ago."

It was clearly only because our *Dumb Bitch Village* show was taking off that I was getting this call. After all, if I was the typist on this incredible Rebecca show, they might as well take their cut of the sales on me, too. I knew I was an afterthought, a client you settle for—but I was an aspiring actor, I had no self-esteem! I was just thrilled to finally have a manager.

All week long we soaked in the compliments about our show and the open bar of Amstel Lights, until finally we gathered at the front of the stage with a bunch of other comedians for a painfully forced Q and A about our film. Near the end, Rebecca grabbed the mic out of my hand.

"One more thing," she slurred. "You New Yorkers think you're so fucking great, but you don't know shit. Chicago in the house, baby. We in the house." She then began jacking off an invisible, quite large penis as she squatted down and caressed it, shouting, "Chicago! Chicago!" The New York comedians onstage with us were pissed, but they also went on to write for *SNL*, so I don't feel too bad. Hopefully they have since confused me with a different brunette.

Onstage I may have hidden my face in faux embarrassment, but to be honest, I loved it. I reveled in the power of a woman who does not give a fuck. And yet, giving a fuck was the thing I was best at! I gave a fuck to my detriment. Around this time I was at a bar with Rebecca one night when I noticed two people in the corner, whispering and looking my way. I barely knew them, but I began to panic and tugged on Rebecca's shirt. "I think they're talking about me," I whispered in horror.

Rebecca turned, barely clocking them, and with a gorgeous wave of a hand she said, "Who cares what they think. Those people...are just furniture, in the play of your life."

I had it engraved on a ring that I wore every day till the metal turned green.

★ ★ ★

After the TV festival, we put together a pitch over the next few months and then flew to Los Angeles to pitch our web series as a TV show. This was it, we thought, this was the trip that could change our lives. Days before leaving, our manager asked if we all wanted to crash together. I remember this as the moment when managers and agents became human to me, asking to sleep on the couch of a free Airbnb, and not just these hidden puppet masters of Hollywood.

I would quickly learn just how "human" they could be over the course of this LA trip. Our manager, who was going to drive us to all the meetings, pulled up on the first day in a loaned mini Fiat. Her license had expired, as it turned out, so she couldn't actually rent a car. All week, I sat horizontally with my knees hugging my chest in the back seat as our manager missed every single exit and drove 40 miles an hour on the freeway because she was afraid of LA traffic. Somehow, our pitches had all been scheduled on opposite sides of the town, so we drove an hour one way, pitched, then an hour back, constantly running late to meetings, never knowing what was happening. I'd been spending all my time learning how to write scripts, but little did I know that studying a basic LA map would've been far more beneficial to my career in that moment.

In the parking lot for one of our meetings, the security guy said, "Chelsea?" and my manager assumed he was referring to me, a nobody from Chicago, still folded in the back seat of the Fiat. She nodded and followed all his directions till we were in line for tickets for *The Chelsea Handler Show* and missed our actual pitch. The next day, as we sped down the highway, already fifteen minutes late to pitch to a large streaming network, we realized she'd missed the entrance and we were headed for the freeway again. Our manager slowed down the Fiat on a 60-mile-an-hour on ramp, came to 5 mph in the turning lane, and yelled, "Jump out! Just go!"

We ran up the side of the grassy hill, laptops in hand, till we got to the meeting. We were giggling so intensely we couldn't stop, as we were ushered into a conference room with three executives who had been waiting for twenty minutes. As we delivered our jokes, they would begrudgingly reply, "That's funny," instead of laughing. When we left, I rubbed grass off my knees and thought, *This will be the story we tell together on the late-night couch when we make it.*

We pitched the show to maybe eight places and took half a dozen other general meetings. General meetings are a staple in Hollywood, or "generals" as they are called in "the biz" where you plan to "get lunch" and never do, continuing to "circle back" and "put a pin in it" till one of you dies or quits and moves back home. General meetings are supposed to be giant hour-long "get to know each other" sessions that instead just make all parties rethink why they wanted to get into this industry to begin with. Rebecca and I had a stock story we'd perform, and then we'd just go from there and improvise our best two-woman show, just without our usual music and lighting.

The exhaustion that came from all the generals that week was intense. Each one felt like an emotional marathon: I watched executives fall in love with Rebecca but survey me with ambivalence. I shouted my quips louder and forced more attempts at small talk, exerting as much effort as I could to get them to love me, too…the exact thing that we all know only works to push people away. In each meeting, the reality of our imbalanced roles was suddenly becoming harder to ignore. Rebecca was the star, and I was her baggage. To me, it seemed like everyone was looking at her as our generation's next female Steve Martin, but in order to hire her, you also had to bring along her loud secretary in an ill-fitting bra.

As a part of our pitch, we'd do a bit about our characters' dating lives and how they "use Tinder like men do." We'd pause and wait for them to ask what we meant. Then we'd pull out our phones and say, "Throw out the net, see what you catch," and we'd start swiping "yes" violently, like our characters would do, and inevitably we'd get an actual match in the meeting. We'd gasp, feigning surprise, and show them the profiles of who we connected with, half in-character, asking the exec what they thought of them and improvising bits from the details in the profiles. Sometimes we'd even send a real message or make plans to meet up later while we were still in the pitch.

Tinder was fairly new at that point, so this comedic setup always crushed. But a tension began to build as we performed it together because Rebecca didn't like that I was the one going on Tinder during our meetings. By that point I had a boyfriend, Caleb, who I'd been with for a while. It didn't seem right to Rebecca that I was pretending to be single in the pitch when I was the one who "got to have a boyfriend" in real life, and suffering on a dating app was actually her reality.

At the end of the four days, we had survived most of the trip, and there was just one more meeting the next day. This particular network had met us at the New York Comedy Festival earlier in the year. They were the most promising meeting of all, set early in the morning so that all the heads of the network could attend. They had told our managers that if we added a younger character and changed some minor elements about the pitch, they would probably buy the show.

That last night in LA we took glasses of wine to the pool of the apartment building we were staying in. I looked over the city and realized we had done it. We were drinking wine, IN THE POOL. The height of luxury! There was just one hang-up. Since the TV network had asked us to add in a younger character as a lead, it meant we needed to rethink the entire setup and all the episode ideas to include this new character. I swam toward Rebecca and suggested that we rebreak the pitch, lingo for "redo the whole thing," but that we do it while we hung out in the pool like Bitcoin billionaires.

"I've been thinking..." Rebecca mumbled. "Do we really want to be on that network?"

Tomorrow's meeting wasn't with the most impressive conglomerate—in fact, they were notoriously terrible to work with, but they were a TV network nonetheless, the one that was most interested in buying our show, and we were dirty improv girls from Chicago who made less than $100 a night performing sketch comedy. The thought that we could be better than that had never crossed my mind. But Rebecca always valued herself. She knew her art, and knew she was special. Rebecca didn't need to settle for less.

I could have drowned her. If I didn't have $12 worth of wine in my hand, I would have tried. Our manager saw the fight between us brewing and frantically called the other, more senior manager on our team. I began concentrating on having a silent and furious breakdown.

The reality was, we'd been fracturing long before this moment. Hundreds of small cracks had led us here.

In the beginning, I was so enamored with Rebecca's lack of need that I hadn't yet considered that she didn't need *me*. She never felt the urge to text back, offer the compliment, or gush affection to her wobbly, overly emotional, often crying best friend. I luxuriated in the feeling of her presence. She eased my edge, and I borrowed from her well of confidence. I became addicted to her personality, feeling as if it was easier to remain in her shadow than to venture out and make my own. That's a long way of saying I was: passionately codependent! And I only grew more entrenched with each year of our friendship.

Despite our disastrous meet-cute on my twenty-second birthday, Rebecca and I had become best friends by the time I turned twenty-three, and she joined me in my sacred birthday tradition of making one wish for each year of my life. Outside the comedy theater in the back parking lot, we crouched behind a dumpster for some privacy to celebrate before running in for our next improv show. She held a pack of birthday candles and lit each one, passing them to me as I made twenty-three wishes. The bulk of the dumpster blocked the wind, and I blew each candle out, willing every wish as if my life depended on it. We were so happy we cried, barely even clocking the trash and rotting corn dogs at our feet.

On Rebecca's twenty-fourth birthday, we threw a massive Lady Gaga–themed party in her apartment. Just before the cops came to break it up, she and I had gotten into a fight because I'd felt she'd spent the party ignoring me. She cried.

We spent my twenty-fifth birthday on the deck of the Second City cruise ship, and by my twenty-sixth birthday we were back on land and celebrating on the porch of the apartment we lived in. My new boyfriend, Caleb, was there because I'd told him about my birthday tradition. Trying to be a good partner, he'd brought the candles. Rebecca eyed him and went back inside as she murmured, "Do it without me." I cried.

On my twenty-seventh birthday, we'd just finished performing an all-female comedy showcase. She'd made me cry by giving me feedback on my set, and I made her cry for doing a full-page interview in the local paper without mentioning anything about our duo, and then we ate a bunch of Taco Bell and laughed as she lit twenty-seven candles for me.

On her twenty-eighth birthday, we sang karaoke all night until I confronted her about preferring to improvise with the men in our cast instead of me. She cried.

The final crack was a year before that LA trip, when Rebecca had decided to move out of our apartment because it had become ostensibly too much for us to live together. She had been bitingly mean for months building up to the move, making comments about Caleb or meaningfully withholding a reply when I expressed an insecurity. To a third party, these digs might not have even been noticeable, but as her best friend, I felt her small stabs as the devastating emotional blows she intended, the type of thing that's only possible with someone who knows you to your core. I sat across from her crying the night before she made her decision.

"Stop pushing me away," I begged. "Stop being cruel to me. I have a line, and if you cross it, I'm never coming back to you." She only nodded, likely understanding that she still had further to go before I'd ever really leave her.

A different night, in between birthdays, at the 4:00 a.m. dive bar across from the theater we loved so much, we both sat across from each other weeping on day four of a fight. Rebecca slammed her fist down on the table, uncharacteristically exploding. "You need too much from me!" she cried. I stood up almost simultaneously with her last word and ran out of the bar because I, too, was afraid of the depth of my need.

It was around midnight, and Rebecca offered up a smile from the doorway of our Los Angeles Airbnb. "Okay, I changed my mind. I want to do the pitch."

She had spoken to the more senior manager, and he had convinced her that we shouldn't bomb the meeting, at the very least, in case they ever wanted to work with us on another project.

Looking back, I don't know if she just valued herself enough to not compromise on the idea and add in a younger character, or if it truly was absurd to believe we could rethink an entire pitch that fast, and the mere idea of it overwhelmed her.

But I can guess the deeper reason for her resistance: this was the pitch meeting that was most likely to end in success, and Rebecca didn't want her career to be tied to me anymore. She was looking for a way out. She wanted to be a healthy person, with a life of her own, no longer in a codependent best friendship that also dictated her professional success. Had I myself been in a healthier place, maybe I would have known to walk away. I chose Rebecca over everything, especially myself. For so long, it was an easy decision. I didn't even like myself, and yet I loved her. But I had seen it so clearly that night in LA: she did not want what I wanted.

The next morning we got into the tiny Fiat in silence. I sat sideways in the back with my laptop perched on my knees. Rebecca and I rapidly tried to think of new things to say, and I typed up the changes the network had asked for. By the time we pulled up to the building, I knew we were doomed.

We sat in a fancy lobby sipping our miniature glass bottles of pristinely filtered Nordic water. I thought of what Rebecca had told me in one of our fights that week—that she felt like I used her in our pitches, making her dazzle the executives with stories from her life while I merely rode the coattails of her raucous anecdotes. From my perspective, I had been cueing Rebecca for a joke so she could be the one to shine. She was the cheerleader flung into the air, dazzling the crowd with a backflip, but I was the bitch below, poised for the catch, blowing out her knees in service of the big finish.

As we followed an assistant into a giant office to shake hands with these four heads of comedy, I thought about what Rebecca had said to me during these fights, and I decided that I was going to show her how wrong she was. I was going to filibuster our way out of this pitch entirely, and I was going to do it all by myself. The executives gestured for us to take a seat. Instead, I stayed standing, and told them every jaw-dropping story I had.

The cruise-ship masturbating story probably took up ten minutes, and I had fifty more minutes to go. I told them about a Second City sketch where I would enter by swinging in on a rope from backstage, and the time when Rebecca swiped her finger right up my ass just as I leaped off the stool for the jump. I started laughing out of shock and lost hold of the rope, tumbling onto the stage, unable to squeak out a single one of my lines.

I told them other wild tales, like when we found out a guy Rebecca was dating secretly had a girlfriend and we broke into his apartment to hide shrimp in the floorboards. I told them about the time I punched Rebecca's ex-hookup when he wouldn't stop harassing her outside a bar one night. As soon as my fist met his face, our friend Mallory ran over and began pummeling him, too, until he fled. Then she turned around and asked, "Who was that guy? Why were we punching him?"

I was grabbing things in the office as props, and the executives were howling with laughter, but every six minutes they tried to pivot me into talking about the pitch and I would keep going. I ignored Rebecca and my manager's small interjections, never even glancing over to clock their reactions. In those moments in their office, I was back to my solo comedy days, too busy treading water to understand that I was thriving, and if only I hadn't let my crushing self-doubt swallow me, I wouldn't have become the secretary to the Rebecca Show.

Finally, there were ten minutes left in the meeting. The president of the network adamantly stopped me mid-rant and said they *had* to hear the pitch, no more stories. I fell silent and opened my laptop, debating if I could ask for another water to spill it all over my keyboard. Rebecca and I half-heartedly read through the notes we'd written that morning until finally it was over. The execs said they'd "be in touch," and we boarded our plane back home.

A few days later, we were back in Chicago getting our nails done with our friend Jo when our managers called. Rebecca and I ran outside the salon and picked up. "Girls"—as they always called us—"they want to buy your TV show!"

I began screaming on the sidewalk. *"They want the show we pitched?!"*

"No," our manager said, "they don't want the pitch. They thought that was very bad, but they want all those crazy stories you told, they want to do a show about your dating antics, written by and starring you."

This was it: no more auditioning to be the cereal lady, no

more fitting into hackneyed stereotypes like the wifey one and the funny one. These characters were based on us, and we were going to bring our specific comedy to television. We were masters of our own destiny, besting an impossible system—and we'd done it together.

There's a picture of me and Rebecca taking this call. We're standing outside the nail salon, three feet apart, each of us leaned up against the window. In the photo Rebecca is looking over at me in sunglasses, her lips slack. I'm in front of her, but I've craned my neck around to look back at her, squinting, perhaps even glaring. Our friend Jo took it to remember the moment we were offered a TV show. She printed it out in black-and-white and gave it to us as a gift. It would be our last photo together.

A week after our official offer from the network, our managers called. I had gone away on a trip with Caleb to visit his parents and was hiding in their basement to take the call. This is where I was when they broke the news to me.

"Rebecca is just in a different place than you," they told me. "Her new acting agent thinks she's gonna hit it big this year and get on one of the splashier, better networks." Her new, supposedly elite acting agent said the network was notorious for underpaying young talent, and it wasn't worth it for Rebecca to take it because she was about to become a bigger star. Rebecca believed him.

I begged for the crumbs. Could I write it alone? Could other people star in it and I'd just go back to being the secretary? Anything for these seven years to not be a waste. But our togetherness had been our undoing. What we had sold was us, and what made us special was the friendship. That's what they wanted, not me by myself.

Rebecca called me afterward, but I don't remember what she said.

I refused to forgive her. I refused to let my soul be present in the same room as her. We had three months left together on the Mainstage, performing eight shows a week. Every night I showed up backstage, I vaguely smiled and said hello to Rebecca, performed with her for three hours, and then politely said good-night before heading home.

One evening backstage, she grabbed my shoulders and boomed, "I'd rather you be mad at me! Just hate me! Yell at me! Anything but this!"

I stared back at Rebecca with the weight of an anger that finally matched how much I loved her. With our TV show gone forever, I felt like she'd chosen the possibility of fame over our friendship. All those hours I had poured into the entity of us as a duo had been a lie. She had never wanted the same future that I did, but she let me toil away in it anyway, using my efforts to propel her own career forward. I shrugged in reply, attempting to wield her weapons as my own—apathy and withholding.

Every time she had ever flicked me away in the past, I always came back. I had always been the friend who fixed things, who did whatever it took to make sure we were okay. But I had finally reached my breaking point. She'd crossed my line, and I was done. I vowed to never return again unless she begged for it back. I wanted her to realize she needed me the way I needed her. I wanted her to do something grand—write daily letters pleading for forgiveness, or show me a terrible neck tattoo that said *Chelsea&Rebecca4Eva*—*something* to show she was very, very sorry. I wanted an offering the size of a TV show.

On my twenty-ninth birthday, the staff at Second City came out with a giant cake for me, gathering to sing "Happy Birthday" while they waited around for free pizza. As they brought the cake over I began to cry, because Rebecca stood across the room in the corner, glancing over occasionally, no longer welcome in my life. Every time I stole a look at her she was whispering with a male castmate she was close with, and she laughed away, seemingly unmoved by the distance between us. Just be-

fore midnight, I lit twenty-nine candles on the roof of the theater and blew them out, one by one, by myself.

The network that wanted our show picked up two others
shortly after ours—it was the year of "the Funny Girl!" Those
two shows both made it to pilot and then made it to air. One
of the shows was written by and starring a comedian, who is
now one of the most famous working actresses of our time. The
other show was written by a now-successful director who has
made her own female-driven comedies and films that are wildly
popular. They both have spoken out in interviews about how
working with that network was awful, underpaid, and both of
their shows were fucked over with only one season. But they
had made it on air. They secured their first credits, and they had
jump-started their careers.

Everyone in my life is sick of hearing me tell that part of the
story, pointing to my own professional successes as consolation.
But it wasn't only about the missed opportunity. I wanted Rebecca. I wanted the path with my best friend, I wanted our own
show on a shitty network, and then another show, and then on
to movies—together. My friends and family urged me not to
look back, but I wasn't, I was looking beside me, at the empty
space where Rebecca would be standing.

For years I thought I was the one in the right, that Rebecca
had fucked me over, that we should still be best friends making each other cry on our birthdays. Our friendship breakup
was the most devastating heartbreak I have ever felt in my life,
far worse than any romantic one. It didn't seem fair: a platonic
friendship doesn't even have to face the normal obstacles that
would inspire a breakup. We didn't have to mesh our finances
together, navigate sex, or deal with any weird in-laws. When a
friendship breaks up, there's nothing to blame, it's just because
someone in the purest form is deciding: no thank you, *not you*.

Romantic breakups have well-worn paths for us to travel

down: nights out at a bar, rom-coms to watch and renew your belief in love, a good cry on the shoulder of your best friend (the exact person you don't have in a platonic breakup). But in these kinds of heartbreaks, there's nothing to soothe your wounds—there's not even a good, iconic, cry-your-heart-out friendship-breakup song to eat ice cream to. There's barely any art about it, period. And there's no one-night stands with a stranger to put a Band-Aid over the hurt. Rebecca had been everything to me, and in many ways she felt like the entire reason my life had been going so well in Chicago.

And yet, as soon as she was gone, things actually got way better. Well, first it got way worse, but later it got better! When I no longer had the option to pour all my energy into Rebecca, a giant space opened up in my life—one that began to quickly fill up with incredible, healthier female friendships that I'd previously relegated to secondary roles. Without Rebecca to follow behind, I was forced to begin the journey to figure out who I was—what my taste was, how to be confident on my own, how to care for a relationship without destroying it with my need. If I had gone into my thirties lacking any of those skills, I would likely still be dating the dude who told me orgasms weren't a "tit-for-tat" kind of thing—or worse, the cruise-ship flautist.

We both became better, happier people without each other, but that doesn't ease even one millisecond of the pain I feel when I think about her. There will always be a piece of me missing, an empty spot with a place card for her. There are thoughts I have and things I see that would only make sense to tell Rebecca, but there's no Rebecca in my life anymore.

When I tell this story, I still feel a little betrayed. But I know if Rebecca told it, she would have a version where you're rooting for both of us to find our freedom, where you're left in awe of her courage to walk away from something that really was bad for each of us. A part of me is dying to ask her to write half of this essay. But I guess that was always my problem: I never wanted to do anything without her. And for the entirety of my twenties, I never had to. I had the most beautiful, beaming light of a human standing by my side for every milestone, every setback, every dickhead, every romance, every Taco Bell drive-through, every promotion, every broken heart, every battle for every impossible dream, I got to do it all with Rebecca.

I never spoke to another psychic again.

DICKS PICTORIA

The worst drag name in history

"Finding yourself" journeys are often advertised with whimsy, as if the antidote to your agony might fall somewhere between a pottery class and a last-minute trip to the gentrified parts of Italy. When I was twenty-nine years old I was in desperate need of such self discovery, so I tried all the known avenues: gratitude journals, vision boards, a drunkenly purchased Groupon to a questionable spa. Yet it was among a pile of makeup palettes and titty tape where I finally found my epiphany.

I was lying on top of the bed in a mesh gown that was completely see-through, except for a swirling pattern of sequins, and since I'd bought the gown for $40 there were not a lot of sequins. If you saw it, you'd be mad I'm even calling it a gown. I was also wearing knee-high boots with six-inch heels. Given the inebriated state I was in, it wasn't just a miracle I had made it home, it was a miracle I had made it five feet in front of me. The real showstopper, though, was a giant black wig embellished with bleach-filled rivers of DIY blond highlights, which had kindly strangled itself into a mess of knots in my sleep.

If my outfit sounds like something Cruella de Vil would wear to her divorce party, thank you, that's what I was going for. This was my attire for my grand finale in the drag queen show I'd been performing in for the past three months. Which is also why there was a dollar bill stuck dangerously close to my asshole.

With the strength of the night's bottom-shelf vodka still coursing through me, I rolled over in bed and peeled my eyes open to see my boyfriend Caleb gently sleeping next to me. Not only was he sound asleep, but he had the audacity to be wearing pajamas, and it looked like he'd even brushed his teeth. As I gazed upon his sweet, peaceful face, all I could think was that he was an absolute fuckhead and I needed to yell at him.

I knew I was mad at Caleb but couldn't remember why, so I voyaged through my drunken memories of the night before until I recovered the moment in question. There I was, towering over him at the bar, two inches taller than him in my stiletto boots. As I fished around in my thong for money to tip the bartender, I told Caleb that when I got married one day, I wanted to have a giant drag-themed wedding. In response, he mumbled something about how he didn't think he could ever marry me.

Now, the morning after, I softly caressed my boyfriend awake with a big smile, and we began the fight.

Caleb had seemed supportive when I told him I, a cisgender woman, was going to start performing as a high-fem female drag queen. He said he didn't mind that I had wig heads lining the top of the fridge, that every outlet was now taken up by a hot-glue gun, or that the apartment smelled perpetually like cheap hairspray. But the first time he saw me perform, he *coincidentally* got so drunk he puked all over the cab, and all over the body harness I was wearing, which is just a nice way to let you know that he puked on my mostly naked body. So I was prepared for him to tell me the world of drag queens and gender-bending was too weird for him. I assumed he would say, you have no time for me, you gave it all to contouring and learning to death-drop while looking like a third-string goblin porn star. I thought maybe he'd say that he felt uncomfortable around me in drag or that the two stuffed Easter bunnies I'd hot glued to my tits last weekend was where he drew the line.

Instead, he told me I was too sad. That my capacity for pain was too big and never-ending and that it didn't seem like it was going to be all that fun to spend forever with that kind of sadness. He was correct, but so what! What was I gonna do, live with my sadness alone? No! He should have to be our third!

"It's just, it's gotten so bad ever since…" he trailed. "I dunno, maybe you should call Rebecca, try and talk things out?"

This was also true. I had been deeply depressed since our friend breakup. Dozens of times around four in the afternoon, he had lifted up the sheet on our mattress with all his strength to create a sort of slide that would roll me off the bed—the only way I would reliably get out of it. The first time I hit the floor, I was so touched. I thought, now this must be love! Look at my sweet boyfriend making sure I live my life even though I don't want to.

In the four years we'd been together, we'd never had an actual fight. I thought it was because we were just that great of a match: me, out of my mind, and Caleb, seemingly not bothered by it. But it turns out he *was* bothered by it, he just kept every scrap of his feelings inside for years because he was a nice, polite boy from a land of cornfields in the Midwest, and instead of sharing those feelings with me when they arose, he had saved them all up for a special occasion, this day right here. This was the day we would break up, though I guess not technically. The fight was such a shock to the system after years of pleasant mediocrity, we just waded around in the wreckage for months afterward instead of ending it. But no matter how much we ignored the truth, the relationship was over after this fight.

The argument spanned the entire morning as we sat in bed. Hours later, just as the hangover was beginning to pave a highway through my skull, we found ourselves in the kitchen, fueling up for more fighting with peanut butter sandwiches, when he said to me, "What if we have a kid? Will you make the kid get you out of bed?" Which was an absurd thing to say, because obviously I'd continue making him do it. Then he quietly, oh so quietly, almost as if he knew that what he was about to say would tremor in my bones for the rest of my life, mumbled, "I think you'd be a bad mom."

Now, before you get too angry, you should know something else: I was also wearing an eye patch. And it wasn't a regular eye patch, either. I had performed with it on the night before, so as part of my costume it was covered with giant red metallic spikes that were sort of a constant threat to my other eye. Now, the eye patch didn't exactly justify what he said, but if you picture what I must have looked like at that moment, I think you might find yourself sympathizing with him. Worse still was that if I took the patch off, it would reveal what was underneath: a red, soupy infection. As gross as that sounds, my eye would look even grosser in comparison to the rest of my face, which held at least a pound of foundation, contour, and glitter. The kinder decision was to just keep the patch on.

Perhaps you're wondering why my eye was infected in the first place. You see, I was fairly new to drag, and I hadn't trained my eye muscles to carry the weight of five—yes, five—pairs of eyelashes stuck to each eyelid with weave glue. You were supposed to start small with, say, two sets of eyelashes on each lid and then work your way up, but true to form, I went straight for the extra credit and glued on as many as I could. After a few performances, my right eye couldn't hack it and got infected. The worst part of the whole experience was that I had to explain to the doctor how I, a cisgender woman, could be performing as a female drag queen.

As I sat on the examining table, pus oozing out of my eye, I told the doctor, "You know, anyone can perform any gender, because gender is made-up. For example, boys don't biologically like blue and girls don't genetically like pink—those are constructs we invented. And drag is an art form, like jazz, or oil painting, or making tiny figurines of your enemies' locks of hair. I participate in the art form of drag, and I perform the gender of female. Though, sometimes I'm like a female-slash-monster, and monsters, as we know, have no gender. Just kidding, they're all men. So sometimes I perform as a female but also male monster, who has no gender."

The doctor sighed and told me I had blepharitis.

So with the blepharitis still raging in my right eye, I only had my left eye to glare at my boyfriend while I was yelling at him. An apt comparison would be that his mom comment had stabbed me with a knife, and then I spent the next hour emotionally running him over with a semitruck. I don't know why I fought back so hard, hurling the cruelest things I could think of, but it's probably because I didn't want to accept the truth of what he'd said: it was scary how sad I could get. Over the past several months, I had been drowning myself in my own sadness; I just didn't realize I was also getting it on others.

But I wasn't going to take that Bad Mom thing! Not because Caleb was wrong about it—after all, that dollar bill was still stuck in my asshole. I wasn't going to accept his attack on my child-rearing capabilities because this was coming from a man who cut his own hair. And not by looking in the mirror, but by bending over so his head hung between his legs, then grabbing chunks with his fist and sawing through them with kitchen scissors. On busier days, he just shaved it all off completely. He was proud of his haircuts, a symbol of his frugality, ingenuity, and lack of vanity. But I wanted a cute boyfriend with cute fucking boyfriend hair. So instead of accepting that Caleb was a hippie sweetheart whose wallet was a rubber band wrapped around a couple of fives and a Quiznos punch card, I watched a bunch of how-to videos on YouTube and then forced those haircuts upon him. Every month for those four years we dated, I would drink a bunch of whiskey (the key to a steady hand) and style it into whatever Ryan Gosling was rocking that month.

Throughout the morning, I continued to yell-cry at him. While my sadness had always gone up and down throughout my life, I was definitely experiencing an upswell, because only six months had passed since Rebecca and I stopped being friends. I was still heartbroken.

After our relationship and TV-show deal simultaneously went away, I had called up my managers and told them that I wanted to move out of Chicago and go straight to LA as soon as possible to take the next step in my comedy career. It was silent on the other end, but I could hear the faces they were making— down-turned lips, scrunched noses, the expression you make when you're the high-school bully and the new girl walks in with a rolling backpack. My managers candidly told me that I couldn't move to LA yet: it was a tough city to start in, and I didn't have any momentum, no work they could pass around, no one excited about me, and didn't I remember that one executive who had said I "came off like a try-hard"?

Here I was, the one in the duo who did most of the grunt work, all the writing, the hustling, the raising of money, applying for shows, finding directors, rewriting all our scripts, producing everything, and yes, that try-hard comment from that executive was also correct… I was absolutely fantastic at trying, and now I had nothing to show for it but those failed attempts. I had spent every iota of my time and energy in the Chicago comedy gauntlet pouring everything I had into Rebecca, into us as a package deal. It was the kind of reckless decision-making that's only possible when the idea of you ever *not* being together is an impossibility.

Every day, I just kept thinking about how before I was even thirty years old I could've had my own TV show that I'd starred in, created, and written with my best friend in the world. And now I had nothing, not even her. After our breakup, I wondered how I would ever survive without her powerful, confident, and momentous force in my life.

I found her replacement in drag queens.

In the months following our friend breakup, I would spend all day in bed watching *RuPaul's Drag Race*, worshipping at the altar of those who'd found a way forward in life by harnessing the power of a craft glitter set and a Mariah Carey key change. Each queen's story of their tragedies and setbacks—how they'd found a way to survive them with a glamorous grace, despite the world telling them they didn't deserve to—moved me to my emotional edge. Bearing witness to their art was my day job, then at seven o'clock I would race to The Second City theater and perform a three-hour comedy set. After that I would head to Boystown and watch a live drag show, take the bus home drunk, go to bed drunk, and start over again the next day at four when Caleb rolled me off the bed.

During season four of *Drag Race* I watched Sharon Needles take the crown—a grunge, trashy vampire queen who'd flipped the drag scene on its head with her garbage aesthetic and goth inclinations. I remember watching her strut down the runway, subtly crushing a red capsule between her teeth so that blood dripped down her bedazzled lips as she walked forward and twirled, posing with the sultriness of a Victoria's Secret Angel. Sharon Needles was a revelation.

Then came season five, and Alaska Thunderfuck 5000 entered the scene. Loud, fabulous, and slightly nervous, she was Sharon's romantic partner, and they had performed together back in Pennsylvania. Alaska was worried that everyone would expect her to be like Sharon, and that there'd be no way to live up to the other half of the duo.

Oh no. I sat up from my depression bed, clutching my chest. I knew that woman. My heart palpitated each time Alaska came on-screen, empathizing with her tortured state as the less shiny half. The shadow of Sharon loomed large over the season, and in the end Alaska couldn't overcome it, crumbling in key moments of the competition. She didn't win her season. The one in the shadow never does.

One night, deep into my drag-queen obsession, I was at Berlin nightclub watching Monét X Change snatch a dollar bill from the crowd and swallow it whole. I was cheering with everyone else when I caught sight of someone in the crowd who resembled a makeup artist named Kat I'd worked with on a web series from a few years prior. The woman in the crowd *looked* like Kat—if you'd turned up the volume on her by a thousand degrees.

I inched closer and closer until we were next to each other, holding up our dollars, standing shoulder to shoulder. "Kat?" I screamed.

Kat's metallic eyeshadow glimmered in the darkness as she turned and recognized me, standing an entire foot taller. She looked down at me, exclaiming, "Hi, honey!"

A few days later we sat across from each other at a downtown hotel. I'd made a reservation for proper high tea, hoping that a cake stand filled with macarons and cucumber sandwiches could hide the fact that I hadn't left my apartment to meet a friend in months. I breezily told Kat I wasn't wearing any makeup, hoping she'd forgive how my face looked. I watched her scrutinize my skin for just a moment, understanding that actually, yes, I was wearing makeup, I was just wearing it badly. Kat chose not to say anything and asked me how I was doing. As soon as our teacups hit the tray, I began pouring my heart out. I cried over tea, cried *into* my tea. She waited a moment before speaking. Often the best advice friends can muster when you're going through a hard time is something trite like *It'll pass*, but that day, Kat offered something much more seismic.

"You should perform drag," she said. "Drag has the power to heal your soul."

Over a pot of lukewarm vanilla rooibos, Kat decided to teach me everything she knew, and as a makeup artist and a drag queen herself, it was quite the gift. She told me about an amateur drag competition that was open to any gender identity, where anyone could sign up, and each week after an audience vote, the queens were eliminated until only one remained. I'd seen both seasons of RuPaul's show, *Drag U,* where RuPaul made depressed cis-gender women like myself into happy female drag queens and it changed their lives. That was what I needed—for everything in my life to change.

I was still performing weekly at The Second City, and we only had Monday nights off. It was a grueling schedule, but one that we had all yearned for, despite not getting holidays, barely any sick days, and even if the president of the United States had invited you over to pet his PR dog, they wouldn't let you out of a show. It was brutal, but should you have a problem with it, they reminded you of the long line of thousands at the door who would gladly take your place. Mondays were the one night a week for you to restore yourself, spend time with friends, or in my case, have a date night with Caleb, who worked a nine-to-five. I came home and told him that on my one night off, I would now be performing in an amateur drag show and using any free time to rehearse or glue rhinestones to the ass-crack of a bodysuit. Perhaps that was the day we actually broke up.

Choosing your drag name is of ultimate importance. It's the first step in creating the woman/creature/monster you actually want to be. I didn't want to pick a silly name or something with a pun—no, I wanted to be *artistic!* So naturally, I proceeded to choose the worst drag name in history: Dicks Pictoria.

Here's how you test if you have a good drag name: announce yourself into the room like an MC, and ask: Is that name memorable? Does it inspire the crowd to gasp in awe or glee? Can you hear it clearly?

The second thing you should do is tell your drag name to a friend and see if it garners a dazzling reaction. Because forever going forward, people will ask you your drag name, and you will have to tell them, and watch their face fall as you say "Dicks Pictoria."

Dicks Pictoria was a take on Dick Pic. Dick pics have a brazen audacity to them. They scream, I am here! In all my sweaty glory! And I'm enjoying myself! I wanted *that* in my name. I also wanted to be called Dicks. It felt fun. This was pre–pink pussy hats at the Oh God, He's The President march, but it had the same energy.

A shame to think I could have been Squirt Vonnegut or Marilyn MonRoe v. Wade, the names I would adopt were I to do drag again, but alas, my fate was sealed. Dicks Pictoria was born. I put together performances where I would duet with a puppet who sang the male parts, and then I mimed the puppet going down on me when I lip-synched my high note, wildly shifting my jaw side to side in soprano ecstasy. I was mixing tracks in GarageBand, walking around my apartment to find out how to balance in six-inch heels, and consistently failing to even come close to accomplishing the splits. With Kat's guidance, I put every ounce of my energy into my debut performance.

By the time the first night of the show arrived, I had rehearsed my elaborate piece no fewer than fifty times. It took five hours to get into my makeup, and I wore three blond wigs I'd sewn together to make one giant colosseum of a hairdo. Kat grabbed my shoulders before we walked into the club and said, "The competition doesn't start when you go onstage, the competition starts the moment you walk in the door."

Then she swung open the entrance of the bar for me to strut inside. The nerves coursing through my body made everything feel awkward and heavy—the layers of makeup, the pain of the shoes, the heat packed into my costume. I stood in the corner

with the other contestants, watching each one go up and thinking *Why the hell did I sign up to do this?*

When my name was called, I walked up the tiny, slippery
stairs onto the 4' x 5' platform they called a stage and launched
into my piece. I'd thankfully rehearsed it so much that I still
knew the moves from muscle memory underneath my fear, but
when the crowd erupted, I gave in to the performance and began
to feel the emotions of the music. Underneath all my drag, I
was hidden, so with Dicks running cover, I began to ease into
a wilder side of me that I'd never met before. It was like a wolf
learning to howl at the moon, only I was snatching dollar bills,
biting off the rock-candy dick I'd sewn onto the puppet and
spitting it into the crowd for everyone to enjoy.

Layers of my costume went flying off as my piece reached its
crescendo. After years of searching through the Target swimsuit
rack for tankinis with an extra set of matching shorts to cover
up on bottom, I was now in front of a hundred strangers wearing nothing but a thong, shaking an ass I had spent my life hating. Of course, it helped that I had two pairs of nude tights on
underneath and that my ass wasn't the main event. The singing
puppet I was currently pretending to fuck was.

We've had a lifetime of culture telling us there's nothing
more important for a woman than being beautiful, but should
you dare to care about the tools that make you beautiful—hair,
makeup, fashion, nails—then you're a dumb ho who expires at
twenty-nine years old, doomed to a lifetime of creating homemade skincare in her kitchen. I'd learned the rules of femininity
from straight white men, as most of us did, since they've been
running society for quite a while now. How you dressed, moved,
and behaved had to fit into the box they'd created, or you were
not a "good" woman who deserved love or respect. Gender was
taught to us as binary, hardwired with rules for girls and rules
for boys, and if you broke them, there were consequences. Hundreds and thousands of brave LGBTQIA+ humans marched in

the streets and suffered through lifetimes of violence and persecution to fight for the rights of queer people, now making it possible for those lucky enough—people of all identities, expressions, and sexualities—to crouch inside a nightclub and witness the truth that gender is a lie, the box is a lie, patriarchal culture is a lie, and none of us have to play by their fake rules.

When I stepped offstage, I immediately began to feel the sharp pains hit my feet again. Clearly I still needed more training in the heels. Kat ran up to me and gripped me in a hug as she whispered into my ear, "You were glorious."

"I need to sit down!" I panted, out of breath. "I have to take all this off."

Kat shook her head no and leaned in again. "Do not show them your weakness, never show them that you hurt, and never ever take your drag off in public."

So I stayed standing in my pleather sweat chamber, and at the end of the night, all fifteen queens scrunched together onstage. They held an audience vote by applause, then announced who had made it to the next round.

My name was called. I was ecstatic. I would get to perform again! In the weeks that followed, I set out to top my debut performance. By performing the character of Dicks, I wanted to take all the things about femininity that I'd learned were weak and wield them onstage as a weapon. I wanted to be so high fem that it was terrifying. I had found my internal campaign slogan: *You will fear my tits!*

Through the eyes of drag queens, I finally saw something in femininity that I'd never recognized there before: power.

The irony of my time in drag is that even though I was up there solo, I was still using it to conceal myself behind another woman, only this time the woman wasn't Rebecca, it was Dicks Pictoria. But over time, something special happened during these performances. Every night when I peeled off the lashes and fished out the glitter that had somehow crawled inside my nipple, I took a little bit of Dicks back with me into my real life. Slowly I started to become the type of woman I had always wanted to be—someone brazen, someone fearless, someone who had shards of glass protruding from the vag area of her leotard, "as a bit."

Pouring all my energy into my drag meant that I was finally focusing on myself, and the results began to show up in my comedy career. Our newest Second City show opened, my third revue and the only one I did without Rebecca. Reviewers wrote articles calling me things like "the Michael Jordan of the cast" and "a more fearless Tina Fey who could outdrink you and kick your ass." I started getting dozens of TV and film callbacks, and casting directors in town told me I had finally found my voice. I booked small shows and commercials, and I was even flown to Los Angeles by a major TV network for the final audition to be one of the leads in their pilot. I knew I wouldn't get it the moment I walked in the room and saw that I was taller than the male lead, but I also didn't have to travel around LA hunched in the back of a Fiat, so overall it was still a win.

The final night of the drag competition arrived. The audience had voted at the end of every show, narrowing it down each week, until there were only five queens left, and I was one of them. It felt like making it to the top five of Miss America, hundreds of millions of eyes on you, hundreds of thousands of dollars on the line, a whole world built up for this one moment when you walked onstage. In reality, the club held maybe a hundred, it smelled like damp pussy, it cost $5 to get in the door, and it was a Monday night.

My first number was *Top Gun*-themed, and I performed as drag king Jessica Simpson in her denim years. I had always loved the movie *Top Gun*, especially its theme song, so I began collecting aviators at thrift stores to see if I could pull off an homage. I wore a blond mullet and a crown of aviator glasses that was ten pairs high. I brought a blow-up guitar onstage and created a piece about a man who was going through a divorce and refused to feel anything. Then the *Top Gun* riff would come on and I'd faux-play the guitar with different parts of my body and dance on top of it. It was serving: Stepdad Energy.

For my second piece I took a risk and decided to sing live. I had written a ballad titled "I Cry Every Day," and each lyric was a joke set up for something that I cried about. Look at her, a woman on the rise, capitalizing on that depression!

I stepped onstage in my see-through sequined gown, thorny eye patch, and that very ugly wig that I had made by wrapping fake synthetic hair around curlers. I looked out into the crowd, and with the mic in my hand, I realized I could feel again. In the middle of mourning the best friend I'd lost, I had made a new one: Kat. In the crowd, dressed in full drag herself, I saw her clutching her hands together, sending all her energy toward me, generously lifting me up and commanding me to find a part of myself that could thrive. I did not care about winning or losing that night because I'd finally glimpsed the light at the end of my depression tunnel.

The track came on, and I began to sing. "I cry every day..."

After season five of *Drag Race*, Sharon Needles's success climbed while Alaska Thunderfuck 5000 began performing on the road. Sharon launched her first single, and soon after she and Alaska broke up and went their separate ways.

Two years of *RuPaul's Drag Race* passed by. Queens were crowned, and others were cut. And then...Alaska burst back into the spotlight. She debuted her album, *Anus*, and club goers all over America devoured her songs—every track was danceable, laughable, and utterly insane. Now it was she who was the revelation. Who was *this* queen? Where had she been? How could anyone have ever overlooked her before? Alaska sauntered on-screen for her music video, uttering her catchphrase *Hiyeeeeeeee,* and a new woman was before us, a woman no longer living in the shadow of the shinier half. Later, when *RuPaul's Drag Race* held its season two of *All Stars*, they brought Alaska back and she snatched the crown with ease, all of us knowing that it should have been hers the first time around, because it was never Sharon who she had to overcome. It was herself.

Hours after the show had ended and the club closed, I floated home in my sequined gown, filled with a 5:00 a.m. burrito, clutching my first-place prize, a thrift-store trophy for youth soccer with the head chipped off.

Two weeks later I was hired to write on Jon Stewart's new show in New York City, my very first break into television. I had to say goodbye to the small drag community I'd been lucky enough to be a part of. I will forever be indebted to the queens whose kindness, courage, and talent brought me back to life, whose generous hearts let me stand beside them, even for just the briefest of moments.

I stopped performing as Dicks Pictoria when I left Chicago. But every so often a morning arises when I just can't seem to get out of bed, and Dicks makes her entrance. She's always at the ready, waiting for her moment to come out tits-ablazing, eye patch oozing, chomping on a puppet's dick, as she picks up the bedsheet, rolls me onto the floor, and shouts, "You'll be a great fucking mom if you ever fucking want to be, okay?!"

BRITNEY BRODY

My sixth-grade savior in the Mormon capital of the world

The sounds of intrusion came in the middle of the night. We were so far out in the wilderness that our only source of light came from the moon, and a lone *Toy Story* flashlight that had just run out of battery. The other sixth-grade girls and I had been asleep for hours when someone outside began shaking our tent, struggling to unzip the front opening. We popped our heads up off the gymnastics mats we were using as mattresses, clutching our sleeping bags to our chests...and in the pitch-black darkness, we began calling for help.

It was an adult—one of the girls' mothers, peeking in through the zipper. She told us to put on our sneakers as fast as we could because we had an important mission ahead of us that would determine our relationship with God. We scrambled to get our shoes on, pushing aside pillows and duffel bags as the clock began ticking down for our important assignment.

Outside of the tent, I followed dozens of other girls in the moonlight scurrying to the center of camp, where the counselors instructed us to form a line.

Then, one by one, they blindfolded us.

At this moment, I began to wonder if attending Mormon

camp was a bad idea. Especially since...I wasn't even a real Mormon. I was pretending to be so I could fit in at my Mormon-
majority middle school. I lifted my blindfold to glance at my
best friend, Britney Brody, who didn't seem at all startled by
any of this. She piously stood in line, ready for the challenge, so
I piously followed her lead, as I always did back then—which,
on some level, is exactly how I got myself into this situation to
begin with.

At the behest of my stepdad, Bubba, my family had moved
to Utah when I was five years old and settled in a city called
St. George, which at the time was considered the Mormon capital of the world. The neighborhood we moved into was filled
with fundamentalist Mormons, the type whose views were so
devout they were just a notch or two away from the church's
former practices of polygamy. I say *just a notch or two* because we
shared a Walmart with a thriving polygamist community who
also lived nearby.

I was one of only a few non-Mormon students in my grade.
When I first started school, I instantly noticed how everyone
treated the one other non-Mormon girl in my class, sweetly telling her she couldn't come to their birthday parties because the
devil lived inside her. And so, I made a quick decision to accept Joseph Smith and the Church of Latter-Day Saints into my
heart and otherwise just lie low—which then escalated into me
faithfully attending Mormon church every Sunday with Britney Brody and her eight siblings.

Britney remains the most symmetrically beautiful human
I've ever seen in my life. She was like a living American Girl
doll, crafted to perfection by Jesus himself in a build-a-Mormon
workshop. Her hair was butter blond, her eyes a bright blue.
She aced the '90s femininity rubric that we all worshipped at
the time, and I was in complete awe of her. Britney was outgoing, but never got angry or took up too much space; she didn't

make jokes herself but was always quick to offer a laugh when others did. She spent her time leading prayer in the mornings, practicing her piano lessons in her giant stucco house, and balling out on our middle-school basketball courts on the weekends, making shot after shot after shot.

My life looked nothing like Britney's, but it was her kindness and lack of judgment that allowed us to form such a formidable friendship despite our glaringly different upbringings. Here's an example: one time my mom gave me $20 to buy anything I wanted from the mall. This was a huge event for me, because it meant I was finally going to get something name-brand from the store that all of America's youth revered at the moment: Calvin Klein. I bought the shirt with the biggest CK logo splashed across the front so that everyone would know I was cool and rich. I loved that shirt. I treasured that shirt. I would have made love to that shirt if I had any idea what that meant, because in our alternative Mormon reality, none of my friends even spoke about holding hands, let alone kissing. Being the genius that I was, I made a plan to wear my CK shirt on Mondays, Wednesdays, and Fridays, and on the other two days I would wear my *Far Side* T-shirt that said *Midvale School for the Gifted*. That way, the Tuesday and Thursday shirt would wipe the slate clean, and no one would know that my Monday/Wednesday/Friday CK shirt was the exact same one. Britney never said a thing to me about it for the full year that I wore it, three days a week. THAT was how nice Britney Brody was.

I began to spend every ounce of free time I had with Britney's family, which, in addition to scoring me some extra time away from the escalating tension at home with my stepdad Bubba, also gave me the social cred I desperately needed at school. As I copied the Brodys' values, style, and ever-wholesome Mormon ways, I found myself successfully cosplaying as a chosen child of the Church of Latter-Day Saints. Next to a respected member of the congregation like Britney, I even became popular. I wore

knee length conservative skirts and got invited to all the hot-
test scrapbooking parties, ice cream socials, and the graveyard
baptisms—which is where the youth group would visit grave-
yards and baptize themselves over the headstones of Catholics,
Jews, and atheists, believing this freed up their tormented souls
in purgatory so that they could become Mormon in the after-
life and float on up to Mormon heaven.

By the time I was twelve, my entire social life revolved around
Mormonism, and unfortunately, so did my public school education. I barely knew geography, US presidents, or anything
about the Cold War, but I could tell you the exact words said
by Brigham Young—the man who laid the foundation for the
entire modern Mormon community and their lifestyle—when
he reached the Promised Land in 1847: "*This* is the place!" That
was right before he discovered that God's chosen water source for
them was filled with salt, hence the aptly named Salt Lake City.

Britney's family functioned like a joyful troop of blondies who
all pitched in for the greater Brigham Young good. They woke
up every morning with a pep in their step, diligently making
their beds and attending to chores. I would be assigned whatever
task Britney had for the day, hustling around, cooking a giant
pot of oatmeal while the other siblings chopped up banana slices
and toasted bread for breakfast. Not thin little sheets of grocery-
store bread, mind you: I'm talking dense, homemade slabs of
bread so thick, it was as if the power of God's love itself had
doubled the size of the wheat molecules in their flour. Eventually I even attended their giant family reunions. To the outside
world, I imagine seeing this family and me was like watching a
gaggle of ducks go hopping across the road in a perfect dainty
row, followed by a little rat traipsing along, blissfully bobbing
its head behind them.

Still, the Brodys always welcomed me with open arms. The
summer after sixth grade was when they brought me along to
their summer camp, which for the most part was just a more

fun, outdoorsy, extended church sermon. Until this particular occasion, of course, when they had woken us up in the middle of the night and blindfolded us for our special mission.

The big problem here was that once the blindfold was on, I could no longer copy Britney as I usually did during these activities, and I lost my confidence in what was coming next. They told us to begin hiking and handed us a rope, warning us that no matter what, we should never *ever* let go of it.

Then, one by one, they sent us up the hill.

I had learned a lot from attending church with the Brodys during their quest to convert me, but I'd also spaced out for much of it, because LDS services are three hours long. However, there is one Mormon story I should've remembered, because it was told to the kids so often that we even used to watch an LDS cartoon version of it at Britney's house when we had sleepovers: the tale of the Iron Rod.

The story goes like this: a Mormon prophet once had a dream where his family had to climb a treacherous hill, but if they just held on to a literal rod made of iron, they would make it safely to "The Tree of Life." As a kid, I was taught that the Iron Rod was symbolic for not straying from the path and avoiding the worst imaginable Mormon sins like gambling, cheating... drinking caffeinated soda. I knew living a Godly life was very important to Mormons, who believe that when you die, God will decide if you are worthy of the highest level of Mormon heaven, or if you suck and belong in the two lower heavens, or worse..."outer darkness."

Somehow, at camp, I had not connected the rope challenge to the story of the Iron Rod. So when another voice offered me a different rope and said there were doughnuts at the end of it, I immediately took it and scampered off the path toward my cinnamon-sprinkled future. The doughnut rope brought me to the top of the hill, where a very stern older man sitting on a rock removed my blindfold and said, "Welcome to hell."

I had failed the simulation. I took my place on a black tarp next to two other crying girls, while this balding man in khakis began a speech that was clearly meant to scare us into choosing the righteous path. He did his best to scorch the fear of Satan into our hearts and minds, but nothing he said really affected me, because I already had plenty of experience with a balding man who acted like the devil: my stepdad, Bubba.

The whole reason we moved to Utah in the first place was because Bubba worked as a river-rafting guide and he needed to be closer to his office, i.e. the Grand Canyon, so after he married my mom, he moved her, my brother, and me to St. George to start our new lives.

Here's what I knew about the story of how Bubba and my mom got together. Before Bubba entered the picture, my mom and dad ran their own construction business. She was helping oversee the construction of a house in Nevada, and Bubba was one of the men on the building crew. She and Bubba fell into a fast and serious romance. He proffered some big juicy promises about their future together, how he was going to whisk all of us away into a life of fun—whipped cream fights, vacations, hot dogs for dinner—while generously paying for our groceries and showering us with gifts and little getaways, as the charismatic baller who's gonna save you does.

My mom had to get out of her first violent marriage, and after the divorce she didn't have any family support to fall back on or even a checking account in her own name. In that moment she needed a hero, and there was Bubba wearing his Oakley knockoffs and holding out a diamond ring.

They eloped. A couple years later I would learn that Bubba spent the night of their wedding in a drunken stupor, pacing and punching walls, angrily wondering aloud to my mom how he was supposed to take care of this whole-ass family of hers. My mom knew hours after she said *I do* that she'd made a mistake. They would stay together for nine more years.

Shortly after arriving in Utah, Jesse was born, which meant another financial burden for Bubba. However, now that the latest kid was his own, he stopped complaining and began problem-solving! He told my mom that her figure "still looked great" after giving birth, and since Las Vegas wasn't too far away, she should become a stripper and really bring home the bacon to solve their financial woes. My mom refused, but every week he raised the suggestion more and more aggressively. So eventually, she left newborn Jesse at home and found a job selling vitamins in Salt Lake City, regretfully taking off for days at a time—and leaving us at home with our delightful new father figure.

On hot summer days, Bubba would take my brothers and me around in his 1950s classic Ford, all of us sweating profusely because old-ass ugly cars without AC seemed to be the obligatory free toy with every stepdad Happy Meal. I remember one time I reached for a bottle of water tucked under the car seat, only to discover it was filled with vodka.

That was the first hint as to why Bubba was beginning to lose his temper more and more. He stopped allowing my mom to leave the house for more than twenty minutes at a time if she wasn't at work. He began pitting my siblings and me against each other, always favoring Jesse. He focused on breaking Lucas, provoking him, embarrassing him in front of his friends, constantly threatening to send him away to go and live with our dad instead, which eventually happened.

But as much as I hated Bubba, I also kind of worshipped him. He had been positioned to us kids as the husband who saved us from an only slightly worse first husband, my and Lucas's dad. Bubba would remind us constantly how he had given us a better life, how much he loved our mom, and that if anything bad ever happened, he'd give us the shirt off his back. The next moment he'd be screaming about how greedy and ungrateful we were, throwing dishes at our heads as we cowered in my brothers' room on the lower bunk bed, wondering what move he would pull next. Bubba went back and forth as the hero and the villain of our household, a greedy little bitch, hogging both lead roles. And whenever things got really bad, he'd whip out his gregarious, river-rafting, party-boy side—the Bubba that had first won my mother over.

There was one especially popular stunt he'd perform for me and my brothers. Every summer, all the next-door neighbors' kids would gather around us as we'd watch Bubba grab the metal ladder from the garage and drag it through our dirt yard. After reaching the side of the house, he'd carefully extend the rungs as far as they could go, step on up, and climb to the roof.

Bubba would look so confident up there, balancing one leg on either side of the ridge, cigarette in one hand, a carton of eggs in the other. The vision of him up above was akin to a disheveled Jimmy Buffet impersonator who was about to attempt a coke-fueled nosedive into the crowd.

After building up to the moment with a rousing speech, Bubba carefully chose a single egg, whacked it against the roof, and dropped its contents from twenty feet above. All of us standing below screamed and cheered: if you caught the egg in your mouth you would get $10; if you swallowed it you would get twenty. It was the financial event of the summer for everyone under twelve.

Even though Britney was my best friend, I never invited her to get in on this egg fortune because I didn't want to risk her witnessing my home life. I didn't even tell her about the things I was experiencing at home. I never gave Britney the opportunity to be there for me. I lived in two separate worlds: in one I was on student council with Britney, sharing her glitter rollerball lotion while we practiced our moves for the middle-school dance; in my other world I spent the weekends doing stepdad-induced yard work and then sat in the dark living room with my brothers to play Bubba's "save money on the electricity bill" game. When Mr. Brody dropped me off after youth group one afternoon, I remember Bubba was out on the porch in my mom's pink sweatpants and a stained collared shirt, barefoot, smoking Marlboros. I probably tried to exit their Suburban while it was still moving, hoping they'd drive away before they could commit the visual to memory.

I was sure Bubba's cigarette habit would be my social downfall at school, not to mention the demise of my mother, whom he had gotten to start smoking, too. My Mormon friends told me that if you smoked cigarettes you would burn in a fiery hell for eternity—presumably lit by that smooth menthol—and I was horrified at the thought of my beautiful mom being sent to the Smoky Gates. I'd recently seen an antismoking campaign in a magazine that said every cigarette takes five minutes off your life. So I came up with a plan to begin stealing their packs of cigarettes. I took some Post-it notes and wrote: *Every cigarette takes off five minutes of your life. This is the five minutes when...* and I'd roll each cigarette up in one of those stickies so you'd really have to think of what you were giving up if you wanted to light that thing.

This is the five minutes when Jesse graduates high school.
This is the five minutes when your first grandkid is born.
This is the five minutes when Lucas gets married.

The two of them continued to smoke, but even so, I never stopped trying to save my mom from those cigarettes. If I had picked up anything from the Brodys, it was their relentless dedication to delivering an innocent soul from doom.

In addition to being a lifelong smoker, Bubba was also an alcoholic, a fact that I did not fully understand for most of my young life—I just thought my stepdad fucking loved orange juice on ice. Even when I learned the term *alcoholic* and realized that vodka was sponsoring our family nightmares, I still didn't really understand what it all meant. Alcoholic parents are a lot like Mary Poppins if, after a particularly off day every now and then, Mary Poppins would beat your ass with that umbrella. But! Just like Mary Poppins, Bubba was also full of spontaneity. When he came home and did things like moving the tattered living room furniture outside to become our new patio furniture, it felt fun. Then he'd surprise the family with brand-new living room furniture—only it was a patio lounge set, complete with two reclining chairs and a table with an umbrella that we kept open. The inside furniture was outside, and the outside furniture was inside, and that tracked emotionally with what it felt like to live with Bubba.

Financial stress was our family's constant chaotic soundtrack, and it grew louder and louder each year. When Bubba's river-rafting wasn't bringing in enough money, he got a job working from home as a network marketer at the vitamin company my mom traveled for in Salt Lake. Bubba was great at this, because the primary job of a network marketer was to sit on the couch all day and sell people on your bullshit—in this case, that customers should subsequently also sell vitamins alongside Bubba, so then he'd get a tiny percentage of *their* commission. If this sounds confusing to you, just picture a sales structure that looks like a nice big pyramid with Bubba perched at the top of it in a half-broken lawn chair.

Shortly after he started this job, we entered our rich years. Now our family ate out at Olive Garden on the reg, took vacations to Mexico, moved into a bigger house, and saw movies in the theaters, purchasing our popcorn fresh from the counter instead of smuggling it from home in our backpacks. Bubba even bought us a Gateway desktop computer, but after discovering Lucas was using it to play video games at night, he chucked it into our backyard.

When Bubba got a taste of success, he drunkenly started to believe he was a hotshot wealthy businessman. He booked dinners for prospective vitamin sellers at the single sushi restaurant in landlocked St. George. He began buying expensive ads in newspapers in London, hoping to rope the Brits into selling vitamins, too! As he was wheelin' and dealin', the credit card bills started growing higher and higher, and Bubba just kept promising it would all pay off soon. But *soon* had come, *soon* was now! We were deeply in debt. None of the advertisements or sashimi had paid off because Bubba was not a wealthy business-man, Bubba was a man with one ball hanging out of his shorts when he crossed his legs.

As the years went on I watched the debt rack up and the ar-guments grow worse at home. I internalized my parents' stress as my own, and the refuge of Britney's house became even more precious to me. All our problems faded away the moment I stepped inside their cream-colored stucco McMansion where paintings of Jesus looked like Brett Favre and a make-your-own ice cream sundae bar was the rager of our Saturday nights. By keeping Britney perfect, I could keep the fantasy intact that ev-erything was okay, as long as I was with her.

That fantasy was obliterated the summer before eighth grade.

There had been a coup in my family dynamic when my mom's half sister, Sharon, and my cousins came to live with us. Aunt Sharon had just gotten divorced, and she needed to save some money to get back on her feet, so for a time we had two full families living in one house. My aunt Sharon is charismatic and wickedly clever, and her presence added a new weight to my mom's opinions since the women outnumbered my stepdad, and the act of having an adult witness around began to deter some of Bubba's rage.

By the time my aunt moved to her own place nearby, my mom had gained some of her own power back. It was around this time when she convinced Bubba that, if he would be so kind as to let her take me on a trip, Aunt Sharon could watch Jesse at her house and Bubba could have a nice, fun weekend to himself, family-free. After all, Lucas had gone to live with our dad, so this could be some nice alone time for him, just like he was always complaining about, right?

For the trip in question, we wanted to visit my godmother Grace and see her son graduate. My mom and Grace were dead set on showing me that I could achieve great things in life, and they wanted her son's graduation ceremony to give me a glimpse of my possible future. Probably because at that point, the only options I'd been exposed to were to either walk the Mormon path of Britney Brody's family and get a good husband and ten kids, or not become Mormon and get a bad husband instead, like we heathens usually did. My mom and Grace wanted me to see a third option: college.

With my aunt staying back to watch Jesse, we set off on our first trip alone together, leaving the state of Utah—and Bubba—far behind.

My mom and I met Grace at a motel and lived it up the first night, lounging in the hot tub and eating out for dinner. Then the next morning, we all began to prepare for the graduation ceremony. My godmother had bought me a khaki linen dress and matching linen hat for the occasion, and I twirled in the mirror, feeling like an orphan who was just adopted by a family who "summers." That's when the motel phone rang.

My mom answered, and immediately sat down on the bed as Aunt Sharon's voice broke through, panicked.

Apparently, hundreds of miles away in Utah, Bubba had decided that today was the day he was getting on the roof. He grabbed the metal ladder from the garage and dragged it through our dirt yard with one hand. He tipped the ladder over, letting it land against the side of the house, and then, he began to climb up.

Only there were no kids below. There was no egg carton. In his hand was a nail gun.

Bubba had just told my aunt on the phone that she'd be taking care of Jesse *forever*, and not to bring him by the house. She said he sounded drunk and she didn't know what to do. My mom began crying—what did he mean? Was he joking? What could he possibly be thinking?

From the corner in our hotel room, I quietly murmured that I might have an idea.

A year prior, when Bubba's business investments had begun failing, he sat me down on our inside/outside couch on the patio. He told me that he was an honorable man and he had come up with a great idea "to save the family" because that's how much he loved us. His plan was to climb onto the roof with his tools, very casually, to do some construction work.

Then, on his way down, he was going to fall off the ladder and die, and once he was dead, his life insurance policy would give the family a giant windfall and we'd become rich again, fondly thinking of Bubba and his sacrifice. My job was to witness his suicide and tell everyone it was an accident—that I saw it happen and that he *definitely slipped*.

Every time Bubba had told me about this plan, he swore me to secrecy, because I guess he felt this honorable act would be better appreciated if it was a surprise! He emphasized how noble it was, how he would be a hero "like a kamikaze," and he told me the grand history of the sacrifice the pilots made on their suicide mission, martyrs for their country, just like Bubba. *Listen*, this is why public education is so important: had I known about the actual events of Pearl Harbor instead of all those stories of Brigham Young, maybe I would have ratted out this plan sooner!

The other large flaw that I later learned was that the insurance company had denied him life insurance because of the state of his liver, so the best we could have inherited was his Utah sushi-dinner debt.

Now, sitting on the edge of the bed in that motel, it dawned on me that Bubba was in the middle of executing the plan he'd told me about. Only I wasn't there, and he had recast my role as witness with a glass of vodka. I broke down and told my mom everything. My godmother and I left for the ceremony while my mom stayed behind to call the cops and find someone to get Bubba down from the roof, where he was eventually delivered to safety.

The drive back home from this graduation trip has disappeared from my memory. I wonder if I perhaps felt happy, the immense burden of the suicide secret I'd been keeping finally lifted off my shoulders. What I do remember is that I felt so sure that Bubba had crossed enough of a line that my mom would finally have to find a way to leave him.

I was wrong. When we came back from the graduation, my mom told Bubba he had a whole-ass *entire year* to get sober, and if he didn't, *then* she would divorce him. So in an effort to apologize for casually almost killing himself during the first trip she'd taken in years, Bubba granted my mom another vacation.

Grace swept through town in her little red Camry, picked my mother up, and took her on their dream vacation. Hawaii? No. Bahamas? No, ma'am. They went down the Grand fucking Canyon! These bitches could not get enough of the river! But I guess the wisdom of the ancient canyon must've gotten through to them, because when my mom came back from the trip, she had changed her mind: we weren't waiting a year, this marriage was over. She and my aunt packed up all the kids, and she gave Bubba forty-eight hours to get out of the house.

We drove to Park City, home to some of the richest people in the entire state. At some point on this trip we stopped at a gas station, where my mom discovered that her credit cards weren't working. We gathered around my mom in the motel as she called the bank and found out that her name had been taken off their accounts, and the only credit cards she had access to were maxed out. Bubba, in a fit of vengeance, had even taken her name off the deed to their car. This was '90s Mormon land where a husband ruled the roost, even while wearing their wife's pink sweatpants.

When we returned from Park City, Bubba refused to leave the house. We stayed on my aunt's living room floor, and I began eighth grade like nothing was happening. *How was your trip?* Britney had asked in a note she had passed me in class. I wrote back *So much fun!!!* and did my best to pretend everything was perfectly normal. I told my classmates that I couldn't attend all their scrapbooking parties because "things were just a little busy lately," as if my family wasn't in a standoff against my stepfather without any savings or a working credit card.

Days turned to weeks, and finally my mom drove us to our house to get more clothes, but she was afraid to go inside. Aunt Sharon went in with me and handed me a garbage bag. "Shove everything you want in here, as fast as you can. Five minutes, okay?"

Bubba greeted us when we came in, like nothing about this encounter was weird at all. He said it was nice to see me and asked us when we were coming back. I ran into my room and began throwing clothes into the bag. When I came back out, bag full, Bubba tried to step in and give me a new outfit he'd bought for me—a pink shirt and matching shorts that were attached on a large plastic hanger. This was the only apology he was capable of.

Throughout my childhood, my mom had never yelled at Bubba. Yelling was not her thing. She was gentle and loving, full of endless kindness. Growing up in Mormon land and going to church with Britney had taught me that my role as a woman was to be gentle and loving, too, but I had watched Bubba take my beautiful mother and ring her dry, so I didn't want to be gentle and loving anymore.

A few years back Bubba had brought home several sets of boxing gloves, including a child-size pair for me. He had declared that all family arguments would be settled the old-fashioned way by physically fighting it out, like his family did growing up. Bubba taught me how to cover my head with my hands and duck, how to stay light on my feet, springy. The first time we had a family disagreement, we took the boxing gloves out into the backyard. Then he punched me in the face and my vision went black as I fell back into the grass.

Fighting was not my mom's thing, fighting was Bubba's. And thanks to him, now it was mine.

I grabbed a pair of scissors and cut up the outfit he'd given me, right in front of him. I yelled everything I wished some-one had said to Bubba all those years—that we hated living with him, that he was a drunk, that we knew he favored Jesse over me and my older brother. I yelled that I had tried so hard to make him love me, and he never adopted me like he'd al-ways promised, and that he was a monster. "Just get out of the house!" I screamed. "We have nowhere to live!"

Soon after that, my mom filed for a restraining order. The cops were called again, and they removed Bubba from the house. My mom and Jesse and I moved back in to try and finish out the school year. When we reentered our home, everything was gone. Bubba had taken the furniture, the pillows, the utensils... all of it. I half expected to see "the shirt off his back" crumpled on the floor, but instead I saw the only plant he had left behind. It now sat in the corner of the dining room propped up in a small stack of dirt, because Bubba had even taken the pot and the little plastic tray beneath that's meant to catch excess water.

The patio furniture was the only thing left in the living room. After school we would lounge on the beach chairs and eat dinner at the patio table with the umbrella up, pretending we were on vacation, because we were—finally, a real vacation from Bubba.

While it was terrible getting lectured at Mormon summer camp for failing the Iron Rod test, far worse was that when we looked over at the other side of the hill, we could also see the heaven simulation. Glowing in the distance was a full-on, lit-up Christmas tree, with music, singing, and a bunch of fucking doughnuts. All the little girls who'd passed the Iron Rod test were now partying "in heaven." Some of them were even celebrating with their actual families who came to meet them, a special touch to really make this simulation pop.

Back at base camp, the heaven group watched us heathens cross down from the other side of the hill, very clearly letting everyone know that we were future whores. As Britney walked down from heaven and I walked down from hell, I knew the chasm of our differences would soon begin to grow far too wide for me to cross over. Within the year I would be spending my days living out of a garbage bag, lounging on a patio chair in our living room as we waited for updates from the divorce court—and no amount of holy God bread could fix it.

Even so, I owe a lot to Britney and her family for the escape they gave me during the Bubba years. When my mom announced that she'd figured out a way for us to move out of Utah, I was secretly happy that I'd be ending my time with Britney on a high point. I feared the worst if I stayed, that one day Britney would finally have to turn her back on me for good after accepting that I would never convert. Her religious life in Mormon land simply had no room for an angry, doughnut-loving, inside/outside furniture gal like me. I believed deep in my bones that eventually Britney and my friends were headed for the Iron Rod to the anointed celestial plane, while I was headed for the dirt in the ground, where I would stay until one of their grandkids baptized themselves over my grave.

Britney and our friends threw me a giant going-away party. We played a salacious game called Baby, If You Love Me Smile, where—wait for it—you sit in a circle…and try and make someone else break a straight face. We took Boogie Boards down to the river, swam at the pool. Before we left, Britney and I promised to write to each other, and we did for several years. Then at seventeen she met her husband, went on her mission, and grew busy taking care of her kids, as I grew busy becoming the type of person who would one day find *whore* a compliment.

Just before we left St. George, Britney drove over with her dad with a quilt she'd made for me, and we embraced and cried. I owed so much of my happiness during these years to Britney, and I tried to convey my love for her through heaving sobs. Then my mom, Jesse, and I packed ourselves into a U-Haul and headed out, just like Brigham Young, toward a new Promised Land. We listened to The Chicks' first two albums, and Gloria Estefan's *Hold Me, Thrill Me, Kiss Me* on repeat through a Discman, with the headphones turned up to the max acting as our speaker. As Mormon hymns were replaced with Gloria and The Chicks singing about the strength of sinner women, my mom gunned it across state lines to our new home in Colorado.

SHITBITCH

Grudge City

When I was fourteen years old, I found out that my dad was not my actual dad.

A bombshell, I know. The man I've referred to as my dad for most of this goddamn book turned out to be, in fact, not my biological father. I wanted you to be just as surprised as I was!

My life changed in many ways the moment I found out, but the worst part was that it forever put me in the "girls with daddy issues" category. I mean, c'mon! We're all sick of this genre! Of all the reasons to be angry at my dad, I'd put that one in the top three. Only, *which* dad am I angry at? The man I thought was my dad, my stepdad Bubba, my biological father? I have no idea/all of them? It's just too bad this book is all about the women in my life, otherwise I could have titled it *Daddies' Girl*.

I was standing in the kitchen of the house we had moved into during my first year of high school in Colorado. The divorce from Bubba was still fresh; in fact, it was far from officially over. I was complaining to my mom about how my dad hadn't spoken to me in ages, and how it was clear he didn't love me but very much loved my older brother Lucas. Perhaps I was upset that he'd forgotten my birthday. Or that he'd ignored my phone call, yet again. Maybe I had tallied up the amount of times I had seen him since their divorce a decade ago (seven).

That's when my mom casually tossed out something like "Well, he's not even your real dad, anyway. Thank God for that."

I said, "What?"

And she said, "What?"

And I said…"WHAT!?"

That was how I found out that my dad was not my real dad, that Lucas was actually my half brother, and that I was conceived with a sperm donor's…*donation*.

To this day, my mom says that she had already revealed this sperm-donor information to me once before. It was after she left my dad when I was five or six years old, and apparently I took the news wonderfully. But my child mush brain had retained none of that information, so when my mom brought it up again ten years later, she thought she was continuing a conversation, and I thought I'd suddenly entered the finale of a soap opera.

After learning the truth about my dad, I wrote a poem titled "Shattered," and it was about being a broken, sad person with no dad whose heart shattered into a million pieces. I then shattered an actual mirror, as if my luck wasn't already bad enough, and glued the shards of glass all around the poem onto a giant 4' x 3' poster board. Let's all pour one out for the teenager in the grocery store picking out art supplies for her identity-crisis poetry.

I'd liken my experience of finding out I was donor-conceived to emotional vertigo: the world flipped upside down, I turned inside out, and every time I looked in a mirror I could no longer see a human staring back. My hands were no longer mine, and my reflection became a mistake. As I stared at myself, every molecule inside my body was suddenly a sneaky little bitch playing me for a fool. I am not of the birds and the bees, I am of the turkey baster and the jizz in a cup. I could have siblings I've never met. I could have hundreds. I have to start over, as a fully formed person. Half of my identity has always been wrong. Half

of my medical information has always been wrong. I may never
know the truth about what's inside me. I'll never have the legal
right to learn who my father is. Every person I ever fuck could
be my brother, cousin, or, worse, my actual dad. I walked into
the moment of discovery a normal human, and I walked out as
an intruder to my own family. My humanity was stripped from
me and replaced with a permanent aching. I am plagued to forever look for my biological father everywhere I go, all desperate-
eyed, veins straining at my temples, the grown-ass version of a
toddler lost in the mall.

My not-dad dad didn't want to have kids, but having kids was
the *only* thing my mom wanted... Ah, a wonderful match they
were. My mom was trying to get pregnant, but it just wasn't
happening, so they finally tested my dad's sperm and found that
he was nearly sterile. Even for men who don't want to have children, there's a lot of shame and secrecy around donor conception for heterosexual couples, and one of the biggest reasons is
because to them, our existence is basically a billboard that says
My dad's dick don't work! Unfathomably, dads don't usually like
to broadcast this in our ragingly patriarchal society that has a
lot of rules for dicks.

I'm not a dick doctor, but if I was, I'd say his sterility was due
to one of the following reasons. First, the most obvious one, he
had a terrible accident as a kid while hopping over a fence on
his father's ranch that left him with only one testicle. There was
also the toll of stress from fighting in the Vietnam War, the fact
that he shot himself up with hepatitis so he could get discharged,
that he overly dabbled in crystal meth after coming home, or
that for a few years in the Bay he ran a successful drug ring until
rumors of a raid shut down his mighty kingdom. Or else it was
genetic? Either way, he and my mom weren't getting pregnant.

As they struggled to conceive, my mom's best friend at the
time saw an ad in a magazine claiming to create *miracle babies*.

This miracle program was run by two doctors at a university who were researching spermatogenesis, and at the time they were experimenting with different methods of artificial insemination. Over the course of the twenty-plus years they ran this program, they wrote and published sixteen papers based on the results of the women they impregnated with fresh sperm from the medical students at the university. I've since tried to read them, hoping they'd provide adorable answers to the story of my birth, but it's really just a lot of dense science about fertility. The doctors told my mom a few baseline facts: they only took samples from medical school seniors who were at the top of their class; each student could only donate three times; and the donors would go through full health scans to ensure that only the most perfect specimens would create their future child. So it was perhaps a shock when I came out with twelve toes.

My mom told me the extra toes were so small that they didn't notice until a couple days after they brought me home. Later, when I was two years old, she had the extra toes surgically re- moved because she was afraid I'd have trouble fitting into shoes one day. Bless that woman, because even without them your girl is still a 9 Wide.

But there was something even more disappointing for my not- dad dad than my extra toes: I was *a girl*. He wasn't a big fan of ladies to begin with or, as he preferred to call them, *females*. In order to even tolerate a woman, she had to meet his very cool list of demands: be thin, don't draw attention, and shut the hell up. This poor guy was sent his worst nightmare of a daugh- ter: I was wide and tall, and whenever my mom left the room I screamed at the top of my lungs till she came back. I'm told I would cry for hours unless she was in my line of vision, mak- ing it abundantly clear that I would not be shutting the hell up.

And since he's not actually my dad, let's think of a new name for him. Dean? Jeff? Dadi with a little heart dotting the *i*?

How about we just go with…Limoncello.

When my mom participated in the miracle-baby program, she wanted to make sure I physically resembled Limoncello so that it would help them pass me off as his own, and maybe he would be inclined to love me more despite not being biologically his. My mom is Scandinavian. Both sets of her grandparents immigrated to the US from Sweden, and she's tall and slender with blue eyes and blondish hair and fair skin. Limoncello has Scottish and Mohican ancestry on his father's side and Irish and Choctaw ancestry on his mom's side. He is short, with jet-black hair, dark brown eyes, and olive skin. Finding a match for him was quite the challenge for an '80s fertility experiment whose scientific foundations have a very dangerous relationship with eugenics.

The doctor told my mom that they didn't have anyone whose genetic history resembled Limoncello's, so instead, they would use one of the Hispanic medical students as my donor to give me the best chance of coming out with some darker features. When I was born with brown eyes, they celebrated…until they saw I was also blonde as fuck. Regardless, one of my best memories of Limoncello is that he loved my brown eyes so much that he would often sing "Brown Eyed Girl" to me when I was growing up. As the years went on, my hair turned a blasé brown, and I began to resemble Limoncello a little more, so at least that part of my mom's plan worked.

When I was a teenager, the donor-baby revelation quickly created an acute emotional strain with both of my parents, because it meant everything about my identity that I thought I'd gotten from Limoncello had been a lie. In that instant, I learned that anything you know to be true can just, suddenly, not be true at all. The aftereffect is that sometimes nothing in the world feels real anymore, especially me.

I'd never had a good father figure in my life to begin with, but now I didn't even know what my biological father looked like, and that took a toll on my brain. I know it's not correct to think this, but I do wonder if I would have avoided some of the abusive men in my life if I had simply given off the impression that there was a big ol' dad around who would take them to task. Of course, lots of girls with daddies also experience abuse. Sometimes it's the daddies doing it, always a fun twist. Nevertheless, I held on to this belief for many years. One time when I was a teenager, I bought a little book at the front of Borders titled *Why a Daughter Needs a Dad: 100 Reasons.* I took it home, wondering if I just memorized all 100 things could I be someone who seemed like they had a father? Years later I was wasted on the sidewalk in Old Town Chicago and wearing a cape for no reason, confronting a fellow comedian for rudely spreading rumors that I'd slept with his friend. I was in the middle of defending my honor, loudly slurring that no, I had not fucked his friend, when he shut down all my protests by snidely declaring, "Jesus, get a dad!"

I'm pretty sure I ran away after he said that, which just goes to show that not only did the book do nothing for my confidence, but neither did the cape! I wish I would have replied: *I did, actually! A few of them!*

But that's the problem with dads… They've also got to be good.

There were so many layers and consequences that came from the sperm-donor revelation, far beyond the fact that a stranger's cum in a lab had helped create me. I couldn't even begin to wrap my head around that part of it, because first I had to deal with the other part: Limoncello, the man I thought was my dad, who is listed on my birth certificate as my dad, who I had called dad and cried why-doesn't-my-dad-love-me tears about for my entire life, was in fact not my dad.

Over time, that part actually became somewhat good news. It was kinda nice to realize that I was no longer tied by blood to Limoncello, the guy who'd taught me that the earth was created by alien dolphins. Yes, alien dolphins. I never quite found out if they were aliens who looked like dolphins, or if the dolphins are the creator aliens? Perhaps it's relevant that when he said this, we were in the middle of burying jars of his money in the backyard, since he also believed that all banks were spies sent by the government.

My first memory of Limoncello is watching him shove my mom up against a wall and hit her across the face, so I was out on him from the jump. When I was just a toddler, I would walk around the house and viciously tear up photos of him. I'd remove him from group photos and I'd shred photos of him alone. My mom would find the shards in horror and scramble to replace the pictures or hide their ripped pieces. I mean, first off, how amazing! Do we love toddler Chelsea? I feel like we do! I never liked him and he never liked me, and honestly, I can't blame him. Limoncello called that shit right then and there.

When they went through that ugly divorce, Limoncello had threatened to fight for custody if my mom tried to take any of the construction business they had built together. She believed him and didn't push for any financial resources, instead retreating toward my soon-to-be stepdad Bubba. Money was always tight after the divorce, and Limoncello seemed to delight in our struggle: it was payback for leaving him. I remember when I was eight years old, I called him up and begged him to pay for the dance lessons my mom and Bubba couldn't afford. In a rare act of generosity, Limoncello promised to pay for the classes, but there was a catch—first I had to memorize his favorite ancient prayer and recite it to him over the phone. I did, and he still never actually paid for the lessons.

Years later I found this ancient prayer tucked into some of the pages of a journal I'd kept. It was very uninspired stuff, like *My limbs are beacons of love made whole by the touch of this universal life.* But the bigger surprise was that when I turned the prayer over, I realized that this *ancient* bullshit had been torn out of a god-damn Scientology magazine. In retrospect, the alien dolphins thing does make a lot more sense.

★ ★ ★

After I found out that Limoncello wasn't my biological dad, I tried one more time to see him and repair our relationship when I was sixteen. I now suspected that perhaps the sperm-donor thing had contributed to our emotional distance, which made me hope it was something we could overcome. At that point, Bubba was out of the picture, and I had taken Limoncello's last name again. What better time to restart our father–daughter relationship? While we had both always disliked each other, I'd still spent my whole life thinking of him as my dad. I still wanted him to approve of me on some level, and I wasn't ready to let that go.

I asked my choir friend, Tanya, to accompany me on the twenty-hour drive to get to Limoncello's house. While at this point, Grace, my mom, Jesse, and I had all moved to Colorado, Lucas was still living with Limoncello ever since being sent there by Bubba. Now Tanya was very into this trip and agreed to come because she and Lucas had struck up a flirtation after he came to visit me and my mom for Christmas. Bringing her would be a mistake for many reasons, but mostly because by the end of the trip Limoncello had told me that I was too curvy, too fat, and that I should eat less so I could look more like Tanya, who was "normal-sized for a woman." Tanya was so naturally thin that her double zero jeans were a bit baggy on her, and once at the mall she was even recruited to model for Abercrombie & Fitch, while I stood next to her seething with rage.

Regardless, I was convinced this trip would be different from the few other times I'd gone to visit Limoncello in my life, because now I had a secret weapon: her name was Jenni Janowiski.

While still running his construction business, Limoncello had been doing a bunch of home renovations for this one client, Jenni Janowiski and her husband, Todd. They became friends during the project, and one day I started receiving little care packages from Jenni, despite never having met her. Easter baskets with themed socks and new lip glosses, boxes of bracelets "just because." According to Jenni, Limoncello talked about me all the time and really wanted to see me again, and sometimes I even found cards in her little care packages that were suppos- edly written by him. Knowing Jenni would be there to help us mend our relationship, I blew across the state at 90 mph, gun- ning toward my fairy-tale ending.

When I arrived, my cool new friend Jenni couldn't wait to hang out and introduce me to Todd and her kids. She knew lots of things about me because I had also been writing Jenni let- ters back. She took me to a play in the city, remembering that I loved theater ever since my wild "internship" living in Grace's trailer. Limoncello was supposed to come, too, but he couldn't make it. Limoncello never made it to any of the things Jenni had planned for us. While my brother and Tanya were tucked away in his room making out, Limoncello was always out working or just simply gone. In fact, it seemed like Limoncello and Jenni weren't actually friends at all, judging by how pissed he looked every time she came to the house to pick me up.

Toward the end of the trip, Jenni dropped me off from a the- ater matinee of the musical *Cinderella*. We were sitting in her luxury SUV in the driveway, and she turned to me in an impas- sioned fit and blurted, "You're probably wondering why your dad and I are so close." I wasn't. I was mostly wondering when Jenni was going to give me more of those nice care packages. Then, without any prodding, she caved. "Chelsea, your dad and I had an affair!"

Keep in mind, I had spent a lot of time with Jenni's family eating pizza rolls on her giant rich-lady suede couch, so I did not see this coming. But her confession had crystallized the logic as to why this random lady was so invested in me: she and Li- moncello had had an affair, and then at some point he moved on, and Jenni thought she could get more time with him by becoming close with me. Only, poor Jenni had made a terrible

mistake, because that was the last thing Limoncello wanted. She
had poured all this energy and money into forming a friendship
with his daughter and was probably confused why it wasn't in-
citing any effect on him whatsoever.

She looked at me for some kind of response to her admission.
I shrugged and replied, "He sucks."

I knew Jenni Janowiski didn't have a chance with him anyway
because Limoncello had recently started dating someone else.
She was an eighteen-year-old girl, only two years older than
me, and he had told me this fact proudly. I think in his mind,
her young age made up for the fact that she wasn't as thin as the
women he usually dated, which he'd also pointed out to me.
I had only ever met two of his girlfriends. The previous one,
Karina, was my size when I met her, and I was in middle school.
The only thing I remember about their relationship was that
Limoncello, sober after his drug-ring days, dumped her when
he found out she was using cocaine. *Be thin, but do it NATU-
RALLY, Karina!* I'm not sure if Weight Watchers was paying
him to traipse around America ruining women, but Limoncello
told me his new teenage girlfriend had a pretty face and he was
going to help her "lose that extra twenty," so let's say a prayer
for wherever that lady is now.

During this trip, Limoncello got off on such a tear about my
weight that at one point he walked naked into my brother Lucas's room where I sat hanging out on a futon. He was cupping
his dick with both hands to cover it and informed me that the
best way to determine if you're a healthy weight was to see if
your thighs touched. I'm not really sure why Limoncello was
this chill about being naked in front of me, but hey, I guess the
silver lining is that we weren't actually related after all? The
funniest thing about his little speech was that when he stood
up normally, his thighs *did* touch: he just kept bending over to
look at them, which then created a natural gap, as every gal on
the red carpet slightly bending toward the camera knows. We

never once spoke about me being donor-conceived, but I did get to see that, by his own definition, his thighs were substandard, and that brings me joy.

When I returned to Colorado, I thought of all the bullying I was enduring in school, the horrors of the Bubba years, the pain of my sperm-donor-dad revelation, and the financial effects of my mom's divorces. I began stewing about how unfair it was that men always seemed to hold all the power. So I wrote Limoncello a lengthy letter. I told him how I never forgot all the times he'd hit my mom, how I knew he wasn't my actual dad, but he'd still been a terrible one at that, and I never wanted to speak to him again. Somewhere deep inside, I was hoping this was the motivation for him to be like *What? I've been a bad dad? Let me make this right!*

He never replied. Even worse, I never got another care package from Jenni.

Years later, when I was twenty-four, Lucas became engaged (no, not to Tanya, to my sister-in-law, Kate). Being the wonderful, very gracious person she is, my sister-in-law asked me to be a bridesmaid, per a tradition that's far better suited to more normal families. I said yes because it felt like I should, and because I really wanted to be there for her and my brother. Yet all I could think about was how it meant I would soon have to face Limoncello again.

Right before the wedding I went on a crash diet to get super thin. I just couldn't let Limoncello see that not only were my thighs still touching, but they also looked like they were spooning each other and both thighs were the big spoon. I wrote in my notebook all the meals I would eat for the month so that I would walk into that wedding skinnier than even bitchass sixteen-year-old Tanya at the mall.

Then, over those thirty days, I gained fifteen pounds.

I mean, obviously I was binge-eating and freaking the fuck

out, but fifteen pounds!? C'mon! A day before leaving for the wedding, I stood on the street in Chicago and pondered throwing myself in front of a car to get out of going. In the end, I just couldn't seem to get myself to jump into traffic in a way that would bring only mild injury, because I also had a very promising improv show in the back room of a sandwich shop that night that I didn't want to miss. I stood on the corner for an hour trying to calculate how I could pull it off before giving up.

Since I hadn't reached my goal weight, I could not fit into my bridesmaid's dress, which I had of course bought in a goal-weight size—something that should be criminally punishable by law. The dresses had these long sashes that you could tie nine different ways, and as the bridesmaids hit the email thread discussing which way they would tie their dress, I joked that I was going to tie mine into a noose. (I have since apologized to Kate for being one of the worst bridesmaids of all time.)

When it came time to put on my dress, I couldn't do the fun twisties and knots with the sashes that made the dress strapless, or haltered with a cute little keyhole right where my Spanx was going to be. Instead, I handled the fabric like a caveman, hand-stitching the long sashes into two large clumps that would cover the shape of my gargantuan bra.

A half-hour before the rehearsal dinner, I began to have some sort of breakdown, sobbing and hyperventilating. I couldn't seem to gain control. Nothing was working to get me to chill the fuck out, and my family was overwhelmed by the episode. They ultimately decided to leave for the dinner and just let me cry it out in the hotel room, where I stayed and ate a dozen muffins left over from the free continental breakfast. Hey, it was too late to get thin!

The next morning, they called the wedding party together to take group photos at the dock where the wedding guests would later board a boat. I was so ashamed of my weight that the photo series begins with me discreetly hiding behind other people, then slowly, you can see me edging behind furniture and various maritime accessories—cushions, metal poles, a shelf of emergency life vests. Five minutes into pictures, I was just entirely out of frame: I had escaped.

When we boarded the boat where the ceremony was taking place, it finally happened. I saw Limoncello. We made eye contact for just a moment, and he looked right through me. It was as if he didn't even know me. My heart split in two, creating the type of cavernous gap that I can only imagine he'd wanted for my thighs. Of all the ways this encounter could've gone, I had never imagined the one that would hurt the most: indifference.

It has now been more than twenty years since I've spoken to Limoncello, but right in the middle of those years, we stood on a boat together. I heard he lives in Thailand now.

Even though most of the hurt around my father issues came from not knowing the truth for so long, I sometimes wish that I had never found out I was donor-conceived at all. It would be so much easier to have someone tangible to project all my pain onto. Limoncello was a known entity, someone with a voicemail I could scream into, a face I could picture when I cried. I was already used to being miserable over him, and instead of continuing to wade into that familiar, worn-down hurt, I now belong to some nebulous stranger. A stranger who, in most people's minds, I should thank, because without him, I wouldn't exist in the first place. You see, that's why they are called sperm *donors*—because donations are gifts! They're just generous dudes, doing something out of the goodness of their own hearts, asking for nothing in return...except money.

I was told to keep my donor dad a secret to protect the family from judgment, and purportedly to protect myself from being called a freak. At first, I didn't mind being told to hide my origins. It was an easy secret to keep because it was hard to explain because it was hard to understand because it was hard to face. I was supposed to be a miracle baby, and instead I felt like a monster.

As I got older, the initial acceptance of my secret evolved into a looming burden. I now knew I was not Limoncello's daughter, but many of my family members and family friends still thought I was. When I moved away to the city and had thousands of miles between me and my family, I began to open up about my father in small ways, and I even made a lot of comedy about not knowing who he was—I just never mentioned the donor part. In one of The Second City Mainstage shows, I wrote a song that would end with me going into the audience to try and find my real dad. I loved this bit so much that I did it again years later when I began stand-up.

But the closer I tiptoed toward my truth, the more questions people asked, and I found myself sidestepping my way out of giving them more details. That part was tough when it came up, but I also didn't spend too much time dwelling on it. I was mostly busy trying to hone my craft, write jokes, pay rent, and determine if the somewhat attractive guy at the bar was the same height as me or just wearing several pairs of thick socks.

When I was a teenager, I would straight up lie about my dad, because telling a shitty lie was easier than telling the shitty truth. In my twenties, I would simply say "I don't know" without elaborating further. Which would infuriate people. *How? How could you not know?* These types of comments were always made by people whose family units were so lovely they couldn't even begin to fathom that not everyone knows who their parents are, and that some lucky folks spend their lives having panic attacks over their ambiguous medical history every time they go to the doctor.

My mom had taught me that you don't owe anyone anything and to say whatever you want to protect yourself and your family. It came from a good place, except it was missing something crucial. While I don't owe anyone else anything, I did owe it to myself to be proud of my story, and being told to hide who I was made that impossible. It began to feel like the very thing that created me was the worst thing that ever happened to me.

Agonizing about it to my therapist years later, I freaked out about how there were people in my teen years who I loved and knew they loved me, and I'd told them my dad is dead so that they wouldn't ask me questions. My therapist joked, trying to make me feel better: "Maybe you didn't lie. Maybe he is dead, for all you know." I started laughing, which then morphed into horror. I hadn't ever really sat with the fact that my donor might not be alive.

After that conversation, I tracked down the doctors who ran the university program and began to search for my biological father. I voraciously watched the handful of find-your-donor documentaries that existed, but almost all of them end in despair. The most positive one closes out with a donor who is eager to meet all his offspring. Once reunited, all the siblings and him play music in a field together. Afterwards the donor tells the camera he's happy his children tracked him down because it turns out he's suffering from some medical issues that are hereditary, and now he can warn them.

As I journeyed further into my poetic Li'l Daddy's Girl quest, I uncovered all kinds of even worse information about the sperm-donor industry in the '80s. The university doctors had told my mom that the money the donors would get for their sperm would go toward paying for medical school, a noble cause. Later, when I researched these programs, I found out just how much money these medical students received. A popular phrase is that you can't put a price on a child, but in the sperm donor world you can. Mine was $50.

After I found out about my dad, I assumed I must be innately smart because I came from a med school student, a soon-to-be doctor. So it was shocking to this inner genius narrative to learn the actual truth: many of us were told our donors were medical students, I guess as a popular story for would-be parents. Some of these medical students were in fact future doctors, but some were other types of students…or not even students at all. Some of these donors were homeless men supporting themselves through donating. Some were mentally ill and living in institutions. Some of them were the very doctors running these studies themselves, who *should* have been in institutions. Those are the psychos behind the scandalous documentaries you'll see every few years: the doctor who made 100 children with his own sperm!

While the scientists and doctors behind sperm-donor fertilization may have successfully created children, they forgot to take into account one of the most important factors in this whole setup: the shame. Particularly, the shame they attached to the whole process by making everything anonymous. Donors were promised their identity would never be known to the kids or the parents. Parents were promised their kids would never find out how they were made. The whole industry was built on a foundation of embarrassment that these parents felt over not being able to "have their *own* kids" as it was said in those days, and the need they felt to lie their entire lives just to cover it up.

These donor programs only cared about creating the children, not what happened to them. They used science and data to create us, but then eliminated all the data that would provide access to what genetics were inside us. In order to convince men to donate anonymously and cover up their own shady practices from the parents, they destroyed or supposedly lost the donor records and did everything they could to make sure the children could never track down the human who helped make them. They had no idea that DNA testing would become commercialized and accessible to anyone by 2012, advertised with discounts each Christmas as the perfect gift for your family, turning winter into what we call *sibling season*—the time of year when thousands of families will discover their true origins with a single swab of their cheek.

They didn't realize that when kids went to find the person who made them, that person would usually have a family and a life of their own and wouldn't want to tell their spouse they have another child and it wants to say hi. They never thought about what the secret would do to us, the kids, the product.

Sperm and egg donation is still a highly unregulated medical industry, even though in recent years some legal progress has been made. In the United States there is no federal law to limit how many children a single donor can father, but now Colorado has passed a bill that will at least outlaw anonymous donation (though that law won't go into effect until 2025). Some donor-conceived adults are working to ban anonymous donation nation wide, making it so that every child has access to their genetic and medical information. But the donor industry makes too much money, and the parents' desire to have children always supersedes the debate of the ethics—because their children who will have to live with those ethics aren't born yet and can't chime in.

It wasn't until a 2010 study when medical researchers even bothered to check on the kids themselves and analyze the effect that being donor-conceived might have on them. The researchers found that in comparison to kids who grow up knowing their biological parents, donor kids are more than twice as likely to struggle with addiction, depression, anxiety, and criminal activity (wow, stop bragging, Chels). The study offered lines of data on why I was so sad, which ironically made me deliciously happy. Turns out this never-ending capacity for pain was not a character flaw of my own, but scientifically someone else's fault!

Of course, I must make it exceptionally clear that not everyone has a negative experience with their donor conception. I am only speaking to my personal lived experience. And there are many donor-conceived people who have healthy and happy lives after learning about their origins, especially the ones born more recently, or the ones who never had it kept a secret from them. But if you were, say, born in the '80s to heterosexual parents who hid it from you, there can be a lot of anger to deal with once you find out.

Nowadays I am open with my secret, but I have donor-conceived friends who still cannot share theirs because their parents would never forgive them. I wish I could tell you that I revealed it on my own timing. That I finally got brave enough or healed myself in therapy and walked out in the light of day and shouted *I'm not keeping this secret about my dad anymore. This is not my shame! I didn't even have a choice in this! I am donor-conceived, and it's who I am!* But that's not what happened.

Shitbitch is what happened.

Shitbitch is, factually speaking, the shittiest bitch who ever lived, and she earned her moniker when she began spreading a rumor about me to all of our mutual acquaintances.

By this point, I had told my friends about changing my last name to Devantez, and I had been open about not knowing the identity of my father. Shitbitch herself had watched me perform jokes about it. Just around then the entertainment industry entered a moment where they pretended to care about representation and inclusion. (Yay, great job, Hollywood! It only took 100 years!) It was the perfect moment for Shitbitch, the unoriginal hack that she is, to snicker to people: *Where the hell did the name Devantez come from? Why is it not googleable? Why would she change her name anyway? Isn't that weird?*

I was starting to get successful as a comedian, and lo and behold, I got a job that Shitbitch herself had wanted, so she decided the only reason I was hired was because I was "diverse." But she didn't stop there! Since I didn't know my dad, she said I was actually an ethnicity-faking piece of shit who didn't deserve all those "easy-pass points" that make people just hand you a job for no reason! Shitbitch then told people exactly that: that I was "a fake Latina." This was an especially bold allegation, because I'd never even spoken about my donor's ethnicity outside of the people close to me! She went out of her way to ignore the nuanced pains, the hell I had walked through to articulate who I was.

Person at Drybar: You're something aren't you? What are you?

Me: Well, if you can find my dad, you can ask him.

Lady with "I dissent" in her Instagram bio: Hey girlie, how do you identify?

Me: My mom is white and my dad is a Hispanic sperm donor, so I mostly identify as someone in pain.

McDonald's Cashier: Would you like fries with that?

Me: Hello, my mom is white and raised me and I don't know who my dad is so my identity is complicated, I can only speak to my own lived experiences, okay?! Extra ranch packets, please!

The thing is, Shitbitch didn't care to know more about me; she simply seemed intent on hating me. Yes, it's likely because I was getting successful in comedy, but the hate had begun long before. You see, Shitbitch had gone out with a guy briefly, and a year after it ended, she complained to a mutual friend of ours that he started dating some dumb fucking slut. That dumb fucking slut was me, and yes, it is devastating that our origin story doesn't pass the Bechdel test.

The whole rumor was a very salacious nibble, so eventually it all got back to me and the gossip picked up like the villagers in *Beauty and the Beast*, storming the castle with old logs chanting, "Show us the dad! Show us the dad!"

In a way, I understood Shitbitch gossiping about me. After all, gossip is very fun. (Do you have some?! DM ME!!!) But Shitbitch's gossip was overwhelmingly vicious. Like, holy fuck, stick to something more noble like "she slept her way to the top," "her boobs are fake," or "all her jokes were written by her tallest ex!" Shitbitch went even further than rumors. She created fake social media accounts and would write things on my page like "Watch your back, Señorita." I know, it was unhinged. Like at that point, just fight me! I would've been down! (Still am.)

If Shitbitch had been genuinely concerned that I lied my way into a job I didn't deserve, she would have had the courage to ask me to my face, or approach my best friends. But, of course, that was never what she actually cared about. She relished in the clout she garnered from hosting this little paternity-mystery soirée. It brought her more attention than her own writing. That's the thing about gatekeepers: they can't get past the wall with their own talent, so instead they offer to guard the door.

Though I'm making jokes about it now, what she did was absolutely excruciating. It still hurts to talk about it. Shitbitch stomped on my deepest wound, the daddy wound, something I couldn't fathom discussing with a stranger, and now it felt like she'd corralled a bunch of them to come stare and point at me, demanding: *What are you?* What was debilitating was the root of what she was saying: *You're wrong. You're a mistake. You don't deserve to be here.* The psychological toll of carrying a secret as a kid burrows deep. So deep in fact, that in response, I only felt one thing: *You're right.*

At the time, it seemed I would either have to 1.) die 2.) find a way to rise above it all by not caring about gossip (hahaha-haha, no) or 3.) out the secret about my dad and pass around my DNA test like it was a flyer for a Blowout Presidents' Day Sale on ethnicity. Now, given that I have to draw a goddamn map just to explain my family history, you can understand why I didn't like talking about all of this casually during small talk. Besides, discussing my identity meant facing complicated questions within donor conception that no one has fully figured out. Race is different than ethnicity, and a large component of ethnicity is your lived cultural experiences, so what does that mean for a lab baby? There are no textbooks about donor-kid identities, no TED Talks, no graduate theses, it's just a big ol' *TBD*. Am *I* supposed to be the one figuring those answers out? I am a gal who, up until recently, thought *crick* was a real word and even tried to put it in this book. (It is, in fact, just the vocal affectation of the word *creek*.) So it really doesn't feel like it should be me!

I have always been riddled with questions. *What box do I check on forms? What do I say when people ask? What part is fucking what? How do adopted kids navigate their identity? How do those who've had a parent abandon them feel about their labels? What if I had been conceived through a one-night stand—would that change my sense of self?* I really needed proper guidance and care to help me understand who I was, but alas, I don't even know where I could've gotten that type of insight from. Oh wait, that's right—*from a dad*.

At one point, an acquaintance I'll call Shitbitch Junior picked up the rumor and repeated everything from Shitbitch Senior, telling people who were complete strangers. The rumors demanded the daddy evidence to clear my name, and I felt so humiliated I thought I ought to give it, but it would mean telling everyone that I changed my name because ███████████████ ████████████████████████ and outing the secret that I was donor-conceived.

There was so much holding me back from outing myself as a donor kid beyond just the embarrassment of it. I had made a promise to my family, and I was in a silent pact with them that I, Chelsea, would be the strong one. You could always count on me. I was resilient; I was a fixer. I was deeply torn because I couldn't stop people from hurting me without turning around and breaking this promise and hurting my family. Especially my mom. For her, I was this incredible gift in her life, a human that she had wanted and worked hard to have, and I worried that if I showed my mom the depth of my agony around being donor-conceived and how angry I was about keeping it a secret, it would break her spirit and push her away from me, and then I wouldn't have any parents at all.

Outing my parentage was going to out my truth: I am very not okay. Often I feel inhuman, I hate that I don't know who I am, that I can't have a nice, short little bio for myself, and sometimes, I want to die.

But as I considered coming out as a donor kid, my therapist urged me toward a different seed in my brain, one which I had been nurturing quietly for many years—that maybe I'd survive it, my family would survive it, and maybe there was a happier existence for everyone on the other side. She talked me through a hypothetical where maybe no one would even really care. She pointed to all the people in my life who already knew and loved me just the same. I had been inching my way there on my own for many years, and now I had been given a choice: I could continue to writhe in pain and be humiliated on Shitbitch's terms, or I could force myself to share my donor conception and own my story before I was actually ready.

And so, one fine sunny day, I threw my family under the bus and told this stupid Shitbitch something very private and intimate about my life that I had previously thought I might take to my grave.

Now to be fair, it's not like I had *never* told anyone my father was a sperm donor before. In fact, I had actually told the secret to many people: my agents, my best friends, some ex-friends, several bosses, a few coworkers, and a random man at a bar across the street where we had gathered when The Second City caught on fire and life seemed so fleeting I thought I should open up to…Carl? Mike? Marcus? But I always told the secret to people who I *wanted* to know, in moments when I felt safe, when *I* felt like sharing. It was infuriating that I would be forced to share this part of myself to anyone I didn't choose.

And even though I had told handfuls of people about my donor status and CarlMikeMarcus roamed the earth knowing more about me than most of my exes, there were still people in my family who didn't know. When I made the decision to come out with the truth, I then had to sabotage reunions with my very fun and cool Maury Show reveal: Surprise, everyone! He is NOT the father!

I've run the math in my panic sweats at night, and there is probably someone who I didn't make it to—distant family members or friends of our family who don't follow me online (rude) and will find out by reading this very essay. One of the people I was most afraid of telling was Limoncello's mother, my grandma. I had a few sweet memories of her from my childhood—making mint tea from her garden, walking out back to pet her horses and feed the chickens on her ranch. After Limoncello and my mom divorced and I had taken Bubba's last name, my grandma and I had fallen out, so I imagined this donor news was going to send her to her grave. I called my mom and asked if she had any contact info for her. My mom replied, "Honey, she died a few years ago."

The news hit me with distant sorrow. Then I was aghast… because part of this news was ridiculously, stupidly, horrifyingly funny. I had been walking around this earth, torturing myself in order to protect my once-was grandma from finding out her son was not my father, and she was fucking *dead*. Aghast, aghast, I tell you!

On top of the struggle to share the donor revelation, to fully explain my name, it meant I would have to talk about an excruciating collision of tragedies—including ███████ ████████████████████ and all the times I'd had my last name changed as a kid. Shitbitch was forcing me to go back and face

██████, and I hated her for it. If you've had something horrifying happen to you, you know quite well that telling people often just makes it feel worse. The only humans equipped to take in your story and offer a reaction that won't make you regret bothering to share are often only those with similar experiences, who've seen enough tragedy to know how to listen to yours. Even the loveliest, most empathetic people are often frozen in their own processing, unsure of what to say, so they'll comment casually like your Really Big Deal is not a big deal at all or, worse, they commit to a string of intense follow-up questions to try to prove that they care about what you've shared. I knew if I opened up about my wounds, I would be headed for hundreds of those encounters for the rest of my life.

I thought about keeping the information to myself, certainly the easier choice if only I could swallow my pride and resign myself to absorbing the sting of whichever Shitbitch I encountered next. But then in a sob-induced shower, I caught sight of the tattoo I had gotten on my twenty-first birthday, a twisty, artistic scroll of letters I had branded across the stitches on my left foot where my twelfth toe had been. The tattoo was the sentence *Walk through the fear* with all the letters scrambled so that it wasn't legible to the outside eye. I had it tattooed on my body knowing that I had to be strong and face the moments of severe terror in my life. To be honest, I thought those moments were gonna be things like *Approach the famous person and give them your script* and *Move to the city with $2 to your name, girlfriend!* Not *Stuff your greatest humiliation into a T-shirt cannon and start the giveaway.* But there it was, the answer, waving to me from my ghost toes: just keep walking.

I told my secret over dinners and drinks and even in some wildly awkward texts. The first time I said it out loud to strangers was onstage, in a series of jokes that wildly bombed. Still I kept walking through the fear.

In the beginning I would get frequent panic attacks, my teeth would chatter and I couldn't get them to stop. At night I would have ugly dreams about all my dads. Divulging all these details about myself made me feel like I had just been pantsed in the cafeteria and wasn't wearing underwear (something that actually happened to me—and I would take that feeling any day over telling this story).

And then, slowly and without fanfare, the burden of the shame began to evaporate. Every time I said it out loud, it got a millimeter easier. Once I'd told enough people, I even felt comfortable with the idea of joining online communities and support groups for other donor kids struggling with their heritage and identity, which was something I'd never had the courage to participate in. Talking with fellow donor kids was the moment I felt saved, as it were. I had been so busy hiding from being a donor kid that I hadn't spent any time actually dealing with it. After years of feeling like the worst, weirdest bitch in the room, I came in contact with thousands of people who were just like me, many of us suffocating, tangled inside our unique grief. I spoke with dozens of donor kids whose families were wrecked by the revelation, who also found out their lineage was different than how they were raised. I even met a few who'd gone on to change their names. Finally, I could feel that I was not alone. I never had been. All my chaos began to make sense.

Oddly, coming out the other side of this so much more fulfilled and at peace meant I could look at the Shitbitches and think, *Ah, my darkest hour led me to the sun!* Yet I'm not thankful to them, and I cannot fathom how I will ever forgive them.

One of the most common obstacles to forgiveness, besides not getting a damn apology, is trying to understand how people could be so cruel. At the end of the day the only thing that I could take comfort in was what my mom told me in one of our phone calls: "Honey, people like to throw rocks at shiny things." And I agreed, singing along with the chorus of Taylor Swift's song "Ours" and thinking *Yeah, I am a shiny bitch, aren't I?!* But then I remembered that on season seventeen of *The Bachelor,* a top-five contestant named Tierra ran around screaming "These bitches are trying to take my sparkle!" and later in her confessional, she tearily told the camera that "People like to throw rocks at shiny things." Now, we know Tierra was the villain that season, so unless I can get the unedited footage of her journey to see if she got an unfair shakedown, that explanation no longer felt like something I could take comfort in.

I am prone to holding on to my Shitbitch grudges, but unfortunately I've scrolled by too many memes that say that *I'm* the one suffering the most by holding on to my hate. I don't want to continue to suffer from Shitbitch because of my own unwillingness to move on, so I've tried to find some ways to let it go. And that's how I ended up toying with becoming a Christian.

Yeah, that's how dark this got for me.

I was searching so deeply for answers about enemies that the only thing that got through to me was a friend of mine telling me about what the Bible says to do about thy motherfuckin' haters. It spoke to me so deeply, I'm telling you—if I'd had a different childhood, this part of the book would be about my adult baptism. My friend sent me a sermon, and I felt so much lighter after listening to it. And not just any sermon, it was a sermon from God's Justin Bieber: Mr. Joel Osteen.

In the sermon, Joel said that God will make your enemy your footstool. That God will put you back together in front of the person that broke you. And that vengeance belongs to God, not you. It is not your job to fight it, defend it, or get revenge. Your only job is to protect your heart and stay strong and graceful, and God will take care of the rest. This sentiment brought me so much calm, it felt like I could finally let my grudge go. In fact, the sermon moved me so much that I had to face something much scarier than outing myself as donor-conceived. I had to ask myself, was I going to follow Joel Osteen on Twitter???

I did.

I know, I know! But he's got some poppin' tweets, and through my scrolling, I realized why this God thing brought me so much peace when everything else about forgiveness has taken zero effect. Because built into that teaching is that while you are forgiving and moving on and being the better person, revenge is still happening. God's gonna fuck some Shitbitches up! My sense of peace didn't come from learning to forgive them, it came from the assurance that they would fucking pay for this in biblical proportions.

At times I've been tempted to take Shitbitch's part out of the book. It's so infuriating that you can be minding your business and then a Shitbitch can lob a rock at your head and suddenly become an inseparable part of your story, and a chapter title in your damn book. The tale of all my dads—donor and otherwise—has enough going on without a Shitbitch taking a role in it. I mean, my God, I told you about that whole twelve toes thing, didn't I?! But I am keeping her part in because while I wouldn't wish this experience on anyone (just kidding, I hope it happens to Shitbitch!!!), it has also resulted in that boring, tedious irony: in trying to hurt me, she made me even stronger. Begrudgingly and angrily, I'm very deeply grateful that I was able to acknowledge the painful things that make me who I am, because that's the moment when I finally got to be myself.

I know that if I wrote this essay again in a year, two years, ten years, I would probably have something totally different to say. I am not at the end of this journey, I'm at the beginning. I don't know if I'm saying the right things about myself and what it all means to be donor-conceived. Every time I start to feel bad, I try to treat this part of myself like a child. The part of me that is living openly as a donor-conceived person did not live through all my earlier years with me; it's still new to this world. The donor-kid part of me is still…a kid, and so I'm trying to be gentle with it.

But I do have a wish for myself. I hope that someday, if I re-read this, I will have forgotten some of the painful details entirely because I stopped holding them so close. I hope one day I can look back and laugh, wondering why it was ever so hard to share to begin with.

SHAYLA

The monster inside

When I was twenty-two, shortly after my godmother had driven me from New Mexico to Chicago and dropped me off to pursue my career in comedy, I discovered I had a 7½-pound tumor growing on one of my ovaries. I MEAN, CAN A BITCH GET A FUCKING BREAK???

The tumor was so large, I was told I needed to have immediate surgery to remove it that very week. The only problem, besides the tumor, was that it was my mom's third wedding on Friday. And honestly, thank fucking God she was about to marry my wonderful new stepdad-to-be, Edward, because he had recently earned himself a Father of the Year award when he had added me to his health insurance.

I had noticed that my lower stomach had gotten bigger, but it was 2009, so I was effectively covering it up with peplum tops, A-line dresses, and stretchy leggings cosplaying as jeans. I'd just started taking improv classes, and I started to feel a shot of pain each time I tried to stand up and move for exercises. Whenever I wasn't performing, I would have to lean my lower back on the wall of the classroom to take the pressure off it.

I assumed the back pain was because I was out of shape and

overweight or that it was just one of the many gifts my big boobs had given me. But then one night, it became impossible to ignore. I had bought a dozen of those cookies that are sold at every grocery-store chain in America—big fluffy disks of white dough, covered in a thick frosting, dyed various colors to match whatever holiday was closest. Each one is two hundred calories, and I told myself I could have one cookie a week. I ate the entire box that night. The next morning I woke up feeling like death, barely even able to open my eyes. I lifted up my shirt to see if I was bloated from the frosting, and I balked at the sight. When I touched my stomach, it felt like I had a watermelon inside of it.

Holy shit, I thought, I must be allergic to gluten! I went a week without sugar or flour, and when things didn't get better, I decided to visit a chiropractor, the only medical expert my New Age upbringing had taught me to consult. The chiropractor simply tried adjusting my neck, which clearly wasn't the issue, and sent me on home. When I showed my roommate my stomach that night, she told me I needed to see a doctor—a real one—immediately.

I googled "doctor???" and got the name of a clinic that was a mile from my apartment. After riding my bike there, I met with a general practitioner who took one look at my stomach and told me I was four or five months pregnant.

Now, I'd broken a nearly three-year stretch of celibacy just a month prior, and I knew there's no way a pregnancy could happen that fast. I told the doctor that it was impossible. He condescendingly asked, "Have you ever had sex, sweetheart?" I mumbled, "Hell yeah," and then he said, "Let's get you that pregnancy test, then."

When the doctor left to test my pee, I began to cry the level of tears you cry when you realize you're the Virgin fucking Mary with an immaculate conception, only you're not a virgin, and the father is a man who made you watch him play video games on your second date.

He returned shortly after, bewildered. "I can't believe it," he said. "You're not pregnant."

He examined me again and said we should take a blood test, because I *had* to be pregnant, but then that test also said I wasn't. He excused himself. Through the door of this tiny clinic I heard him on the phone. "You need to see her today! Get her an MRI and a sonogram. It's an emergency!"

By the time he came back into the room, I was a wreck. In one hand I was urgently sending texts to my mom letting her know she was about to be a grandma, and in the other hand I had wadded up my medical gown and was using it as a Kleenex to catch my sob snot. When the doctor caught sight of me, he must've tapped into his requisite training on bedside manner, because he forced a tight smile and asked, "Is everything okay?"

I told him I could hear him through the thin wall of his stupid clinic declaring this was an emergency, and also his dumb ass had made me believe I was pregnant for twenty minutes.

He gave a little half laugh. It was no big deal! Then he said I should get myself to the hospital immediately.

I got back on my bike, pedaled my protruding gut to the Illinois Masonic Medical Center, and spent the afternoon getting more tests. Nothing was coming up at first. You may recall that one of the worst parts about being a donor kid is that you're missing half your medical information. I could fill out the history of my mom's side, but my dad's side was blank. This made it much harder to check for conditions that might have been hereditary, so they volleyed me between tests using their best estimated guesses.

It was almost 8:00 p.m., and my phone was dying by the time I finally went to see a lovely technician who administered a not-so-lovely intravaginal sonogram, where they stick a giant wand up your vag and fish around from the inside. She was moving the wand around when she let out a sharp gasp.

"What is it?" I yelped. She said my doctor would tell me because it was illegal for her to give any formal diagnosis. I said, "Who the fuck is my doctor?" She said it was that guy who I saw that morning. "Oh, no thanks," I said. "I didn't really like him. You can just tell me, yourself." The wand was still inside me as she explained my medical rights, which included the fact that the patronizing doctor from that morning would be in charge of delivering my diagnosis, and absolutely no one else would be able to. Then she pulled out.

I called a new friend who I'd met in improv class, and he picked me up from the hospital and put my bike in the back of his car. I would never get that bike back again.

When I returned to my apartment, "my doctor" finally called me back just before midnight and said they'd found a large mass, probably a tumor, and by the looks of it, it was really fucking huge. He gave me the name of a surgeon in Chicago and told me I needed to see them immediately.

It was Tuesday.

On Friday I was supposed to fly out to my mom's wedding.

My mom and I quickly decided that I would get to New Mexico and have the surgery there so she could be with me and I could still make the ceremony. She set up an appointment with a gynecologist who could operate on me, and all I had to do was make it on the plane.

It became more and more apparent I was going to have some trouble riding the L train to get to the airport for my flight. I'd already used up a favor with my brand-new improv friend, and the only other person with a car whose number I had saved was the guy I'd broken up with a couple weeks ago—the one whose super sperm I worried had made me four to five months pregnant. Let's name him WorldOfWarcraft, because I think he'd like that.

"Call him up, ask if he'll bring you to the wedding," my mom suggested.

WorldofWarcraft was still hoping we'd get back together, so

he eagerly drove me to the airport and booked his flight for the next day after he got off work. Only, I was still new to the city and had assumed there was just one airport in Chicago. There are two. He drove me to the wrong one, sped back across town to the right one, and I didn't make my flight. I had to put a new $350 ticket on my emergency credit card, where it would remain for the next four years as I paid it off in $5 increments—an everlasting reminder of my mistake.

I arrived and spent the day before the wedding in the Santa Fe hospital alone, getting routine blood tests before the big surgery, while my family was running around picking up desert shrubbery centerpieces, bottles of wine, and freshly pressed suits for the big day. In order to get in fighting shape for major surgery, we decided I should visit our family's favorite type of doctor: that's right, a chiropractor!

At the clinic, I lay on the table as he put my body in alignment to help prepare me for the operation. He then took me through breathing exercises and tried to release the tension in my shoulders as I told him all about what had happened at the hospital. He walked to his bookshelf, where he kept a giant medical volume filled with the spiritual reasons behind every physical ailment and disease. He paged through his book looking for ovarian tumors, then asked me, "Is the tumor on your right ovary or your left?"

It was on my right ovary.

He read my diagnosis out loud. *"Abandoned by your father."*

Apparently, had it been on my left ovary, this would have meant abandonment by my mother. I laughed. The chiropractor said, "What, you don't believe it?"

"Oh no, I believe it," I said. "I just wonder which father it was."

On Saturday before the ceremony, I began drinking the neon-colored liquid you're supposed to ingest while fasting for 24 hours before the surgery. About a third of the way into the bottle, the surgeon called to let me know that one of my blood tests had come back with indicators that my tumor could be cancerous. I would now need my surgery to be done by a gynecological oncologist, who specialized in ovarian cancer. My newly anointed stepdad, Edward, had a sister who was a doctor herself, so she called around to find a new doctor in Albuquerque, and the surgery was set for a week later.

In the meantime, my poor mom cried off all her wedding makeup as we contemplated my fate. I put down the neon liquid I had brought to the wedding and reached for a champagne flute instead. Word quickly went around that I was dying, so when I gave my speech that night, I absolutely crushed, generating the amount of laughs that can only come when the entire audience thinks you're at death's door and that this speech may be your last.

The surgery was rescheduled at Presbyterian Hospital in New Mexico. My new doctor had told me that there was a chance I was about to have an entire hysterectomy, depending on whether it was cancer and if it had spread. The hits just kept on comin'! As I was wheeled into the operating room, I told the anesthesiologist that I had a history of not doing well with drugs, and I'd needed extra anesthetic when I had my eleventh and twelfth toes removed as a kid. The anesthesiologist leaned in, looked solemnly at me, and whispered, "I always win," and then I blacked out.

When I woke up from the surgery, the first things I asked were if I still had a uterus and if I would live. I was still very out of it—that anesthesiologist had really given it his all—but someone told me that the tumor was benign after all, and I had kept my uterus and my left ovary. Relieved, I promptly went back to sleep.

The doctor had cut vertically through my stomach lining since the tumor was so big, and consequently sliced right through my abdominal muscle, so I couldn't walk for six weeks. I recovered at home in New Mexico. I spent those weeks in so much pain. Not physical pain—no, no—but the pain from the acute stress that I would fall behind in my newfound comedy career! I had just moved to Chicago, only recently started all my improv classes, and was just beginning to make friends. I writhed in misery, wondering if all the students in my conservatory class would bond and progress without me. My solution? From the hospital bed, I made a six-minute long video about the tumor debacle and used it to audition for a solo comedy competition in Chicago. They accepted me into the show, one of eight performers, and I began to plan my escape back to the city.

Thank God that WorldOfWarcraft and I got back together—I couldn't make it up the stairs of my fourth-floor walk-up for another six weeks, but WorldofWarcraft lived in a building with an elevator, so I broke the lease on my apartment and moved into his. He was of course thrilled by this development and eagerly hoped we could have sex again, apparently very unafraid of busting those stitches back open.

Instead, all we did was fight. My only reprieve was when he went to work so I could be alone in his apartment until my conservatory comedy classes started, where I'd go and watch from a chair in the back, waiting for the day I could participate. I still didn't know many people in Chicago or have super-close friends. I'd quit my job and had no money to pay the rent. I needed somewhere new to live, I needed a job, and I needed my stitches to heal so I could finally break up with WorldOfWarcraft and his video games.

After five weeks of healing went by, I figured that was close enough to six, and I made plans with a girl I barely knew in my improv class who had a car. When she picked me up to go hang out and see a movie, I urgently hobbled out of the apartment building with my rolling suitcase and told her "Go! Go! Go!" I'd left a note for WorldofWarcraft, who was going to be home any minute, letting him know that I had moved the fuck out.

I couch-surfed and house-sat for one of my teachers, Anne

Libera, the woman who had started the college program I attended. Her mentorship was so lifesaving that I began calling her my comedy mom. While taking care of her dog and her plants, I applied for new jobs and wrote sketches for my precious comedy classes that I'd refused to miss. Two months after my surgery, the solo competition show I had applied for began, and I got up onstage and performed my first-ever solo comedy piece, an assigned song parody to rewrite Patti LaBelle's "New Attitude." Every week I would present a new comedic bit that the heads of the show had assigned, all the while healing a little bit more from the surgery. At the end of the eight weeks, I came in second place, but under the pressure of each comedic assignment, I had also discovered that maybe I wasn't just a performer, maybe I was a writer, too. After the competition ended I kept writing pieces for myself and began performing solo all around the city, until the night when I received Rebecca's email about working together.

After my surgery, the doctor told me the tumor was 7½ pounds and it was dermoid, which means because it's growing off your ovary, it develops hair and teeth. (I'm sorry for making you read that, but imagine living it. Do not look up pictures of a dermoid tumor. You're going to want to, but I'm telling you right now, don't fucking search that thing.) At that weight with teeth and hair, I had essentially been carrying a tumor the size of a newborn child.

The tumor was the biggest dermoid New Mexico hospitals had ever seen. An honor. I named her Shayla.

DELTA, DOLLY, TINA, CAROL, JANE, AND RACHEL

For all the early 2000s Tree Girls

I learned to read when I was very young, and like most early readers, I was incredibly annoying about it. Whether we were moving to a new house or a new state, books were my constant when I was growing up, and I'd lug them by the pound wherever we went. As a teenager, that love parlayed into magazines, and I can remember shamelessly standing in the aisle of the supermarket to read all my favorites while irked shelf-stockers nudged me out of their way. In one particularly inspired issue of *O, The Oprah Magazine*, I read a quote that said, *The cure to insecurity is education*. I was insecure about everything, and all I had to do was *learn* my way out of it? An early advanced reader's dream!

In high school, I took in every book I could get my hands on, yearning for something to fix me. I read *The 7 Habits of Highly Effective People* (I could only master 5), *Women Who Love Too Much* (rude), *You Can Heal Your Life* (can you, tho), *Never Eat Alone* (surprisingly, not about eating disorders), and *The 48 Laws of Power* (too many laws! Even the Lord has less). I read *Rich Dad Poor Dad*, and honestly, both dads? Losers. I read all of Suze Orman's books, and now I taste blond highlights and a bold blazer whenever I sip a $4 latte that could have gone toward a house. I read all the spiritual books around our house, Osho, *The Four Agreements*, *The Alchemist*. But none of them held the answers I was looking for.

At the same time that I was reading these tomes, I had somehow taken all of the agony I had experienced in my life and focused it solely onto the scale at the Curves gym, where I worked out for a free-trial month alongside the moms of the high-school boys who called me fat. Ah, *sisterhood*! I felt that if I could somehow get thin, all my problems would disappear: my classmates would respect me, my mom would get rich, and I would fly off into the sunset on a teeny tiny magic carpet made out of a dELiA*s S/M corduroy crop top. I began dieting, then bingeing, throwing up, and on my worst days, chugging ipecac, because as great as I was at the bingeing, I was not so great at the purging.

My magazine obsession soon narrowed into fitness magazines, and I dove into a manic phase where I would only read the Before and After stories and the little diet graphs at the bottom detailing the two Oreos they would eat for dessert. A cup of plain nonfat yogurt as a treat. A tablespoon of peanut butter. A half of a frozen banana mashed up so you can pretend it's ice cream. Or how about when Kelly Clarkson told a magazine that she sucked on a frozen grape to cut sugar cravings? I am technically a millennial, but perhaps a more accurate label would be: all the people who grew up sucking on an ice-cold ruby seedless every night.

I toiled away in these miserable days where I would count perfect sets of calories before crashing and eating an entire carton of ice cream, six ham-and-cheese sandwiches (if you remove the top piece of bread, you're in The Zone!!!), or at a particularly low point, seven bags of dark chocolate Milanos while I was still inside the grocery store, promising myself that tomorrow would be better.

I was in the midst of one such spiral when I saw her: Delta Burke, smiling up at me from the glossy cover of her half-memoir, half-style book. I was perusing a yard sale, waiting for my mom to buy yet another wicker basket, when the subtitle on Delta's book caught my eye: *Eve Wasn't a Size 6 and Neither Am I!*

It was a distressing line, because first we must ask ourselves, where did she get Eve's size information? I'm pretty sure the only measurements of Eve in the Bible are that she came from a single rib, which I assume is the equivalent size of those girls who wear colorful handkerchiefs tied around their chest as a shirt. And yet, what other cultural icons were there to stand with Delta Burke in 1998 and say *I'm not rail thin, and that's okay!* Delta didn't have anyone to stay by her side, but thanks to her book that I'd bought for 50¢ at a yard sale folding table, I now had Delta by mine.

Delta said what I needed to hear: that it could feel excruciating to not fit the idealized norm of a woman's body. For context, this was a size 4 when her show, *Designing Women*, was on air in the early nineties, and by the time I read her book in 2002, the preferred weight for women had shrunk so much that the ideal body had become a heroin-hospitalization-chic size 0. The other option for women's bodies at that time was Mandy Moore, but only if you *insisted*. Mandy was very thin, but she was also tall, and tall in that year was body diversity, baby!

Delta had been widely admonished in Hollywood for her weight gain and tried every diet including meth. (Delta is the one who called meth a diet, in the same chapter she also swore she didn't do drugs. Listen, these were desperate times.) Delta struggled with her beauty when she had it, and struggled even more when she didn't. She knew how valuable she was to men when she was thin and how they punished her when she gained weight. She ended the book with several tips on how to dress for a short torso (leggings and tunics, babyyy!), and then she left Hollywood for good. Delta felt my exact struggle, and the moment I scooped up her book from that table, my eyes were opened to a world of women who were suffering as I was, except they were successful, and surely that was better than suffering and being *unsuccessful*. I had found the help I needed: female-celebrity memoirs.

When I got to college, I agonized over when I would lose weight and how I would ever make money in the entertainment industry when my acting class was assigning me roles like "Tall Man" and "Tree Girl." I tried everything to slow down my bingeing, but not much helped. Growing desperate, I began buying tubs of low-fat yogurt, freezing them, and then chipping away at the tub all night long with a spoon so that it took me longer to eat it. Please, don't make this your Kelly Clarkson grape moment. Do not freeze that yogurt! DO NOT FREEZE THE FUCKING YOGURT. Don't freeze anything unless it's a goddamn frozen pizza, and even then—why wait?—make it now!

There were so many mornings I woke up and thought this had to be rock bottom, and once you reached rock bottom, you could only go up! But apparently I have terrible depth perception, because there was always somewhere lower I managed to go. When I read that cayenne pepper speeds up your metabolism, I popped a couple cayenne pills just before I went to bed, only to wake up in the middle of the night thinking my body was on fire. I raced down the hallway, desperate to get outside into the cold air, and ran straight into the sliding glass door and passed out. When I woke up, I promptly weighed myself.

In high school, my mom had tried to tell me that if you're emotionally eating, it's not about fixing the food, it's about fixing your relationship with yourself. I ignored that advice and instead stole her credit card so I could order a little machine that velcro-wraps around your waist and "does sit-ups for you" through the power of electronic pulses. Each sharp stimulation created a nonstop cramping, which I ignored. *Constant cramps are just part of being a gal!*

I was sure that if I could just get thin, then I would be happy. But! If I had to get *happy* in order to get *thin*, that was going to be fucking impossible. I searched intensely for diet tips that would fix my life. After exhausting every option available to me—from the South Beach diet, to the Mediterranean diet, the just-the-dollar-items on the Taco Bell menu diet, to the fat-free diets of the '80s, the glass-of-milk diet I learned about from our hot-ass neighbor, a dropper you put into your water to make you less hungry, a dropper you put into water that eats up fat molecules, a dropper you put into your water to make it taste like lemonade so that you could pretend you were drinking lemonade instead of having dinner—I gave up. I accepted that I wasn't going to fit into single-digit sizes or play the ingenue roles, or stroll up to my enemies and make them all jealous with my ass. The wittle bitty butt that would make men repent and women apologize would never be mine.

This wasn't a euphoric decision for me—it was pure depression—but either way, I no longer believed I could skinny my way into happiness. Giving up was soon followed by my discovery of comedy, and as I began taking classes, I found myself becoming actually, truly happy for the first time in a while. Before I knew it, I had lost a lot of weight.

And I was *livid*!

Nothing is more rage-inducing than putting in so much effort and time only for not caring to be the thing that finally healed my relationship with food. What kind of Bitchass-Cool-Girl god decided those rules!? The problem with not caring is that it's not an option you can choose when you're in the middle of caring a whole fucking lot. You can't fake not caring, you can't will it, it simply has to be true, and it took me seven years of eating-disordered agony before I could stop berating myself under the false pretense of *getting healthy* and form an actually healthy relationship with my body. If, when I was struggling, I had read in someone's book that they cured their torturous dynamic with food because they'd simply stopped caring about being thin and found their true happiness elsewhere, I would have burned that book...till it had a nice crispy skin on it, and then I would have eaten it.

Delta Burke's struggle with beauty had led her to write a book, and my struggle with beauty had led me to pick it up, and because of this fortunate collision of low self-esteems, it felt like Delta had personally walked me into the section of the library that would bring me endless joy: the memoirs. Shortly after first discovering comedy at NYU, I focused specifically on those by female comedians, or comediennes, or comedien-etties, if ya nasty. The first comedian memoir I read was Carol Burnett's, a fellow Tall Man/Tree Girl, then shortly after, I read Roseanne Barr's memoir, and then Brett Butler's, who was the star of *Grace Under Fire*. After reading these books by three vastly different humans with wildly different comedic sensibilities, I knew one thing to be true: I had been a comedian my whole life, I just hadn't had the language for it until now.

When I was in my first year of high school, I remember a girl on student council explaining an *SNL* sketch she'd seen—something about cheerleaders and a *Tostito, burrito!* chant. Again, we did not have TV, so going off her description, I rewrote the words to fit details about our high school and subsequently performed it during a pep rally. It would be years before I saw a clip of Will Ferrell and Cheri Oteri performing the original sketch themselves.

Even so, my rendition was a huge hit. People laughed and cheered and screamed, but then later they also whispered behind my back that I was weird. They seemed a bit repulsed by the fact that I was constantly cracking jokes and writing funny performances. Joking around was a gig for people like Chris Farley or the popular girls' twenty-five-year-old brother who hung out in the parking lot crushing cans on his forehead.

Yet, as I read Carol's, Roseanne's, and Brett's experiences of trying to make people laugh in a cascade of sexism and rules that were enforced around anyone fem-presenting, I began to understand that *weird* might really have meant *funny.* Especially if you were a Tree Girl in the early 2000s.

I trudged through college with fluctuating moments of artistic success. I was also fully celibate. Technically it was involuntary celibacy, because actually being celibate requires you make a formal vow, and the only vow I had taken was to forever find my self-worth through boys who wore thick flip-flops with jeans. After high school, I was celibate for almost two years before I eventually scored a couple of sexual encounters that could only be described as utterly pathetic. The second chunk of celibacy went for about three more years. Not that anyone was counting (me, like a medieval prisoner, etching out the days with my own blood on the stone walls as I waited to be set free with dick). At the time, everyone around me would say things like "Sex is so easy when you're in college" and "Especially if you're a girl," but not for me. I couldn't get someone to fuck me if I tried. And I did try! A lot!!! I'm pretty sure I was the first female incel.

The only thing I wanted was a passably average relationship to prove to myself that I was a "normal" girl. The more that men didn't find me attractive, the more I became sure it was because my hips were torturing the stretch on the Old Navy low-rise jeans I'd bought four sizes too small. I have the wisdom now to know that it was never my weight that took effect on my appeal—the real issue was my self-worth, and as much as I wanted to find my self-worth in men…I also fucking hated them?

I was so deeply scarred from the men of my childhood that it kind of ruined the whole genre for me, yet I couldn't stop being attracted to them. I would read magazine tips about holding eye contact with a man and smiling as a way to let him know the clit museum was back in business, and in my most celibate moments I gave it a try. These poor guys would be drinking a beer with a friend and then glanced over to see the literal fucking joker, seething with self-hatred and smiling ear to ear. It was a slight hiccup in resetting the ol' sex clock.

It took 560 pages of Jane Fonda's autobiography, but when I closed the book I finally understood why I was so mad at the world. My mom had given me Jane's memoir because it had helped her understand herself, and she'd hoped that maybe I'd find more understanding for her through it. Instead, I found *me*! I believe her book is like a Rorschach test: read it and you will better understand your own soul.

Jane introduced me to a vocabulary I had been lacking. Whatever I knew about feminism by that point, I had learned from my mom's divorces and honestly by just existing in the world. It wasn't called feminism to me, it was called "Damn, men get everything, don't they!" Jane Fonda not only taught me about feminism but also inclusion, climate activism, and antiracism, while still being a woman who participated in all the frivolous things I did, like acting, makeup, dresses, and—our favorite pastime—torturing our own bodies and dating terrible men.

Eventually, when comedians became my community, I felt myself starting to get more male attention, as the guys started wondering *Whoa, who's that girl holding up a chicken wing and pretending she's gonna make out with it? She seems like a fun time!* My dating life began to pick up.

When I was twenty-five, I started dating a man who was thirteen years older than me. Perhaps that makes you think he was a mature businessman of some sort, but no...he was a magician. Can it get any worse? Yes, because he wasn't a successful magician, he was an *aspiring* magician. It was his side hustle. His main career was much more respectable: improv!

When we started dating, I thought his age and career trajectory were admirable qualities and the fact that he would risk his reputation to date someone young and barely starting out meant that I was just that special. I had a pretty bad track record in choosing partners up to that point. In baseball you would call my batting average a 10 or "please go back to beading necklaces." So when this older, successful improviser man showed interest in me, I thought maybe the problem this whole time was that I had been dating people my age, when instead maybe I should have been dating a middle manager!

The power imbalance was so large that it took me a few months to realize how odd it was that he insisted on becoming director of my sketch shows…that…*I* was currently the director of. Or that I had somehow paid for dinner on our first few dates. Or that between the two of us, I was the one with stable housing. You know, I guess things started to feel a little off when he broke down in tears after I didn't use a joke he suggested in a monologue I had written.

Once I met his parents, he told me he needed to know if I would marry him, and he needed to know now! We were on two different life journeys, and it was time I "stopped being immature" and joined his. Around this time I was reading Rachel Dratch's memoir, *Girl Walks into a Bar…* I was initially pouring through it for any crumbs of how to be a performer at The Second City theater in Chicago, where she got her start, but I soon found myself drawn to something else instead: the art of manifestation.

Rachel writes that you can pose a question to the universe and then ask for a sign to determine if the answer is *yes* or *no*. Apparently, the best way to practice manifesting is by first asking for something small. So while sitting on the bus-stop bench waiting to get to my second job as a nanny, I gave it a whirl. I closed my eyes and said to myself, *If I am supposed to dump this magician, I want to see a white feather, and if I'm supposed to stay with him, I want to see a butterfly.* These signs seemed to choose themselves as I whispered my little prayer to the Universe, the divine, and Rachel Dratch. I meditated on this ask for a few minutes, and then the bus pulled up.

The door whistled open, and out stepped a woman in an ankle-length muumuu. The fabric of that dress was black and fully embroidered, head to toe, with a pattern of small white feathers. I mean hundreds of white feathers, just cascading toward me as she exited the bus. I had asked for a subtle signal, and this woman appeared in a dress that said RUN, BITCH.

I called him from the basement of the house where I was nannying and quietly, politely began breaking up with him. I whispered that I thought he was like, so amazing and just deserved someone who could, like, give him what he wanted, be that marriage or the opportunity to direct his girlfriend's student sketch show.

"Okay," he said. "But you gave me an STD."

Now, at that point in my life, due to the whole ovarian tumor thing, I was very diligently getting gynecological checkups, and as recently as three weeks prior had a full STD panel come back clear. So I knew this was scientifically impossible. But that's the thing about dating a thirty-eight-year-old: my brain was malleable, and he was a balding authority figure, so in my heart I thought, maybe I *did* give him one! Maybe it was a *super* STD?

Everything about sex can be so scary in your twenties, that I thought that even though I'd only been monogamously dating this dumbass for months, maybe I had a long-term STD that had escaped the panels. Or it was a dormant STD that I got in those hot springs when I was sixteen and it was just now showing up. I thought back to the last guy I had slept with before my old-ass boyfriend. I did meet him on a cruise ship, which feels like the first sign someone has an STD, so maybe it was plausible?

Saving this STD information until now was a genius move on his part, because instead of breaking up with him, I demanded to see him as soon as possible. With the power of Rachel Dratch's 1,000 white muumuu feathers behind me, I sat this nearly 40-year-old man down and said, "Show me your dick."

As I pressed him for details, I found out he hadn't taken a test but had just "seen something strange" on his penis that he had a *feeling* was an STD. There I sat, very platonically inspecting my older boyfriend's dick on his bed, which wasn't so much a bed as it was an old mattress lying on the floor. Somewhere in the back of my head I heard Rachel Dratch laugh, *Bitch, how many signs do you need!?*

My boyfriend pointed to the STD. It looked like…a small freckle. Not even a raised freckle, but a tiny, slightly darker spot on his dick. When he saw the look of incredulity on my face he snapped, "It's *new*."

A week later, we got the full panel of his test results back. His super STD that his young whorish girlfriend gave to him was *an age spot*. In retrospect, I do believe my vagina caused it.

He might've been the magician, but it was up to me to make this beautiful woman disappear. I called him during one of his shows so that it would go to voicemail, then told him after the beep that it was over and refused to answer my phone when he called back. He left me two voicemails where he's crying and screaming vengeance at the top of his lungs. I freaked out to my friends as he promised I'd never work in this business again, frequently reminding me that he was in a higher position in our comedy community. He had all the power in the relationship, which is ironic for a man who did not even know where to get an STD test since "boys don't go to Planned Parenthood." I thought of him when I sold my first TV show and whispered a thank you to Rachel Dratch.

But my time with Rachel didn't end there. Years later, I was in a totally different relationship with Caleb, the man from my drag era. He still thought I'd be a bad mom but I guess not bad enough to break up with me! Instead of ending things after our huge fight in Chicago, we made the natural decision to move together to New York City for my new TV job. But the moment we got to our new apartment in Brooklyn, it became wildly apparent that not only were we not supposed to be dating, we probably didn't even have enough in common to be polite neighbors.

After almost five years together, I turned to my old Rachel Dratch trick. I asked the universe for a sign as the C train rumbled through the tunnel. If I was supposed to stay with him, I wanted to see a flowing red ribbon—a standard, pretty easy object to see in the world. If I was supposed to break up with him, I wanted to see a golden orb in the center of two golden petals—a symbol that would obviously be a lot more difficult to spot, making it clear to the universe which option I was hoping for. I gave my little prayer a deadline: I wanted to see one of these signs in the next four months but before May 1, when we would have to renew our lease.

That very night, sweet, lovely Caleb was rubbing my feet, and we were talking about each other's days. It was January, but we still had a small Christmas tree perched on top of our microwave, which was intended to fill the apartment with joy and instead only underlined and italicized our 420 square feet of shared living space. I laid my head down on the couch, and when I looked up I saw it. At some point, one of the golden ball ornaments had fallen and landed into the wings of a golden snowflake, folded just so, in a way that resembled two petals. It was my sign. I never would've seen it if he hadn't been rubbing my feet while I lay down at just the right angle and if the couch wasn't positioned almost directly underneath our microwave.

Are you allowed to break up with someone who is giving you a foot rub? It seems like that should be illegal. But I had just asked for the sign a couple hours ago, and shocked that I'd seen it so quickly, I sat up with the power of Rachel Dratch and I asked Caleb if he was happy.

He moved out a couple weeks later, because clearly symbols

from the universe have no sense of how hard it is to break a lease four months early in New York City.

Many years after that breakup, I was on a girls' trip with everyone from my main text thread, which we called Roger-Roger. The vacation had taken us two years to plan because we couldn't figure out one free weekend between all of us, except for Valentine's Day in 2020. Everyone in this group worked in entertainment, and since we could barely find one weekend off, we agreed we would also be using it to nap as much as we wanted.

That first evening, my friends had retreated from the hot tub to take a predinner nap, and that's when I cracked open my latest celebrity memoir: Jessica Simpson's incredible gift to the world, titled *Open Book*. Under the influence of alcohol, the hot-tub chemicals, and Jessica's prolific offering within the pages, I began to recap her memoir on my Instagram story. People wrote back in droves: either they couldn't believe there was any substance in celebrity memoirs or they, too, were just as obsessed with these books. Inspired in equal measure by both responses, I began recapping all of my other favorite memoirs on Instagram.

As DMs poured in on that Valentine's night, I sent my manager, Jordan, a one-sentence email: *I just had an idea for a podcast. A podcast, ugh, I know…*

I was not looking to be yet another comedian with a podcast, but the premise of this one felt so innate, it was hard to ignore my desire to do it. My pitch was a show where I would recap, discuss, and celebrate female-celebrity memoirs. It was sent out to buyers on February 19, 2020, and an offer came in immediately to put the podcast on a top network. We began the months-long process of sorting through the contracts…and then the pandemic hit.

Quarantine started, and the world was forced to face itself in a new way. In my downtime from work, I began doing Instagram Lives and connecting with strangers all over the internet about these women's stories, which offered a brief escape from our new shared reality. The idea of recapping these books online grew into something deeper, forging a path for us to make it through the quarantine together with just a bit of our sanity still intact.

Despite how much joy the digital book club was bringing me, I almost backed out of the whole thing right before I was set to start recording episodes for the podcast network. Sitting a CDC-recommended ten feet apart on the porch with one of my best friends, Kenzie, I told her that I didn't know how to talk about how much these books meant to me without also relating them to specific moments in my life.

That's right, I didn't want to share details about my life—a hilarious sentence to be writing in one's own memoir. A podcast felt so much scarier than stepping out onstage, because at least then I was in person and physically with the people listening, so I felt I had some sense of control. Stand-up and TV shows are curated and scripted and go through rounds of feedback, which helps eliminate the chance that you'll completely fall on your face. A chatty, off-the-cuff podcast would mean there was no artifice, no script, no acrobatics to hide behind. I simply had to be myself. That did not feel like a formula I could count on. I had never fully been myself in my art. I made comedy about other people and events in culture, and even when I was talking about myself, I was creating a fictional piece or a joke with a clever twist, not telling you deeper details about my life and... that's it: no punch line...no fireworks...just *me*.

However, as intense as my fears were, I had also confronted a different possibility in these books. Almost every single one of these memoirs implored its readers to tell their own story: it would set them free. Loni Anderson said write it on a napkin, don't even share it with anyone if you don't want to. Brandi Carlile said don't wait, don't judge your experiences as interesting or not, just tell them. Jane Fonda and Dolly Parton wrote that everyone's story is important. All of these women knew first-hand the power it held. And the stakes for celebrity women to share were so high—they had shaped our culture and were often then destroyed by our culture. Their lives and sometimes their paychecks hung in the balance of whatever narrative the male paparazzi or tabloids wanted to spin. Then, when they took the time to tell their own story, it had healed them, and society oh so conveniently branded the books as trash literature so that we would ignore their power.

Quarantined at home, speaking into a microphone with a producer over Zoom, I felt a sense of intimacy and safety settle in as we began recording the podcast. I talked about how Demi Moore found out as a teenager that the man she called her dad was not her dad, just like me.

I spoke about how Rue McClanahan helped slow down my people-pleasing fervor and habit of rushing into terrible decisions with the simple phrase *Let me think about it.*

I talked about how Gabrielle Union's book so deeply understood the depths of my humiliation that it helped me walk my ass into therapy, and how Gabourey Sidibe's book helped me stay there.

I recapped Tina Turner's book, in which she wrote about her abuse from her husband Ike Turner and the two drive-by shootings that occurred after she left him, and how she'd survived by moving in with her female best friend as she worked to build her career back up. Tina had run across a four-lane highway without a penny on her to get to freedom. If she could be brave with the whole world watching her, in a generation that hadn't even opened its eyes to abuse, sexism, and racism, then what the hell was I waiting for?

I shared as much as I could, and I would sometimes even shake the whole way through those first podcast episodes, speaking as fast as I could to get far away from the moments of vulnerability. As I processed those women's lives out loud, I began rapidly processing my own, and it really is true: telling your own story can heal you.

Shame wraps itself around our throats over time, slowly choking us, and we don't cry out for help because we think we're the only ones suffocating, and we don't want to be a bother. We are all taught to be sweet, be polite, be normal, don't rock the boat, so that those at the top can hold on to the power that doesn't belong to them in the first place. We grow up siloed in our fucked-up memories, and we walk around feeling helpless and alone in our pain. And as long as we feel alone, then we'll never realize how many of us there are. That there's more of us than them, should we want to fight back.

You're told that you're the only one who wanted to disappear, you're the only one who was raped, you're the only one who was shot at, you're the only one who has been humiliated, you're the only one who had enemies, you're the only one who had a weird family, you're the only one who has made a mistake— no one else. Every time someone shares their story, the lie that we are alone in our pain is shattered, and the more I read these women's stories, the more I begin to reach the surface myself.

SOPHIE

Searching for The One

I could no longer ignore that something was horribly wrong, because a giant red flag was literally staring me in the face: I was bleeding out of my asshole. It was a terrifying discovery, but I handled it well. Assuming it would stop on its own, I ignored it for several days and then, in an anxious 2:00 a.m. spiral, scoured the internet for doctors who offered payment plans and had more than two stars on Yelp.

The next afternoon, I lay in the exam room as little medical tools scrounged around inside me, gloved fingers felt for masses and lumps, and the poor nurse's eyes were surely scarred for life. One thing was for sure: my butthole blood was not a result of Nairing all my asshole hair off, because that was something I had never done—but it certainly would be now after making eye contact with the nurse and witnessing her witness my butthole. When all the tests were done, the doctor and the nurse said they couldn't find anything wrong, so there was only one other reason my butthole might be bleeding.

The doctor closed his folder and asked, "Are you stressed?"

I burst out laughing.

Had *stress* shown up on WebMD when I searched *butt blood* I wouldn't have even bothered coming in. Of course I was stressed. We are all stressed! I was so stressed that my life at that moment didn't even feel that stressful; it was just another day as a twenty-nine-year-old hairy-buttholed woman seeing the doctor for her stress-induced butthole bleeding.

Then, the doctor started running a new series of verbal tests, which were clearly designed to find out if I was severely depressed. Mental health practitioners need better quizzes. The questions were things like *Do you ever feel like canceling social plans? Do you have frequent nightmares?* Try some subtlety, my friends! Throw these questions into a What Love Language Are You? quiz, and at the end your diagnosis will be *Surprise! You're all about gift-giving and panic disorders. Get some fucking help!* I answered defensively, trying to prove that I was mostly fine, ass blood aside.

The doctor told me he thought I might have complex PTSD. He gave me the name of a book I could order that helps you begin healing, the subtly titled *The Complex PTSD Workbook: A Mind-Body Approach to Regaining Emotional Control and Becoming Whole*. Desperate to feel some peace again, I ordered the book, but I couldn't make it past a page or two without having a panic attack. I guess the doctor knew enough to know that I had all the signs of c-PTSD but not enough to know that sending someone off on their own with a workbook like that was the exact opposite thing that someone with c-PTSD needed. But it was cool of him to realize that I was struggling, and he gave me a push toward finding the help I *actually* needed. That, and a handful of Klonopin. Each time I took one, lo and behold, the ass blood stopped. What I really needed was more Klon— sorry, I mean, I needed to focus on my healing.

That should have been the moment I set out to verify his diagnosis, but instead it would take me three more years before I'd give my mental well-being the same level of attention I spent making sure the guy at the Taco and Burrito Palace put enough cheese in my quesadilla. I brushed off the doctor's words, assuming his Yelp star spoke for itself. The Klonopin provided some fabulous reprieve from my recent mental dirge, so after the blood disappeared, I quickly rebounded to my default mindset: assuming the answer to my problems was trapped inside my own hectic spiritual aura, and one day I'd self-improve my way into a calmer brain.

As I'm sure you've picked up on, I grew up very New Age—crystals, incense, and all that jazz, i.e., Enya. By the time I was twelve I knew that the moon in my astrological chart was my real obstacle in life. Even now, when I take my bra off, you'll hear a bunch of rocks clack onto the floor, because I still stuff a couple crystals in there before I go about my day. I've seen more psychics than I've seen doctors, more astrologists than dentists, more iris-readers than pediatricians, and if you've met me, you know that it shows.

When I was in middle school, my godmother Grace came over one day with a present for me and Jesse: a kit full of sacred ancient teachings passed down from aliens. The "technology" of aliens was supposedly life-changing, and being extremely nice aliens, they had given their elite tech to a man named Tubby Miller, who said he was willing to share it with other very lucky humans on the basis of a strongly suggested donation, which Grace readily gave.

We took this ancient technology into our home in awe. We couldn't believe someone was letting us in on this life-changing magic. And even though that technology was quite literally a 4' x 5' laminated sheet of paper, it seemed like some real thick, convincing lamination. On the plastic was a bunch of geometric shapes and lines using every ugly color of the rainbow: neon green next to a brownish-orange and highlighter pink, because despite being very smart aliens, they were apparently blind to color theory.

Grace explained that you were supposed to stand on a specific

shape on the laminated-paper mat while holding an ancient magnet, which resembled a very heavy hockey puck with even more
ugly colorful triangles on it. The power of this magnet could send
forth energies and communicate telepathically with the universe.
We would stand on the mat constantly, thinking about what we
wanted in life and who needed to hear about it through our brain
waves.

Of all the signs that should have let us know that we were
wielding office supplies as telepathic wands, the name of the
technology—the Gentle Wind Project—written on the corner
of that mat in a cursive, downloadable free font, is what really
should've clued us in on the scam. It turns out that Tubby Miller
was running a cult with all his lamination. He was later sued
by all the people in his cult after they escaped (by telepathically
communicating through the hockey magnets for help, I assume).

I've been brushing up against cults for most of my life, so with
much wisdom I can tell you that the biggest problem with cults
is that they are fucking awesome. It's an instant community, the
rules are clear, rewards are always promised, and there are usually
drugs. At any second I could fall into a cult because I love self-
help. I'm always eager to find all the ways I'm terrible and try to
improve them. And, like a fabulous, help-seeking people-pleaser, I
am willing to put in the work, so I will definitely dig your ditch/
massage your hands/do a sensual and questionable dance with a
turtle for the lead guru's pleasure. To be honest, I didn't even realize I was sharing common spaces with cults my whole childhood until way later, which is an ideal quality for someone you
want in your cult.

I simply cannot ignore the validity of some of the woo from
my upbringing. I once bent a metal rebar in half using only my
neck while a crowd stood in a circle around me chanting. I was
fifteen. Grace's friend Amy lived with us as a temporary roommate at the time, and she was taking a holistic-nursing class up

in the city, so she enlisted my help for her presentation about the power of the mind. Several times at home, we'd practice by placing each end of a rebar in the divot at the bottom of our necks, right above the sternum, and we'd attempt to walk toward each other and force the rebar to bend in half. After many failed attempts, the metal just *bent*, and we went soaring toward each other in the inertia of the snap. With a single success under our belt, Amy drove us up to the city for her master's-class presentation. She guided her fellow nursing classmates in a chant, and then…we did it again. We bent *another* rebar. It was spiritual. It was miraculous. It was the unknown science around the mind. It was…interesting how this exercise was *always* done with rebars and never something else—say, a 2' x 4' or an old mop. But it had happened, and I can't unsee that shit.

Yet, despite all the tarot cards I had pulled for job interviews or crystals I'd stuffed inside my cleavage for a walk home after dark, by the time I was in college, it was apparent that something was deeply wrong with me, and it wasn't going away, despite no longer being in Mercury retrograde.

I was in a dark place my sophomore year of college—these were the chipping-of-the-frozen-yogurt-tub years—and I spent all my free time on my twin bed, eating and sleeping. At one point, my roommate Ali used the last of her cash to buy me a $5 alarm clock from Kmart on Astor Place, thinking that would help get me out of bed. When the alarm clock didn't work, Ali did something that I'll forever be grateful for. She called up the mental health services at our college, pretended to be me by reading the number on my student ID, and told them she was a fucking wreck.

Ali took me to my first appointment, and the moment I sat down, I began sobbing. The only thing I remember from that first session was that at the end the counselor told me that I only had nine sessions left, per the school's policy, and I realized I had just wasted the first one by crying through the whole thing.

That semester, I used all ten. They didn't fix me, but after a dime piece of therapy, enough of the fog had lifted that I became convinced our dining hall's frosty machine was worth the trip outside my dorm room, so at the very least, I stopped spending all my time in bed. Therapy had now become a possible tool I could reach for, whenever the tarot cards failed me.

Later in my early twenties, I hit another emotional rock bottom: I became a comedian. I was performing free improv shows at night, auditioning for commercials during the day, working in restaurants for rent money, and silently telling myself I was an untalented piece of shit for sport. It was time to start seeking out counseling again.

I first saw a kind, lovely woman through the Catholic Charities program because I had no money. After she asked if I was aware my bra was always showing through my clothes, it was clear we weren't a match. Then I found a program that was pay-what-you-can for grad students logging in their hours to become therapists. My new therapist was really cool and closer to my age, but I usually left our sessions feeling much worse than when I went in. This was likely because she was attempting some sort of new technique that gave the power back to me so I could process my own problems. Our sessions would go like this:

"Maybe I should break up with my boyfriend."

"Maybe you should."

"What, why? Oh my God!"

"Well, why did you say it?"

"I don't know! Do you know?"

"I think you know."

"You're the expert, *you should know!*"

"I don't know."

"Then, why am I paying you?!"

"You're not, really."

Unsurprisingly, I wasn't even spending my therapy sessions discussing my past. Instead, I talked about the drama going on at the comedy theaters. A dozen sessions went to discussing how a male director had told me I was "too confident" in a way that was "a little much" and would ruin my career. And apparently I didn't discuss it enough, because I'm still mad at that director! Years later he sent me a congratulatory email on my first TV writing job, and I ignored it. A couple months after that, he resent the email, wondering if I hadn't gotten the first one. I would have written back, but I guess I was...too confident.

After about six months of sessions together, my grad-school therapist confessed to me that she too had been an actor but she'd quit because of all the same things I was struggling with—asshole directors, unfair casting, jealousy, insecurity, and terrible material, like when that one male castmate kept writing me into a sketch where I only had a single line of dialogue, which was (and I am quoting this directly) *That's the man who rapes me every night!* It was to be delivered, per his note, "with a big smile" on my face.

While I should have found my therapist's confession empathetic and endearing, I instead decided that I couldn't be taking my acting advice from a goddamn understudy and quit going to therapy. Listen, I know I had issues—it's why I had signed up in the first place.

After that, I returned to the woo and began seeing an intuitive that everyone in the comedy community recommended. I had a few sessions where he told me I was very special and talented, that I would go far and had nothing to worry about. Then I talked to my friend who had been told the exact same thing...and then another friend and then another, and I realized that either we were all coincidentally the biggest talents alive, or this man's main customers were actors, and he'd just learned exactly how to secure a very validation-hungry fan base.

As my twenties wore on, I began to think that maybe I was

just a lunatic and that perhaps that would never go away. But that thought didn't scare me, because we all think we're nuts sometimes. Right? Right, guys??? Only, I would continuously freak out at the smallest things in my life and then feel nothing during situations that actually mattered. When boyfriends would raise their voice in an argument, I'd feel like I couldn't breathe. When my mom would tell me about a minor financial concern, I'd feel as if I might pass out. If a guy didn't want to have a second date? I destroyed my tear ducts and several journals. But when my mom called me to let me know that Bubba had died, I didn't feel a thing.

My day-to-day emotions weren't in line with the actions around me, and my responses were incredibly heightened or wildly delayed or sometimes absent entirely. The only times I felt happy were when I was performing or working on a professional project because it would take up so much of my energy that my brain became too busy to turn itself on me. Inside a script or a production, I thrived, powering through obstacles one by one as the effort to defeat them calmed me down.

When I wasn't performing, I would sometimes stare into a mirror and wonder if I should be here. One time, I voiced the thought of killing myself from the back seat of my friend Jo's car. She hit her brakes, pulled over, and physically shook my shoulders, yelling at me in such a stern, loving way that it snapped me out of the spell I was in. I could hear her voice echoing in my brain every time those thoughts appeared again.

I went back and forth like this, pouring myself into work, stitching myself together just enough to get by each day, until it would all become too much and I'd try more therapy or woo techniques to mitigate my emotions.

One time, I thought maybe a nice suburban therapist would do the trick. We went through our first session where you do the intake, which is where a therapist asks you a thousand basic questions about your life to get a better picture of your history and mindset before the real therapy can begin. Every time I answered one of the questions on her form, she'd look back at me and loudly exclaim, "Huh. Okayyy?"

Afterward, I sent her an email letting her know I didn't think we were a match. She wrote back two words with no punctuation. *Good luck*

Things were not looking up for me.

When I turned thirty, I started to feel my brain escape from what last bit of control I still had over it. I was finally in a good, loving relationship with healthy communication. I'd "made it" in show business and was working as a TV writer to pay my bills and no longer worried if I'd make rent each month. I had an incredible group of female friends. I was creatively soaring. But the panic inside me was bubbling up stronger than ever before. Trauma kept spilling out in small talk and jokes, no matter how hard I tried to put a lid on it. I was so confused as to what was happening, because my life *felt* better than it ever had. Now, looking back, I can see that I finally had enough stability to make room for a messy, flamboyant breakdown. After all, it's very hard to tell your boss that you can't finish the breakfast shift because *I'm just like, really in my feelings this morning*—it's the type of thing you typically need a salary and sick days for.

My full breakdown arrived one evening when I was standing in a parking garage, talking to a new friend from work. As we were saying goodbye, I very quietly, very nonchalantly started crying and couldn't stop. When I tried to explain why I was crying, I spiraled further and ended up telling her my whole life story as a man twenty feet away was charging his electric car. When I finished, she gently pushed me to see a therapist again. Hey, I had a theme!

This time, I had something special going for me: health insurance that covered therapy. With the power of my writer's union insurance, I was able to look for a therapist who special-

ized in the areas where I thought I needed help. The voice of
the Klonopin doctor from years prior rang in my ear, and so I
looked for someone who specialized in trauma. Whether it was
because I was finally ready, had upped the amount I could pay
per session, or simply ran out of white sage intention candles,
the gentle winds brought me to Sophie.

I love my therapist Sophie so much that everyone who knows
me should be making sure I don't sign my bank accounts over
to her or invite her to my wedding (just kidding, already did) or
put her in charge of my estate. I don't have an estate, but if I did,
she would be in charge of it. Luckily, I know Sophie wouldn't
allow any of that (she refused to come to the wedding), but I
still put her in the seating chart, just in case.

After I found Sophie online, we had an introductory phone
call where I told her I would be spending six weeks with her
max, and that I just quickly needed to stop feeling like I was
going to suffocate from my own thoughts and then I'd be on
my merry way. I told her I didn't fully believe in therapy because it had never worked before, I'd just simply run out of
other options, and all the memoirs I was reading kept promising its many benefits.

Sophie agreed to my six sessions. I asked her if I could skip the
intake. The intake was the part of therapy I hated the most: it's
basically like regulated small talk, asking all the simple questions
that I'd spent my life trying not to answer because my life didn't
have simple answers. *Are your parents married?* No. *Are they divorced?*
Kind of; my mom is divorced from my dad. But he's not actually
my dad. *Who is your dad?* I don't know. *Where are you from?* Nowhere? *Where did you grow up?* All over. The basic questions that
come after *Nice to meet you* are landmines for me, and I'd learned
to leapfrog my way past every single one of them in polite con-
versations. Except, you can't play leapfrog with an intake form.

When I began seeing Sophie, I told her that ███████

████████████ wasn't that bad, my dad stuff was stupid, and that I was mostly over all of it, but I did need help with some flashbacks, nightmares, panic-inducing intrusive thoughts, and the constant, ever-nagging feeling that I shouldn't be here. You know, small stuff! Somehow Sophie saw past my hyperfunctioning grin and worked a rebar-bending-level miracle, because we did the intake and it wasn't too bad. After the six sessions were up, I kept coming. And after each one, I started to feel a little better.

I remember one session where I explained to Sophie it often felt like my organs had been replaced with work. If I was working, I was alive, I could breathe, I was happy.

I told her how when I was performing at Second City, the shows were essentially elevated sketch revues, so each scene lasted three to four minutes and you would take breaks backstage in between the scenes and transitions that you weren't a part of. Sometimes those breaks were thirty seconds long, and sometimes they were three to seven minutes, and then you had to jump back onto the stage or hit a cue at just the right second, to keep the flow of the show going. Most people took this time to laugh with a castmate or think about what they were going to order for dinner during intermission. But I would finish a scene and run backstage to my open laptop, sit down, and work on a screenplay or script for those one to two minutes of downtime, then run back onstage to perform some more. This continued throughout the night.

Throughout the years I have heard many compliments, as well as many more tastefully shared concerns, about my work ethic. Not only could I take on a workload and amount of creative projects that should crush someone, but I felt ecstatic while doing it. My drive to create and produce projects was endless, and I never took breaks. I would fall asleep while working and wake up in the middle of the night and continue. If I ever had a moment that wasn't fueled by a deadline, my mind would drift and suddenly I'd be back in ████████████████████.

In this session, Sophie changed her position in her chair, catching my focus, and asked, "Where did you just go?" I said, nowhere, what did she mean? She gently said she wanted me to see if I could start noticing when I was checking out. I tried to retrace my train of thought: I had just been talking about relaxing, and taking work breaks, and how I have to keep my mind busy or it'll go back to ███████████████.

Her voice cut through and brought me back. "Like again, just now," she said. "Where did you go?"

Over time, with sessions like these, I learned how to notice when I was dissociating, which turned out to be constantly. I had somehow developed an elaborate system to almost always keep me outside of my own mind. In fact, before you tell someone they are *so strong* or *so brave*, you should probably first check to see if they are just routinely sending their brain to the moon.

I'd only ever seen overworking as a positive thing. The idea of relaxing had never been enjoyable in practice. On vacations I would feel sick and panicky, sometimes emotionally spiraling and picking fights with whoever I was with just so my brain would have something to do. I was most relaxed when I was under siege with a deadline, bringing my laptop to a pool hangout as if I was Katherine Heigl in a rom-com where her stupid little job was getting in the way of falling in love with the ugly, affable lead, who would eventually teach her about the meaning of life during one scene where she finally shuts her computer and sings karaoke.

This time, when Sophie diagnosed me with c-PTSD, I listened. I still cared a lot about whether there was enough cheese in my quesadillas, but now I made room for my mental health, too. When I actually began to learn about what my diagnosis meant, it felt like Sophie had placed my hand on a light switch and revealed that I'd been sitting in the dark—and there was something I could do about it. Then the next week, she'd show me the light switch again. And then again. And then again. And then after some time, I'd be in a session saying, *I'm so happy the lights are on! How did I ever live like that before?* and she'd point over to the light switch and be like, *They're actually not on right now*—because I had accidentally turned them off again.

My whole adult life, I thought I was suffering at the hands of my own shitty personality, but it turns out those flaws weren't personality traits at all, they were symptoms. Workaholism. Hating new situations. No curiosity to travel. Panic after a meditation. Hypervigilance for safety. Even some of the good parts of who I am—my go-getter energy, my overfriendliness, my sixth sense about which asshole was going to approach us in a bar—were fueled or even created by this disorder.

Sophie reminded me how *c* in c-PTSD stands for *complex*, and it basically means that you have experienced several large traumatic events in life and that your brain and body are working through all of them together, which creates multiple trauma effects instead of just one. Things get even more complex because in order to survive the traumatic events, your brain does this thing where it shuts some of it down, or blocks it out, or sends it away to summer camp, hopefully a real nice one with horsies, so that you can keep plowing through the day-to-day in survival mode.

After doing some deep trauma work with Sophie, sometimes I revisited my memories and they began to look different. None of them were new to me—instead, it felt like suddenly noticing something for the first time even though I'd been staring at it every day. As if each morning I'd used the same hairbrush for twenty years, but one day I looked down and realized that I'd been holding a pinecone the whole time. It's very unnerving, making it sometimes hard to process events because I don't know when to trust my own brain.

I could describe what the process of healing felt like, or I could throw in another handy therapy metaphor! I would have these sharp moments of clarity that felt like waking up from a coma and realizing that I was currently at the wheel of a car, driving 120 miles an hour. And as I look behind me, I realize I've actually driven hundreds and thousands of miles. And then I have to figure out what the hell happened during those thousands of miles, while simultaneously continuing to navigate the current road I'm on, a daunting task even with health coverage and a trauma-expert therapist offering suggestions from the back seat. We made a lot of progress that first year, but I was still having intense physical episodes where I couldn't stop feeling like the world was ending or that, at the very least, I shouldn't be in it. My current life had become so wonderful and filled with love and stability, but my body couldn't seem to accept that I was no longer under attack. Even though I was safe in my present moment, it didn't matter: I was stuck inside my own mind with my memories, boxing a ghost.

The first time Sophie brought up the idea of going on medication, I freaked out. "I don't want to be that bad," I told her. I thought medication would mark me as someone who was out of control, who lacked the drive and discipline to better themselves, who settled for the easy fix. I didn't want to get hooked on it and never be able to come off. What if one day I couldn't afford it or access it anymore? Or if I'd have to live with this thing I thought of as a crutch and become dependent on something outside of myself? I grew up thinking medication like that was for the weak and that it would change my personality or, worse, dim my creativity. The only thing I could cling to for happiness was my ability to write and perform, and I was afraid the drugs would dull those skills or take them away entirely, and then I'd truly have nothing.

After a lot more talking, research, and panic attacks, there was one thing Sophie said that made me feel like I might want to try it. "Going on the right medication is not a magic pill that will heal you. It's more like a cast on a broken arm. It's a hug, holding your nervous system together, so that you can have enough brain space to do the difficult work of healing yourself." She also told me that the right medication wasn't something that changed your brain or your personality. It would help restore deficiencies and bring me to the same level playing field that other people got to experience. That kind of offer was hard to ignore. Hadn't I always wanted to be normal like everyone else?

I set up an appointment with a psychiatrist to discuss going on medication.

A choir of newborn angels sing! A bus pulls up and the door opens—it's full of puppies! The puppies hop out and begin doing a choreographed dance! Whoa, the dance is Beyoncé's "Formation" and they're fucking crushing it! Why the hell had I been so afraid of medication?

All brains and bodies are different, and you have to do what's best for you, but what was best for me meant trying out a few different medications under the supervised care of Sophie and a psychiatrist until I eventually found the right one. My personality stayed the same, and—*gasp*—it got better! I didn't lose the ability to be funny or creative, and while the medication didn't fix me or heal me, it did something else very important: it held my nervous system together so that I could begin to heal myself, exactly what Sophie said it would do.

Once my nervous system had restored itself enough, I was able to do so much trauma work that, as I am typing this, I can say that the panic attacks have gone down significantly. The sobbing spells are still there but a little less scary, and my once-bleeding asshole? That's been doing great, too. The c-PTSD is not gone and likely never will be, but now I have the tools to mitigate some of the negative effects when it flares up.

I've learned to feel the difference between when I am present and when I have checked out and entered a dissociated state. I never seem to catch myself on the way in, but I can now catch myself in the middle of a horrific thought, or a false panic that I've convinced myself is a premonition, or a deluge of images that I wish would go away, or a looped memory that I watch as if I was floating in space, looking down on a little haunted Chelsea planet, detached from gravity, with no control over what I'll see next.

Now if I recognize myself in a spell, I start doing all the things that Sophie taught me to bring myself back. I physically shake my body, I use the smelling salts in my purse, I run little somatic balls over myself, I try to engage in a conversation with someone nearby, I sing, I do little *vss* sounds on my out breaths, I put my hands in ice water or rub ice on my face, or I pick a color and start naming all the things in the room that are red or green or blue. The funniest thing about my tool bag is that everything inside it is similar to a lot of the tools in the New Age world. I just had to travel the right way to find them.

I was told many times in my adult life that I was an intensely sad person when I wasn't performing—from Caleb to my theater director in college to the doctor who diagnosed my butt blood. And while I think that big ol' bag of sadness will always be with me, when I was able to lift some of the trauma off my back, I began to feel cheerful. I became the purple Teletubby in a bold lipstick and bangs, eager to giggle and roll around in a field every now and then, pawing at dandelions and giggling at cloud shapes.

Trauma-informed healing is what I attribute much of my joy in life to, and I'm the happiest I've ever been. It took years of striking out with the wrong modalities of care, but I'm so glad that I didn't give up on finding the right therapist.

Or... I'm in a cult. The leader is Sophie, the psychiatrist is probably an alien, please come get me and these magnets.

ROGER-ROGER

A gathering of Le Trash

I am, and will always be, a woman of the trash. *Trash* is said with love and care, as a 7-Eleven vanilla latte balances in my purse and an Olive Garden breadstick perches between my lips.

A Chanel bag will always be as good as a *Channel* bag to me; in fact, I'd prefer the one that says *Channel* because I'd feel more at ease when I throw it on the floor, which I'm absolutely going to do. I will also be shoving a burrito into it, so that I can eat the other half of my Chipotle lunch while out with my friends at a nice restaurant where they all order meals. Please know that I will still tip the server, because those of us who are trash know how finances in the service industry run, and those of us who are not trash believe the tip amount should directly correlate to how often the server laughs at your jokes.

Growing up, our family motto was Champagne Taste, Beer Budget. We presented and acted like fabulous women who deserved only the finest things, and there must simply be a problem with the mail because those fine things just hadn't arrived yet. My mom and I would traipse through the open houses of giant, beautiful homes, imagining a day we could live in one while also telling the real estate agent we were really looking for a kitchen with bay windows, so sadly, we'd have to pass. Our dream dish set was multiple colors, bold blues, oranges, and purples, making it the ultimate sign of wealth: mismatched, but on purpose.

Instead of a TV, my mom had found an old treasure chest and placed it in the corner of the living room. She then filled it with coins, jewelry, actual cash, and, yes, Mardi Gras beads, as she believed it would feng shui wealth into our lives. We awaited the day we'd be so rich our living room would be covered in department-store tassels—tassels on pillows, tassels on curtains, tassels on rugs—while in the meantime my mom would DIY our lives. She could sew any outfit and decorate any room solely from the clearance section in Walmart. Our prized piece was a giant, gorgeously framed painting of a woman in the desert, chilling on a bench, braless, with a shotgun resting on her knees. My godmother had procured this fine art by stealing it in the middle of the night from a hotel and leaving cash on the hook it had hung on.

Our particular brand of garbàge was fabulous. In that way, you would never have known we were ever struggling unless you truly knew us. We were not just trash, we were *Glamorous Trash*. Everywhere we went, we carried ourselves with aggressive esteem, our tits pushed up and a drugstore lipstick sparkling across our smiles, plus a little dabbed on the cheeks as blush.

I was not always proud of my Glamorous Trash heritage. I spent most of my life running from Le Garbàge, seeking out a life filled with the very thing that had made my family miserable: money. On the scale of struggle, we had always been okay, or else okay was always on the horizon, but certain moments from childhood still pull up in my mind like a Tacoma with a subwoofer, blasting a playlist titled Fi$calHAUNTING$$.

The playlist begins with a banger: me dropping out of soccer in seventh grade to avoid burdening my mom with the $50 uniform fee, that she would later get sad-mad at me for not telling her about. Then it skips ahead to watching my brother

Lucas eat a pastry for lunch because in high school all his friends would go off campus, and he could only afford to eat the 75¢ Danishes from the Smith's grocery store. The bridge hits and I'm listening to my mom trying to find a way to get him a bigger weekly allowance from Bubba, who says no. Then, the beat drops, I'm wearing my mom's black high heels out for New Year's Eve when I'm nineteen years old. A friend points out that my shoes keep slipping off, and I spend the night wobbling across the dance floor to go stuff more toilet paper in the toes. The playlist closes out with a crescendo of toothpastes. In my later teen years, I became a toothpaste kleptomaniac, believing each pocketed tube was $3 saved that I would desperately need in the future. Then one day I looked in my bathroom drawer in horror to find a dozen toothpastes in various states of use, collected from friends' houses, motels, and stores, all lined up for oral execution, praying I would come to my senses soon.

None of these Fi$calHAUNTING$$ were the end of the world, or even close to the worst that it could get, but my body held on to those memories as if they were, in fact, both of those things.

The urge to seek a deal never left me, no matter how much money I was making. When I started performing in my first Mainstage Second City show, I took over the locker of a woman who was leaving her final show just as I was getting started. She was one of the most radiant, powerful, successful women to ever grace the stage.

I opened it and began to fill it with my things, when I saw that she had left a pair of sneakers stuffed in the bottom shelf. I recognized them as a part of her costume for an old sketch; she had worn them every night onstage for a year. They were battered up, dirty, and...actual Nikes with the big black logo swooped across each side. After discovering we wore the same size shoe, I did some calculations and realized we would probably never be in the same room together again, and these sneakers could become part of *my* shoe collection—ahem—my now-name-brand shoe collection.

I was on year three of wearing these sneakers around when I was standing at the ATM on the corner of Bergen Street and Fifth Avenue in Brooklyn, and I froze, suddenly in awe of my own checking account balance: I had finally achieved that illustrious thing called savings. There it was, a juicy $3,000 that was just going to sit in my bank account month after month, untouched unless emergency called. I was thirty years old, writing for Jon Stewart on a show that was soon supposed to debut on TV but would never actually air. I didn't know that yet. In that moment, standing in New York City, with savings, a job in television, health insurance through the writer's union, and a goddamn pair of Nikes—I thought to myself, I've fucking made it.

But the road that led me there? I'd say it was akin to the path less traveled—if someone had turned it into a theme-park ride, operated by a nervous preteen who forgot to hook up your seat belt.

In college, an acting professor of mine who was as equally inspiring as he was problematic once said to our class, "If you let money stand in the way of getting what you want out of life, just quit this business now. You are not guaranteed money. In fact, you will likely never ever get it. The only thing you are guaranteed as an artist is art." At the time it was inspiring advice, which is wild considering it was delivered at an arts college that played to the maniacal tune of $25,000 a semester. But hey, a scam only works because they get you to emotionally buy into it! Two years later in Chicago, one of my comedy studies professors said that the best way to succeed in this business was to bring a blue-collar sensibility to everything you did and, quite simply, find a way. If you didn't have film equipment, borrow some, or buy some and return it within thirty days. If you couldn't rent out a theater to put on your show, perform it on the sidewalk. If you couldn't afford a prop, make the prop yourself, or write it out of the script. I memorized these two pieces of advice when I was starting out: this was how I could make it in entertainment.

I had been aching with worry that not only would I not be able to participate in my dream career, but I would never be able to eat off the entrée section of the menu, or that one day my mom would need a place to retire and I'd have to build it for her by hand out of all my monologue books for females, 20-30.

I didn't come from money like so many of my drama school peers, so I didn't have a backup plan. Once I was in the city and had a little bit of education, I quickly surveyed my odds and determined them to be grim—I had naively arrived hoping to be scouted on the street like a model, only in my case I was hoping for some man in a suit to shout, "You there! You should be the Affable Best Friend with no lines in a commercial!" When I surveyed the other ways in, it seemed I would need some sort of connection, but I didn't have a cousin who had a cousin who had a cousin who knew the accountant for Jennifer Aniston.

But now, with the gravity of these two pieces of advice, I could see the way forward: it would be hell. It wouldn't get easier. I'd have to quit following the paths of those who came before me and make my own instead. I knew I could do that because that sentiment was present my whole life—blue-collar grit was where I came from.

In the final days of leaving Bubba's grasp, we were trying to move all our belongings in a single day and drive off before he noticed. There was a large dresser holding us up, an antique that was coming in the U-Haul, but no one was there to move it, and my mom was calling a male neighbor to come help. I no longer wanted to believe things could only get done with a man around; in fact, I never wanted to wait for another stupid man ever again in my life. I walked over to the dresser, lay on the floor, hoisted my legs up against the wood, and began pushing it out the door myself.

Shoving furniture by myself was my default mode. Now all I had to do was apply it to my entertainment career.

Since my family wasn't nasty-rich, that meant most of my time had to be spent at jobs I wanted nothing to do with to support myself as I pursued (high falsetto) *The Arts!* But I had been working gigs for extra cash since I was a kid, so that part wasn't daunting. In elementary school I would weave potholders and make sachets and sell them around the neighborhood. When I was eleven I began cleaning houses, until one by one they fired me on account of my being very bad at cleaning. When I was twelve, I put up flyers at the local shipping store, offering to do, honestly, whatever. The flyer probably said something like *Incredible helper. Skills include: being cheerful, putting dishes away in low cupboards, recently typed three full paragraphs in my computer class.*

It clearly worked, because I ended up becoming a personal assistant to a wealthy lady who had just gone through a divorce and needed an extra set of hands. For a full year, I watched her son while he napped, prepared him little lunches, and lent a hand when she was cleaning out the garage and making donation piles. I was very helpful with that particular task, because I would take every single item home with me. That job ended when we moved away, but thanks to her, several high-end cardigans and a nice electric razor came with me. At fourteen, I became a barista at a coffee shop. This is still my favorite job I ever had, even though I almost got fired for giving my mom the employee discount long after they had told me to stop. In my household the deals never stopped, baby!

Waitressing is the job I did the most, at way too many restaurants for me to remember them all. There was the Italian restaurant when I was fifteen and made bank all summer with the tourist crowds. One night I stood out front after working a double shift when a customer exited the restaurant. As he walked out, he pointed to the sky and asked me if I had ever seen the full moon. Having just discovered I could take home $50 per night before I even had a driver's license, I crisply replied, "I'm too busy for the moon" and headed back inside to collect the tip he'd left. There was the seafood restaurant where they held bikini contests every Friday that inspired all my binges and diets. There was my second job as a posh hostess for a four-star brunch restaurant. It was there that I saw my first sugar baby and sugar daddy (hey, another available employment option!).

Then there was the hot spot in downtown Chicago during the semester in college I spent in the comedy studies program, where "the skinny girls" were cocktail waitresses in tiny black dresses and "the fat girls" were in white suit jackets working the buffet floor. The guy running the place wore $10,000 suits, and he told us at orientation that we were a family—nay, "a tribe"—and yes, obviously, this man was white. He told us we'd all split our tips evenly among each other (as tribes do?). One time we split the $20 we'd made that night, and after realizing I was going home with less than bus fare, I hung up my white suit jacket in the basement and never came back.

Summers in between college, I'd waitress at a diner in Santa Fe, New Mexico, where my mom had moved during my last year of high school. I'd quit with no notice, vowing never to come back because I was surely now on to "better things" only to return the next summer or holiday break and beg for my job back. Once I was out of college and had moved back to Chicago, I got a job at a fine-dining restaurant. I'd lied to them about my level of experience by memorizing different features of the wine using homemade flash cards, and I was soon fired after one of the owners stood in the corner watching me massacre the opening of a bottle of Moët. Then there was the coffee shop on the corner in Wicker Park that had about two customers a day, and which I also think was a front for something shadier, because all we served were muffins from Costco, and I was instructed to tell anyone who asked that I baked them myself that morning.

That's not even close to my full résumé. When I wasn't waitressing I was doing admin jobs, interning, working at summer camps, answering phones at call centers, nannying, and I once hosted trivia for a few months for a company that made you lug your own amp around to bars, and I then used the gig to try out my own stand-up comedy in front of a bunch of begrudging trivia players. I worked multiple jobs a year, sometimes two or three at once, and I would get fired or quit without notice when there was even the slightest chance I was about to be cast in a show, even when it was for free and when that show was not held in a real theater, which was the case with most of them when I was first starting out.

The very first paycheck I ever received for performing came when I was a sophomore in college. For some reason, NYU didn't mention in the admissions catalog that they had become the number one school in student suicide. The administration came up with the perfect solution to combat the rising numbers: a musical comedy show during Welcome Week, featuring twelve drama students singing songs about STDs, unprotected sex, and not killing yourself. This may sound like a very dumb show, but as one of the few paying summer acting jobs for drama students—and a *musical*, at that—it was the gig of the century.

The auditions lasted three months where a hundred of us would attend "optional" workshops twice a week and present little songs and sketches that we wrote, as the director decided who had the funniest rhymes for *herpes* and *condoms aren't that bad*. She eventually chose her final twelve, and I didn't make the cut. I cursed the director to pieces and cried into my notebook of genius ideas I'd written for the show. The next week, I performed a sketch in the director's class that involved me playing the bongos while pretending to be Jesus on the cross. I had tapped the sweet spot of religious parody, and now I had a hit on my hands. Afterward, the director grabbed my elbow and pulled me aside to offer me a role in the cast. "I think I was wrong about you," she said. And with that, I got my first paying job in theater! It also probably helped that my good friend Dana had dropped out of the show, leaving an open spot.

We were given free housing for the summer and a small monthly stipend, and in return we'd spend all day working on the show we'd be performing for the incoming class. The very first day of rehearsals, the director announced that the biggest solo of the show would be about suicide. It would go to the best singer because suicide was a topic very close to the director's heart, and it was really important that this two-minute song be able to do the gargantuan work of preventing any future student deaths. Dana had an incredible voice and this was likely to have been her solo, so in her absence we all began vying for the crown. After weeks of rehearsing, the director announced who the suicide song would go to. It was me! I wasn't the best singer there, but she said it helped that I'm so loud.

I was euphoric. I hadn't been cast in much during my first two years of college and was making very little headway with the idea that I was any good at acting, but now I was singing the biggest solo in the show! Over those first few weeks, the director began to choreograph my song, shouting "Louder! Louder!" as all my castmates glided around, acting as my dancing inner demons. At the end of the song, I was supposed to curl up into a little ball for the finale. Only, I am tall and thicc as hell, and I have really long legs and a laughably short torso, so tucking my legs up has never worked for me. When I went to curl up in a ball, it looked more like I was posing as a small table. The director was a naturally minuscule human and couldn't figure out why I wouldn't just do it. "Get small! Make yourself really small!" she'd shout, but a table I would remain.

One day, after rehearsing my solo, the director came to the center of the room with a grave announcement. In front of everyone, she said that I would no longer be singing the suicide song. In an effort to be candid, and possibly offer feedback to encourage me to choose a different profession, she plainly stated that I "looked too ethnic" and "seemed like someone who actually would want to kill themselves," and the song was just too depressing coming from me. She was widely known—and widely beloved—in the drama department for her intensely honest personality. So I simply nodded and tried to keep my face neutral and very not-depressed. Shortly after, the director recast the role to someone more "happy looking"—my very wonderful, very thin, blonde, and blue-eyed roommate.

Ironically, instead of saving lives, I can say with certainty that the suicide song made at least one student want to die.

My second paycheck in entertainment came when I began performing comedy in Chicago. Well, technically it was on the Pacific Ocean—the cruise ship for Second City. Reports came back from the high seas that I'd done a great job during my contract, so before we even docked I was offered another position performing a six-week show in Baltimore. This was part of their new custom traveling shows where casts would show up to cities and plug-and-play city-specific references to only mildly tepid enthusiasm. But something very important happened because of that show. I got an agent.

In an exceptional act of kindness, one of my castmates in the show, Brooke, offered to send in my materials to her agent, which she did, and even though they never reached out, her vote of confidence made me believe I deserved representation. Then, her husband Josh, who worked in a casting office, came out to visit her and watched our show. A few weeks after we returned, his casting office announced a new TV sketch show and began auditioning every comedian in the city, including people without agents. Josh brought me in for my very first professional audition.

Since it was for a sketch show, we had to write our own material, so I was able to fill my audition with jokes and twists and reveals that, altogether, were more a display of my writing than my acting. After I finished my piece the head casting director said to me, "Who are you, where have you been, and who is your agent?" I weakly offered up that I didn't have one. She thought that was unbelievable and picked up the phone on the spot and called the best agent in town, who immediately signed me on her recommendation. My life in television had begun.

One of the first big commercials I booked was for an electronic device for a big brand that I won't name, in case I signed something saying I wouldn't! I beat out four hundred other Chicago improvisers for the job, as well as others from New York and Los Angeles, and was told I'd be flying out the next day to film it. At six that night, my agent called and said that while the marketing team (who had cast me) had loved my audition, the execs of the electronic brand saw my video and were convinced my hair was a wig. They wanted me to prove it was my real hair before they'd close the contract.

I have told you a lot of terrible things about myself, so I don't mind telling you that I have a nearly perfect head of hair. It's incredibly thick, it dries in easy, nonchalant waves that can be styled curly or straight, and it will stay in place for days and sometimes a full week. The people at Drybar fear me, and my hair stylist uses two blow-dryers when I'm in the chair. So I guess I kind of get why they thought my hair was a wig, but also, fuck off? The commercial was offering the most money I'd ever seen from a gig, so I promptly sent over a bevy of photos that depicted my hair styled in all different ways, plus a video of me shaking out my hair and proving it was still attached to my scalp. Satisfied, they agreed to fly me to New York City.

When I arrived for the gig, they put me in a 1970s cab for twelve hours with the windows rolled up and no air conditioning. These producers were shooting on a 97-degree day in New York City, so inside the cab was far beyond 100 degrees. Behind the cab, a very air-conditioned van with the director and producers followed, watching me through the monitors as they shouted directions into my hidden earpiece. Never ever give a people-pleaser an earpiece. Every three minutes, I'd hear the director say, "Stop responding to what I say. Pretend you don't have an earpiece in," and I'd say, "I'm so, so sorry," and then he'd repeat, "Stop responding!"

After each ten-to-fifteen minute lap around the city, the cab would stop and escort more random passengers into the back who had presigned waivers to be in the commercial. As the cab drove down the street I'd pop into the little cab window and ask the passengers, had they ever seen an image so crisp on such an entertainment device before?! Then I'd attempt to improvise funny, positive, PG-rated responses to their reactions over this new device, all while being trapped inside a boiling-hot car.

One of the first routes the driver took during the shoot was right by my old dorm room, the only freshman building that had offered low-cost housing. As sweat poured down my face, I looked upon my old discount dorm and drowsily thought, Look at me now, NYU! The Tall Man/Tree Girl has officially booked a commercial!

The cab was so intensely hot that production assistants began strapping ice packs to my body to try and cool me down—not because they cared about my well-being but because they needed my sweat to stop "ruining the shots." Eager to please on my first huge job, I never complained. When I walked out of my hotel the next day on my way to the airport, I immediately passed out from heat poisoning and missed my flight home.

The commercial eventually went up online, and all the comments said things like *Lol no*, and more than one person wrote something like *Is that Aubrey Plaza? Why would she do this??* which I took as a huge compliment. I used the $11,000 check from the shoot to make the first massive payment on my student loans, and it was worth every second.

When I wasn't earning money from sporadic commercials, I was spending my time trying to come up with a five-minute comedy set that would get me on TV, on the one show that regularly cast comedians out of Chicago: *SNL*. Every year the *SNL* and casting executives would come through the city to scout talent. Since *SNL* was either everyone's legitimate dream job, or simply just the only legitimate entertainment opportunity that came to the Midwest, our comedy community lost their minds during the lead-up, execution, and fallout from these visits. The head of one popular comedy theater got the idea that they should hold some preauditions for the actual audition for the *SNL* showcase, and that these auditions should be open to every single human who ever delivered a well timed *My wiiiiiife*.

When I showed up to my time slot, they were running four hours behind, and the list of comedians ahead of me was a hundred names deep. It had been haphazardly decided that everyone in the city auditioning would stay and watch their competition, because there simply was nowhere else for them to go. When it was finally my turn, I had already swallowed my own nerve-vomit at least three times. I walked to the little platform in the classroom that was operating as a stage and began my set.

Fifteen seconds in, the theater owner picked up my headshot between her two fingernails, holding it like a chicken bone in your minestrone, and tossed it onto the floor. She was less than five feet in front of me. I was close enough that I could've picked my photo up and put it back on her lap (which is probably what Andy Kaufman would have done, so wow, what a missed opportunity).

Unsure if I should continue, I sort of slowed my pace and looked to her for direction, but she'd already started checking her phone. I knew I'd lost her. She always had these two large dogs with her, and they came over and began licking my head-shot on the floor—probably because during this time of my life, I carried my headshots around in a flattened pizza box. (Relax, not the giant pizza box from delivery, but a frozen grocery store box that I had pressed down because it had real thick card-board, similar to a folder. Only, it wasn't a folder, it was a grown woman's headshot pizza box.)

All of this might have felt survivable, except 150 of my peers were also watching it happen. There were a few ways forward, but the one I chose was to stop myself thirty seconds into my first monologue and loudly say, "Thank you!" Then I took a small bow and ran the fuck home.

College professors and concerned adults had always told me that this career will rip your soul up. They'd spout the familiar *If you can do anything else in life, do that*, and I'd grit my teeth and tell myself I could handle it. Could it really be that bad?

A thousand times, yes.

I've received an email at 5:00 a.m. from a cocaine-fueled executive writing threats about my audacity to take a differ-ent job, including a long monologue about 9/11, which they somehow tried to thematically weave into the situation. I've gotten dream jobs only to take phone calls for my own salary negotiations while curled up in the fetal position on my office floor, wondering if maybe it would be easier to quit. I've had actors take credit for jokes I wrote and pretend to our cowork-ers that they improvised them off the top of their heads. I've had a semi-famous starlet tell the executive producers of a show that I couldn't play the three-line role that they wanted to cast me in. After she'd leaned in and whispered this to a bunch of producers—one of whom was a close friend of mine—she made her way over to the table of us scriptwriters and, no joke, began to braid my fucking hair.

I've had grand successes, moments where I'd be so proud of my own work on a TV show that I'd find myself choking up over it, only to have my boss ban me from talking about the show because she worried people would find out I was doing most of her job for her. I've had a coworker try to make out with me at a bar, to which I attempted to gently push them off. They were later fired and then told people the reason was that I had stopped talking to them and that my reticence towards them (ahem, *boundaries*) had been a form of bullying! I've worked on scripts for twelve years that my managers had told me would never sell (too female, too niche, too dark) only to watch someone else sell the exact same idea, and I had to live with the fact that I never even got the chance to try.

Trying to "make it" in this business felt like hurling myself at a brick wall, day in and day out, and then one moment, after years of running full speed into layers of shale aggregate…the wall gave way and crumbled. Unsure of what to do next, I kept hurling myself at it anyway.

When you get your first monumental break in the business, the energy and momentum that comes from chasing the dream starts to dissipate, and it becomes time to steer a different ship: *living* the dream. Actually, that last sentence is the entire concept of the book *Rich Dad Poor Dad*. Rich people expect wealth and success, they are especially equipped to navigate it, entitlement is real and very helpful, and poor people wah wah wah. I knew how to labor, budget, and scrape by. I was in an intimate relationship with the struggle: how to withstand the setbacks and keep walking through all the moments that were begging you to quit. The struggle is where I had learned to thrive. I did best in the middle of the climb, in the part where you're dreaming of the moment, finagling a way to the top. Once I actually got to the moment, I no longer knew how to go forward.

When it came time to start doing things like negotiating a salary or turning projects down, it felt impossible. Without exaggeration, I can tell you that I have said the following sentences while on business calls:

I don't care. I'll do it for free.

I'll just wake up at 4:00 a.m. to get it done, I don't want to turn something down.

I'm not really a fan of that genre or that writer, but yes, tell them I'd love to!

When my agent told me I'd sold this book and they wanted to publish it, he asked me how much I would do it for, and I replied, "I dunno. How much do they want?"

Then, one day, a new text thread appeared on my phone.

There were six women in this group message, including myself. The six of us were not an established friendship group. We all knew each other from working in the business, but while I was close with some, others I would have described as more like awe-inspiring acquaintances. We hadn't ever all had dinner together or even attended the same party. The first text said something like *WHAT'S UP! Do you guys want to chat about some shit!?!*

And from there it grew into my constant phone-a-friend and the executive branch to the center of my heart, helping me navigate all things in life.

Of all the text threads in my phone, I don't know how this one became such a North Star, but I think it's partially because everyone included in it had four things in common: they all started out as comedians; they are currently a showrunner; they grew up working-class, so no Hollywood bullshit would ever compare to the actual hardships they'd already made it through; and finally, and importantly, they all genuinely love other women. It's a gathering of Le Trash, the women who, if the occasion arises, would not hesitate to throw a punch, would never pay full price for a shirt, and would show up to a four-star restaurant and order a Belvedere and Sprite without a hint of embarrassment.

We named this thread Roger-Roger.

Sometimes I wake up to two hundred messages and save it for coffee and read through it like it's my favorite book, taking in news updates, home-life updates, bits and jokes. Roger-Roger has solved emotional problems, relationship issues, family arguments, and one time everyone sent a picture of just the bottom folds of our boobs by holding the phone under our shirts, because one of the Rogers was having a bad day and we thought it might cheer her up.

Sometimes I turn to Roger-Roger like it's a WebMD who can actually be trusted, where I can feverishly type a problem into the chat and await my diagnosis.

How do I reply to this awful and aggravating email?

They tell me:

You never have to write an email back. Remember that.

And:

Here, I've copy-pasted the response I use for people like this. Now it's yours.

One time I texted the group, *I'm taking on another script, and there's no money, but the people it's for could really help me out in the future.*

No, you're not!!! they replied, delivering monologues on boundaries, survivor mentality, and reminders of where good art comes from—i.e., not from overworking yourself.

Another time one of the Rogers texted, *I was offered a gig speaking across the country, but the flight, the time, the ask, it's all way too much, given everything I have going on.* We all told her to turn it down, to value herself, to respect her time. Then she told us how much they were offering her. *GET ON THE FUCKING PLANE RIGHT NOW,* we wrote.

During a difficult negotiation for a new job, one of the Rogers texted that she had accidentally been forwarded the correspondence between her lawyer and the TV network with whom they were fighting for more money. That Roger took a screenshot of an actual sentence their lawyer had proudly typed about them. *It seems you've been misinformed as to the stature and talent of my client.* Two of the Rogers fired their lawyers, realizing they also deserved lawyers who would say crazy shit about them, too. I had the sentence printed up on T-shirts and mailed them to the group like it was Roger-Roger merch.

When someone has a larger, more difficult situation in her life, we call a Roger-Roger court. A text will appear. *Is court in session?* Then, the texter waits to see if, across several different cities and sometimes internationally, enough Roger-Rogers are currently looking at their phone to form a jury. Someone will reply, *Court is in session.* I assume this little charade is as close to Dungeons & Dragons as I will ever come, and if it's anything like it, then fuck, that game rules!

Once everyone is present, the case is presented via text: the issue, the pros and cons, the logistics. We then wade through the discussion together till we figure out the right call. At times we disagree, and if the issue is escalated, the texts will turn to voice memos as each Roger-Roger pleads their case into their phone, hiding behind desks, whispering through hallways, or while slurping spaghetti in bed. My favorite court case began with one of the Rogers texting, *I'm hiding in a closet at work...* followed by the most epic of all our debates over a $200 swimsuit someone was considering purchasing.

We'd all fought our way into the business and hoped to make the climb easier for people like us, so that more of *us* could be in it together, toppling the patriarchy and the assholes. We made an Excel spreadsheet of talented writers without representation who were seeking jobs and added names to it regularly. The Rogers would hire from this spreadsheet and pass the names on it to showrunners looking for recommendations, and we joked about starting our own agency when this spreadsheet worked over and over again to get people jobs. When one of us received another *Can I pick your brain* email, we started a Roger-Roger Google Doc where each of us dumped in every piece of wisdom, link, and book recommendation, sharing it for whenever someone emails one of us looking for advice.

I used to think that in order to truly live the good life, I'd need access to experts in marble buildings with expensive hourly fees to tell me what to do. But I now know, after gaining access to some of those marble buildings, that those places are filled with everyday losers just like us, their Chanel bags don't mean shit, and there is no one more powerful, wise, and impactful than a team of best friends in your phone. Roger-Roger taught me how to be a better boss, how to stand my ground, and how to decide when it was time to walk away. They taught me how to tell someone to fuck off nicely and how to tell someone to fuck off in a way that would haunt them forever. Without them, I think I'd still be swinging a sledgehammer at an invisible wall, still stuck in that first moment I'd stormed the castle, but with no actual plan once I got inside. With their guidance, I've found new walls at which to swing the sledgehammer, and best of all, I'm not swinging alone because Roger-Roger is always with me.

I'm so thankful to the person who sent that first text message years ago, who thought enough of me to include me in it, who started this joyful, momentous, ongoing heartbeat in my phone. It was the woman who left the dirty sneakers.

ASHLEY

From three-day-old leggings to red carpet gowns

Ashley and I plowed through the crowd of famous people in shiny gowns as we searched for the exit of the LA Convention Center. We had another party to get to, and it was very important that we leave immediately so we could get in the car and take off our excruciatingly painful heels. I was thirty-two years old and had just attended the Emmy Awards as the date of my best friend, Ashley, who had been nominated for her writing on the TV show *Full Frontal with Samantha Bee*.

We finally escaped into the warm dirty evening Los Angeles air and began our hobble-run down the grand staircase to the spot where the town car chartered for Ashley was supposed to meet us. After finishing the several dainty appetizers we'd swiped on our way out, we made it to the street, where hundreds of limos, black cars, and expensive SUVs crowded every open space for blocks. Ashley and I scanned limo after limo, each one with a stressed driver waving their arms and talking heatedly into cell phones in search of their passengers, until Ashley pointed far off in the distance to a man in a black suit jumping up and down.

"There, that's our car!" she shouted. It was a full block and a half away. Ashley looked at me, resolved. "I'm not gonna make it."

She then proceeded to peel off her heels, holding the shoe straps in one hand and her purse in the other, and lifted the front of her mint green dress so it wouldn't get dirty. But she still had a long train and sashes hanging in the back of her gown, too, which she couldn't reach. As I surveyed her, I knew what I had to do.

I joined Ashley, removing my heels, and picked up the back of her dress and sashes, stuffing my shoes and purse into the folds of my armpits. Together, we zigzagged through a sea of luxury cars, barefoot, starving for real food. Right before we reached the limo, I looked down to see my feet were already covered in asphalt filth, and I thought to myself, this is better than I even dreamed.

I did not grow up around museums and boho art houses showing black-and-white Woody Allen films about teenage characters who found him attractive, only to be received as "great art" instead of utter absurdity. We did not have *cinema*, we had *movies*. Actually, for a time in Colorado we had *movie*, singular—since the movie theater in town only had one screen and it was open strictly during the summers, on Saturdays. Most of my window into the outside world where I could dream of a life beyond the one I was living was through the entertainment magazines waving to me from the grocery-store rack.

I lived for buying issues of *Us Weekly* or *People* the day after awards shows, flipping through all the dresses with reverence. My mom and I would discuss our favorite actresses and their style choices as if we were paid to do post-show glamour analysis for each event. I would cut out pictures of the gowns I admired, including a clipping of Halle Berry in her sheer maroon Oscars gown that had strategically placed florals to cover her cleavage. She was my one-woman vision board.

When I got older, I never missed an awards show on TV, even the second-rate ones. I was always hoping someone who won that night would be brave enough to use their thirty-second speech to say something actually meaningful and that I would be gifted a moment of inspiration that I could tap into the next time I doubted my career choice. If they couldn't be inspiring, then I hoped for righteous anger, and if they couldn't be righteous, then I wanted the complete opposite—a glimpse at their dirty, raw, uncurated humanity so I could lap up a moment of *Stars, they're just like us* (and often worse).

I know most people look at Hollywood awards shows as ridiculous, overblown, elitist parades of wealth…and that's exactly why I wanted in! These events had everything I craved from parties: fancy gowns, free food, structured activities, the pressure of speeches, and velvet couches upon which to dangle a martini and talk shit while pretending your smudged lipstick makes you Helena Bonham Carter.

I've often found that the kinds of people who work in Hollywood and hate these events usually overlap with the kinds of people who were raised with easy access to such nights. Awards shows mean nothing to them because growing up they had more occasions to dress nice than just Kaylynn's virginity-pledge ceremony. But if you do hate dressing up, awards shows are still a token of prestige in the field to which you chose to devote your life, so if you can't even get hard for the free pasta buffet the size of a Slip 'N Slide, then I think you should give up your spot to someone else. Which is why when Ashley Trojan-horsed me into the Emmys as her date, I vowed to violently enjoy every millisecond of it.

I wore a crimson red gown I'd procured with Ashley in a literal alley downtown for $100. It was made of an incredibly comfortable stretchy fabric that hugged my curves, and while I did later find a burn mark on the strap, that just helped make a hair decision for me: I'd be wearing it down!

When we arrived, I strutted behind Ashley through the security scanners as if the man demanding I put my phone in a little plastic tray was asking for my autograph. I forced several annoyed strangers to take photos of us on the tail end of the red carpet, where non-famous Hollywood citizens can attempt to pull one off for the Gram. I watched the show that night like it was Shakespeare's finest, even though the host was an animated *Family Guy* character (I think? Only the viewers at home could see it; we were just staring at an empty stage with a voice-over). During all the commercial breaks I checked Ashley's lipstick, ran for refills, sat down at the touch-up stations meant for nominees and asked for a powdering, and said hi to friends I'd known throughout the years, marveling at the fact that we were all there together. Before the night had even really begun, I'd already shoved a champagne glass in my purse as a keepsake, which immediately shattered. I turned up the volume on each moment because I didn't know if I'd ever be back at the Emmys again. I mean, I hadn't even earned my own invite! The only reason I was at my first Hollywood awards show was because I was lucky enough to be loved by the talented, radiant, kind, generous genius that is my friend Ashley Nicole Black.

The one instance in my career that stands above all others, the one with no explanation other than luck and the divine, is the moment I met Ashley. It was the very first day of our very first class of The Second City Conservatory, when I was twenty-one years old. We were in the bathroom on a break, and when I walked out of the stall I saw one of my new classmates, Ashley, who asked me if her makeup looked okay. I assured her, "It looks great. If you want to add some lip gloss, I have some in my bag." As I fished around for it, she said, "Could you apply it for me?" and so I touched up her lips and added some mascara, too, and we had an adorable bonding moment.

Ashley has a different version of this story. She swears on her life that I came out of the stall, washed my hands, and caught her eye in the mirror, declaring, "Let's fix your makeup."

Ashley's version is probably the correct one. However, in her version, she also says she was having a tense moment in the mirror because she had arrived for her first comedy class full of the previous night's cheap rosé and was exhausted from her PhD program. So when I started pulling glosses and mascara out of my bag, it was a kind gesture, if not also a little psychotic. Then I spun Ashley around, as you do after a successful makeover, and we walked out of the bathroom and back to class together, looking as much like comedy glamazons as one can when both your outfits are three-day-old leggings and loose hoodies.

Historically, I had looked for friendships I could hide inside when I've been too scared to try and live life on my own. One can easily play Freud with this pattern of mine: I grew up watching my mom team up with my aunt Sharon when she came to live with us in Utah, and later as my mom teamed up with my godmother Grace, so I was always trying to recreate a female power duo of my own. There was me and Britney Brody, then me and Rebecca, and they always seemed to sing the same tune of glorified enmeshment.

Ashley wouldn't let me shove this friendship into a codependent sinkhole.

And trust me, I tried. I was headstrong and full of need. But Ashley had a secret weapon that stopped me in my let's-wear-matching-sweaters-to-the-party! tracks. She had something in spades that I did not: boundaries. These foreign, unfamiliar things were established really early on in our relationship when, late one night at a bar after class, Ashley got up to go home, and I did that drunken thing where you squeal, "Nooooo! Stayyyy!"

She looked back at me so centered, so grounded, and firmly said, "I need to be able to leave when I'm ready, or I won't want to hang out with you at all."

She so clearly stated her own needs and her own rules that I instantly followed them because I didn't want to give up a single moment with her. Ashley was, and still is, the smartest person

I have ever met in my life. I'm talking everything from calculating the tip without looking at the bill to knowing both the Ohio senators by name to the exact anecdote each personality type needs to hear to finally accept that trickle-down economics is not really a thing. She's so smart it makes no sense that she's also incredibly funny, stunningly gorgeous, and kind. I should be able to stop right there, but somehow this woman is also a master of family dynamics and once solved a problem I was having with a difficult coworker by correctly guessing what was behind the issue: he was the oldest child of an alcoholic parent so he "lashes out at authority under the guise of protecting those around him." With this new empathetic view of the situation, I was able to fix our communication.

From the moment I started pursuing a career in comedy, Ashley was right by my side, also pursuing hers. We finished our comedy conservatory in the same group, in which we wrote a sketch together about working at UPS that got so much attention we would continue to reprise our characters for years after. We did more and more sketch shows together as part of big-cast ensembles, where sometimes we'd perform together, but more often apart. Either way, we always warmed up to En Vogue's "Don't Let Go." We knew lots of the same people but had different friend groups. Ashley would go off and start projects that I had nothing to do with, and I often did the same. Sometimes we'd go weeks without checking in, but whenever we really came up against an obstacle in our careers, we'd always reach out to each other.

After my preaudition for the actual *SNL* audition flopped, I called Ashley in tears, and she helped me decide to create a one-woman show with characters who you'd want to watch for longer than the length it takes to say your coffee order. I knew there was only one person who could direct my show—Ashley, of course. A little while later, when she wrote her own one-woman show, she turned to look for her director and...asked some stupid boy! She was already directing *his* show, so she told me it made more sense this way: they were going to perform their shows on the same night at the same theater, so everyone who came would get to see both their acting and directing skills on display at the same time. That did make sense, which was annoying. I was used to all-or-nothing friendships, where even the slightest rejection was to be dealt with for days…and reprised on birthdays and special occasions. But Ashley was full of those boundaries, and they weren't budging. I was forced to either walk away or accept that we could have space within our friendship and still love each other, which was a new concept for me.

When I was hired to perform in The Second City touring company, one of the people who helped cast the shows said to me, "I want to hire more women to perform comedy, I do, I just can't find any." I called Ashley, who unfathomably hadn't yet been hired at the theater herself and relayed what I'd heard while probably adding a string of obscenities.

"Well, let's show them where all those women are," Ashley replied. She pitched me an idea for a solo comedy showcase that we'd call "Solitaire," where ten women would do their best seven minutes of material, and we'd pack the house and invite the town. I had already been hired at the theater and had an agent by this point, so we came up with a strategy. Half of the women we chose for the show would already have representation or employment at comedy theaters, and we'd entice them to perform because we'd do all the nitty-gritty producing work, while they'd get some free stage time to work out new bits with a packed house—all they had to do was show up. The other five women would not have agents or jobs at the comedy theaters. Then, the half of the women who did could invite all their reps and contacts, and the other half could benefit from it. Ashley got an agent that night, as did every other woman in the showcase.

We did the show a couple more times and then passed it down

to other women who carried the torch. This do-si-do of helping each other out continued for years after we left, and while I would love to believe we cracked the legacy code, I think what I'm describing could also just be called *what guys in frats do.*

Ashley and I traded tips and education like that constantly—podcasts on how to create a screenplay, books on writing, and at some point, one of us got ahold of a PDF of Liz Meriwether's pitch for the TV show *New Girl,* and we volleyed it back and forth like a two-person relay as we swapped ideas for shows we had, emulating the style of this pitch PDF.

Other times, the information we shared was just talking shit or which restaurants had good happy hours. One time in Chicago Ashley needed a therapist, and so I recommended mine to her, since they'd already be caught up on all the Second City drama and Ashley would have less explaining to do! Another time we even shared a crush on a guy, except I didn't know it till after the fact, and neither did she. He and I had dated "in secret" because we didn't want it to "affect our improv careers," which, I must remind you, was not a career but actually a hobby you pay money to participate in. After we broke up and I told everything to Ashley, she confessed that she had also liked him, and I felt so bad I had just ruined him for her with all my horror stories. Had I known Ashley liked him, she could've had him! Then, she would've had to endure all of his bullshit instead of me!

The next year I fell out with an acquaintance of mine, and I was complaining to Ashley that they only seemed to care about people with "status." Ashley replied, "You just noticed that? They've always been that way." I asked why Ashley had never told me, and she laughed and said that it seemed like I genuinely liked them. There was that space again, the space afforded to let each other make our own mistakes and not force our own agendas and thoughts so strongly that the other person had to take them on, too. I had always wanted a fortress of friendship, a multileveled conglomerate of two-minds-become-one, but Ashley was too wise to allow it. We were like two little Starbucks on the same corner—stick with me on this—and I thought we had to merge, baby! Make a fortress of coffee together, or one of us will perish! Ashley taught me to stand still on my damn corner, work on myself instead of putting my attention on the bitch across the street. She taught me that she would thrive and I would thrive, but we'd be stronger if we built our own foundations than if we leaned on each other. She was right, of course. Anyways, down with corporate espresso, support your local coffee shops.

During our time in Chicago, our true love was always work. When Ashley and I began trying to get hired to write for television, we both began writing something called *packets* for late-night shows because those were the only script opportunities that got passed around in Chicago. A typical packet varies in what it asks for depending on the show, but it's usually a couple pages of monologue jokes, and several pitches for sketches or desk pieces. Basically, it serves as a trial run of writing a script for the show in question, which you write for free, while working your other job(s), with no access to guidance or direction unless someone in the writers' room reached out and gave you the information themselves, which is why most comedy writers' rooms have always been filled with dudes from Harvard and their little brothers. Ashley and I did not have the help of nepotism, nor were we nepo-adjacent with dads who could be like, "Guess who I just ran into in first class? His son works on the *PhilJohnMr.Magoo Show* and…"

But Ashley and I didn't need those connections because we had each other. When we worked on our packets together, one of us would pitch an idea, and the other would gauge if that idea had legs and if we were on the right track, and as we refined and honed our writing over and over again, finally we became better writers than all the little brothers.

CHELSEA DEVANTEZ

There's a particular piece of advice that I always give out to newbie go-getter comedians. For years I thought Ashley taught it to me but later realized she thought I taught it to her, so somewhere together in our friendship one of us coined this highly effective and potentially very unhealthy way of dealing with anticipation. Here it is: when you're in the middle of creating a project, a pitch, a script, or an audition, before the moment comes when you will find out the answer to the thing you want so bad, you start a different project, script, audition, or venture. Then, if the answer to the first one is *no*, you already have the momentum of the other thing going to keep your spirits up and you won't fall into complete depression. If the answer is *yes* to the first thing, then that momentum can now fuel your second thing, and now you have two things! This is quite possibly how you become a workaholic Scrooge with no family or friends, but aside from the advice to "get a friend like Ashley" that's the best thing I've found for dealing with the emotional roller-coaster of the entertainment industry.

About eight months after Ashley had moved to New York City to write and perform on Samantha Bee's late-night show, *Full Frontal*, I got the call that changed my life.

"Jon Stewart wants to meet you," my manager coyly stated on the other end of the phone. It took me a minute to catch up to this news. I had dedicated almost a decade of my life to comedy at that point. I'd applied to write on Jon's show, spending hours and hours on the packet, but I had not allowed myself to actually think I could work for or around Jon or really even that I'd ever have the honor of delivering him a sandwich. He is one of the greatest comedians and political philosophers to ever live, and I am a trashy go-getter who was destined to become the manager of a going-out-of-business Claire's.

For years I had wondered if anyone had ever read a single one of the packets I'd sent in, and now I'd gotten a call saying that not only had Jon himself read my submission but he wanted to meet with me. The submission process had been blind, meaning they only reveal the names of who wrote the packet after they had been chosen as the best, so my self-worth skyrocketed like I had just won an Oscar. My manager told me that I needed to fly to New York City, where I'd spend a day writing with him as a sort of working interview, and then I would find out if I had the job. She told me to buy a ticket to New York City "immediately" and to do whatever it took to call out of my current show for the weekend. I told my boss at the theater I was horribly sick and had lost my voice and then booked a nonrefundable ticket on Spirit Airlines to my dream job. I called Ashley and told her I would be in New York City the next night so could I crash on her couch? She screamed with glee—could we possibly both be TV writers working in the same city together, in the exact same genre of comedy?

That's when my manager called me back, and I switched over to the other line. "Hey, so Jon didn't realize that you live in Chicago, and he doesn't want to make you fly all the way out here, so they'll just set up the interview over video chat."

"But you said...you said to buy the ticket immediately," I stuttered. "It's nonrefundable. Just tell him I'm coming."

But my manager replied that she didn't want to "make Jon feel bad," which I think was code for *admit she made an oopsie*. I called up Ashley and told her I was not coming after all.

The next day, I opened up my computer screen, and there he was. Fighting the urge to black out, I tried to look sane and smart for the interview I'd spent every second of the day prior preparing for. The moment the video chat was done, I wrote down every single thing that I had said and everything that Jon said, too, because a castmate had told me if you do that, you can't second-guess anything that happened later. After I finished, I looked down at what I had written. Jon had offered me the job. I wasn't fully ready to believe it until I had been given an official contract, but in the happiest daze I called Ashley and said, "Actually, I *am* coming...to celebrate."

I couldn't get my money back, and I'd already called out of my show, so I got on my nonrefundable flight and flew to New York City. To commemorate my break into television, Ashley procured us all-you-can-drink tickets to a four-story warehouse concert featuring an NSYNC cover band. All I could travel with on the plane were the clothes I was wearing because Spirit Airlines charges for carry-ons, so I showed up in an outfit that I felt I could both party and sleep in. Ashley and I had spent so much time hunched over computer screens and improvising in small black-box theaters, instead of living out our twenties going to concerts, bachelorette parties, festivals, or even nice restaurants. This night in New York City was a new dawn, the life in entertainment we had always wanted, the day we started living our glamorous life with our glamorous TV paychecks. Sadly, yes, I am still talking about being at the NSYNC cover-band concert.

Ashley and I spent the whole night dancing, taking pictures together, and sporadically grabbing each other and screaming, "We write for TV, motherfuckers!" And even though it was a new dawn, I was still so broke that the $80 I had spent on the wristband to get in had brought my bank account to nearly zero, so I spent the whole night making sure I at least got my money's worth of gin and tonics. I made it to eight.

When we got back to Ashley's apartment I threw up in her elevator, then took off all my clothes, and despite the fact that she'd dressed her couch in pillows and sheets and a blanket for me, I crawled into her bed instead.

Earlier that night we had both been given some Adderall, but having tried Adderall before, I knew that I was not someone who needed uppers, so I gave mine to her. As I lay passed out in her bed, she was riding all four elevators in her building up and down until she could find the one I had puked in and begin cleaning it. She then did my laundry and washed my vomit clothes. That meant she picked up my clothes, went down to the laundry floor, used precious laundry quarters, then came back an hour later and repeated it for the dryer cycle. I will never be able to repay this. It's too grand of a gesture! Around sunrise Ashley finally crawled into bed and nudged me awake. She said, "I've got it! I figured out how Hillary can win the election!" And then we fell asleep.

In the morning, Ashley's genius election solution had disappeared, and I firmly believe it's going to come back to her the next time she does Adderall, and she'll be forced to write a book about the campaign strategy that should have been. I got out of Ashley's bed fully naked, only to discover that at some point during the night I'd thrown away my phone, keys, and wallet. I know for a fact I threw them away, because the next morning I found my ID in her bathroom trash can and never found anything else. I can only assume I felt so successful in that moment that I thought I could forever get through life simply by showing my face and dropping the name of the soon-to-be-titled TV show I was going to work on. Then I got on the plane without a phone or money, left to just sit there with the thought that I was going to write for Jon Stewart.

My manager told me I had two weeks to get out to New York City because the show was starting right away. I had left New York City years prior feeling like the city had slapped me in the face and then thrown my own piss on me as I left, and now I was coming back, a TV writer! Only, for my grand entrance back into the city, I was driving a U-Haul through the crowded Manhattan streets and very intense traffic, and now it felt like the city was doing a real deep squat as it dumped on my new shoes.

The night before the job started, I got an email with the address…only it was in New Jersey, not New York City where my manager had told me to move. Too afraid to ruffle any feathers, I figured I would ask questions once I got there for my first day. One train, a ferry, and an Uber ride later, I found myself standing in front of a gate to a farm. It had taken me more than two hours to arrive, and now it appeared I was in the middle of nowhere. As I walked over to the house, I passed some stalls where three horses peered out at me, and two of them had only one eye, and I began to wonder if my high-school bullies had somehow pulled off the greatest prank in history. I knocked on the door and texted Ashley the address, preparing for my murder, then after a minute Jon Stewart himself opened it. I should have prepared for death by full-body shock instead.

I followed Jon into the dining room where the writers were going to be working. The farm was the animal sanctuary run by Jon and his wife, and for the first few months it was to be our headquarters. I looked around the house—aside from the showrunner, Shannon, and the head of research, Max, there was no one else there. I was the only writer he had hired because he hadn't decided on any others yet. I saw a pile of hundreds of packets on the table. On mine he'd written *This one*.

Jon talked to me about the concept for the new show— animated, topical, satirical shorts that would have a spicy take on the morning news, and we would air brand-new shorts every night. Jon then pulled some paper out of the printer and handed me a pencil and told me to write down some ideas because he had to go pick up his kids. I sat there, taking in the enormity of the moment, and texted Ashley, *PEP TALK PLZ*.

After the rest of the writers were hired, we would take the ferry to Jersey together, drinking the beers they sold on the top deck. When fall was upon us, my friend and fellow writer Robby bought a car, and we would all pitch in gas and toll money, and he'd drive us down together. I couldn't help but think about how Ashley was flourishing, now a frequent guest star on her show, going on the road to create funny field pieces, while I was stuck in the Jersey tollway. The commute back and forth every day eventually became too much. I realized I wasn't going to be great at the job unless I just moved closer, because I was losing four hours a day that I could have been spending doing research or working on scripts. I didn't even care that I never saw my friends, because the whole reason I was even there was suffering. I was not doing my best work.

Somehow I figured out that if I could switch the state of my tax residency to New Jersey, I would get $600 more in my paycheck each week, and I could use it to get an apartment there since I would save on paying NYC taxes. I had to have this extra money, because most of my paycheck would still have to go toward my half of the rent on the expensive and extraordinarily small apartment I'd moved into in Brooklyn.

The town we worked in wasn't very big, so there was only one place for rent that was less than $600—an apartment across the literal train tracks being rented out by a man named Hal. Hal said I could take up residence in the second bedroom in the apartment and have the place to myself, provided I move all the utilities into my name and look after the space while he was gone. Hal had recently met the love of his life on eharmony, Melanie, and he was moving to Florida to be with her. I didn't tell Ashley the details of where I was about to live because I was too afraid she'd talk some sense into me.

I turned on the electric and water, then shut off everything else. The only piece of furniture in the apartment was a broken futon, accessorized with an old blanket covering up the rips in the faux leather, and a light-up Budweiser clock on the wall. I ordered a $60 mattress off Amazon that was like a compressed egg crate and would inflate a few inches once it was out of the box. I put that on the floor, and with that, my move was complete.

I would stay at work for as long as I could, then I'd walk across town listening to the audio of cable-news shows on my podcast app before going home to make a giant plate of broccoli for dinner, because spending the day at the animal sanctuary had turned me into a vegetarian. Only, I didn't know how to

cook, so I'd eat a pound of vegetables and then a case of peanut
butter cups, while scrolling niche blogs for work. When I woke
up, I'd start streaming *Fox News* on my phone. I'd text Ashley
as I'd walk back across town, running ideas by her in hopes of
a desperately needed thumbs-up before pitching to Jon.

It was during this time when Ashley became the closest person in my life, the keeper of all my work successes and dramas.
She could have been the keeper of my social life and love life,
too, only I no longer had one. I rarely saw Ashley those days,
but she lived in my phone and on my G-Chat, powering me
through this amorphous time spent on Hal's futon watching *Fox
News* as we dished about our days at work and whatever non-
sense just went up on *HuffPost*.

Two months into my new living situation, Hal showed back
up—things apparently hadn't worked out with Melanie, and he
was back for good. And so, this 68-year-old man and I became
roommates. He seemed nice enough, but every night I still
made sure to push the dresser in the room up against the door
and sleep with Mace in my hand, which actually made me the
biggest threat to my own safety.

After almost exactly a year of this routine, Jon decided to
cancel the show. The technology required for the quick turn-
around animation just wasn't ready when we needed it. I was
crushed that I wouldn't see the show we'd been striving toward
come to fruition, but I knew it was the right call. It felt like I
had lived an invisible year, disappeared into Jersey, and experienced the most epic job that no one would ever know about.
There was nothing tangible to show for it, but I had also had
one of the best years of my entire life by getting to work with
Jon. My time with him on that show had been the equivalent to
four master's degrees in comedy, writing, politics, and fucking
around. Even though I was torn up to not get to work with the
writers and crew anymore, deep inside I was thrilled my stint
with Hal had come to an end.

Back in the city, Ashley took me out for drinks on a Friday, a night of the week I had not experienced outside of my apartment in a while. I was now unemployed in the city that had already spit me out twice before. We sat at a wooden picnic table on the rooftop of a bar whose vibe was dirty-park-bench, but like, ironically. Ashley bought me some $13 fries and a martini. Here we were, finally hanging out in person, but we couldn't be in more different places in life. Ashley had become a star on her show and had gotten promoted for her writing, while I was being told by my manager that they couldn't really help me get another job without any credits, and working on Jon's show for the past year "didn't count" because it never aired.

In the past, such disparate life outcomes would have mucked up a night of friendship for me. I'd have been shoving fries down my throat, grinding through the conversation while wondering what was wrong with me and what my friend had that I didn't. But sitting across from Ashley at that table, I just felt joyful to have her company again. I knew ups and downs like this were inevitable, and I was grateful because I had a friendship like ours to see me through all of them.

Ashley got busier and busier with her work, and I returned to submitting packets to late-night shows, since no job offers had appeared. After I wrote several impassioned emails to my managers begging for an opportunity, they put me up for a position to be the head writer on a new comic's pilot. I knew I was woefully unqualified but beyond ready to do it. Recently, a successful writer had said in an interview that they got their showrunning job by wildly overpreparing for the meeting and even brought in a giant binder of ideas laying out the entire season. I set out to make my own binder. I created a stunning presentation that laid out 1,000 pitches and arcs and ways to reinvent the late-night format. I spent $43 printing three color copies at FedEx with binding and all. I walked into the meeting in a floral jacket that I was going to return the moment I left and began to take the star of the show, their manager, and the two male executive producers through my binder.

Two hours later, just as I'd returned the jacket, my manager called me. I picked up excitedly. "Should I rebuy that jacket? Will I be needing a powerful jacket for my new job?!" My manager took a breath, and I quickly knew the answer was *no*. Since I was a comedian, they must have thought I'd laugh when they told me, "Yeah, so they said you made the producers in the room look bad, like they were unprepared to run the show. They called you Tracy Flick."

A few years later, I would finally meet the writer whose interview I'd taken the binder advice from, and I'd find out over the course of the night that they were a pathological liar who no one in the industry respected. They'd likely made up the binder thing as a way to signal to their peers that they had ideas and thoughts, but the truth is that they probably got their job by glad-handing. Networking. Pretending to be cool and chill. Like the goddamn Tracy Flick that I was, I took notes: *learn 2 b chill.*

As I searched for a job, I spent my free time dating anyone on Bumble who seemed mostly alive and even medium-nice. Ashley would meet me for drinks and dinners, and I would show up in full glam, on the prowl. I wore a minidress to meet her at a bodega once, because I'd learned as a child from Grace and my mom that the grocery store is your stage, baby! Ashley showed up in full glam, too, rolling her eyes. "I put on makeup because I knew you would do this."

Soon enough, I was hired to write on another late-night show, for Comedy Central. I had gotten hired on another blind submission. In the final interview they told me they had read through six months of my tweets and received a call from Jon recommending me, so I was hired.

Ashley and I restarted our two-besties-writing-TV-in-New-York-City dream. We went dancing, we went to spas, we hosted

Oscar parties in her fabulous apartment, we shot sizzle reels for pilots we wanted to star in. As we were setting out the appetizers one night, Ashley caught a glimpse of my phone and drunkenly exclaimed, "Why am I your phone background?" It was a picture of Beyoncé from one of her music videos.

Mistaking a picture of Beyoncé for a picture of yourself was proof that we had definitely leveled up. Years ago we were drinking $2 shots of well vodka in the same Empire-waist dress that we had both bought coincidently, because it was flattering for curves and less than $25. We used to have to call each other up and ask, "Are you wearing the lavender dress tonight, or can I?" We had come a long way.

A few years later, I was living in Los Angeles again when I walked into an interview with Liz Meriwether, who told me she loved my script, and I wisely did not tell her that I was obsessed with her work and that she'd single-handedly taught me how to pitch TV through a leaked PDF. I wrote on the first season of her ABC show, *Bless This Mess*, and when the second season came around she asked me if I knew any other great writers who would be a fit for the show? I said I knew just the one.

Ashley had recently moved to Los Angeles, and even though she had four other offers to write on TV shows that season, she thankfully chose *Bless This Mess*, and we shared an office in Le Grand Hollywood together. Season two was one of my happiest times in television because I had my best friend in the room, backing me up early in the morning when an upper-level writer stated that "technically, Woody Allen didn't molest his daughter...she was adopted," and I began yelling, "Not before 9:00 a.m.! I will not do the Woody argument before 9:00 a.m.!" At lunch we would run to our office, lock the door, and gossip the entire hour about our other projects, our love lives, our plans that weekend, and that one writer who really fucking loved Woody Allen.

One time we were in the writers' room trying to break an episode, which is where you come up with not only the idea of the episode, but also all the detailed story moves and scenes and the order they go in to make the story work. It was taking days for us to crack the story because television has a lot of dated rules about what makes a female character "likable," and we were trying to incorporate a cheating storyline and still keep the woman "likable" to network TV's standards, which is like attempting an archaeological dig at the North Pole while wearing a bikini. (Something that would also definitely *not* be likable, you guys.)

I was at the whiteboard, writing down the various story beats, Ashley was sitting at the table, and our showrunner, Liz, was on the couch pitching out ideas. Suddenly we all hit a wave and began pitching, and at the exact same time Ashley and I thought of the final scene. We shouted word for word at the exact same time, "And then he comes back and kisses her!"

Liz laughed in disbelief. "Did you both really just say that at the same time?" Then, scrutinizing the whiteboard, she nodded. "Yep, that's it."

A week later I stood on set as actress Lennon Parham was kissed by a handsome stranger we'd written into the episode, and I thought to myself, this is why I tried so hard to be here, because some moments just take your breath away.

On top of writing on a show with me, Ashley had been a lead in HBO's *A Black Lady Sketch Show*, which she had shot months prior and was now finally airing, so she started getting a lot of invites to sexy-ass parties, and sometimes I'd attend as her date. One night there was a red carpet with fifty or so paparazzi. As she walked down the carpet, I held her bag, looking on, a valiant keeper of the goods from gown sashes to keys to lipstick. Through a sea of photographers, I watched her face peek through, posing and smiling, as cameras flashed. I caught a glimpse of Ashley, feeling like we were in a movie moment, as she glimmered against the lights and smoothly navigated re-porters' questions.

In the sponsored photo booth later that night, we recreated a picture we took backstage of our conservatory graduation show a decade prior: tits forward, jaws slack, smizing, wishing for a time machine so I could run the picture back to 2009 and shake it in our faces screaming, "Don't worry! It's gonna happen! Try to enjoy the ride more, okay?!"

In an industry whose tagline for women might as well have been *There can only be one!* Ashley and I always lifted each other up and shared opportunities whenever we had the chance. When a high-powered feminist organization reached out and asked Ashley to run a series of politically inspired interviews during a two-day gala at a fancy resort, she recommended me to be her cohost, and I accompanied her on the trip.

Our interviews took place on a small stage, live, and would later be published after the event. We were told to be as funny as possible, but not to upset anyone. During our first interview, we were joined onstage by a famous actress, someone who had notably waited till feminism was trending before she hopped aboard the ol' Girl Power train. We'd only just begun our con-versation when she interrupted me and said, "Why don't you define *feminism* for the audience."

I mumbled, "Oh, I mean I could, but that's not really where we're at, you know? No one needs that definition. We know. They know."

Ashley nodded along with me. "We all know."

The actress whispered back, "I don't think they do. You should tell them."

So, I spoke into the mic and start defining the ideology of feminism. Then I pivoted into intersectional feminism, and hey, since we're here, how about we talk about male feminists, spe-cifically the kind who tell you they're feminists within the first five minutes of meeting you, in which case you should run for your life. The actress shook her head and said, "That's too much, just define feminism, let's start small." At one point she also asked me to define *harassment*. I began to wonder if all this was simply because she herself just didn't know these words.

So far, each workshop at this gala would begin with one of the women who worked on their team thanking another woman for their work for the gala, and that woman would demur and shoo away the applause, until finally caving and grabbing the mic to give a speech on how much time and effort it had required. As I sat there, taking part in what was supposed to be an elite, impactful event for female empowerment, I realized it was actually one of the least inspiring talks I'd ever been to, and all I could think was *So this is why all our movements fail*. I once had a female boss who would wear shirts that said things like *Antiracist!* and *This Is What a Feminist Looks Like*, while she actively hated women and was a huge racist. This gala felt a lot like that.

It was so cringey to listen to their ideas of feminism and girl power as they skirted over any conversation around the actual struggle for women, fem-presenting, and fem-identifying people to be treated with the same financial and political equity as men. I often find that people confuse feminism for treating all women equally in relation to each other, somehow homogenizing a 3.8 billion-person gender and their complexities, plus the varying degrees of struggle that arise when you throw racism, classism, homophobia, and transphobia into the mix. In their quest to "like all women equally" rather than fix these financial and political inequities, we erase all of our differences, and for what? So that we could give every single woman on earth a T-shirt that says *YES, QUEEN*. It's an odd phrase to monetize for a movement, because not all of us *are* queens. I know a couple of "queens" who are straight rotten! I will still fight for their right to equal pay, but they are rotten. What people also seem to ignore is that being a queen is a one-person gig:

the whole singularity of the position is what makes someone a queen to begin with. Its very label implies someone who is above others, not equal to them! The rest of us? We're milkmaids. (New merch?) On the flip side, I know many a woman who thinks that because she wants *herself* to succeed, and she is a woman, she is therefore a feminist, when really she cares nothing about the respect and rights of us all, and in fact even *benefits* from the inequality so she can be the only woman at the boys' club and get more attention, which in her eyes is feminism! Because when there's an equal number of women and men at the table, she can no longer stand out as the one person who meets the rubric of *Good*, i.e., acknowledging there's a silent qualifier, *as good as a man*. But once you get into all the details and nuances needed to successfully define what feminism is about, people are half-asleep, and it's no longer fun. And while we'd like to believe people will put their energy into the pressing issues of our time, the sad truth about human nature is that it also needs to be easy, or not enough people are going to make time for the movement…

I then turned to the actress. "There, I defined feminism, are you happy?"

She shook her head and looked over to Ashley, who was trying to hold in her laughter. "Dear, would you try defining it for us, please?"

After the workshop ended, the organization did not invite us back and instead wrote us an email that said something like *You take care, now.* The interviews were never published.

Four years after working for Jon Stewart the first time, I was sitting on my porch, writing a pilot for a show I'd sold, when my cell phone rang. I looked down and saw it was Jon. He told me about a new show he was making on Apple TV, and he asked me to be his head writer.

I was equally as thrilled as I was in shock. This was the job I'd always dreamed of, and not only was I ready for it, I had been ready for years. But the other part of me was in the middle of a life I'd built in Los Angeles, currently wearing a coffee-stained tank top and sweaty flip-flops, and I had just made a post on Instagram about how I owned the same dress that one of the *Real Housewives* had worn on last night's episode, because Le Trash shops at all the same hot spots.

I called Ashley, spiraling. "I am made for this job, I would be incredible at this job, and also…what if I *can't* do this job?! What if I let everyone down? What if I'm missing some niche part of history that I'll need for a key moment in the rewrite and it wrecks the whole show?"

Ashley replied with a laugh. Then she put on her serious tone, the tone that says *Honey, don't throw your wallet and ID away in the trash can tonight when we go celebrate.* Calmly and firmly, she said, "Chelsea, you're the only person who can do this job."

We'll never know if that was true, but I did do it. Sometimes you just need an Ashley to remind you that you can. I packed up all my belongings with my then-boyfriend, now-husband, and with our dog in tow we headed back to New York City, this time on a plane and not with the U-Haul, thank God, and as I looked down on the city I thought, Just try to shit on me from this angle, you beautiful asshole!

I'll forever treasure every moment of working on *The Problem with Jon Stewart*. The show was brand-new, so we could create everything with a clean slate. Jon gave me the chance to change the hiring process, and I did away with every idiotic, classist, sexist, racist, time-wasting part of the packet process I myself had suffered through, and what do ya know, the room of writers we hired included some of the most talented writers in the country, and not one of them was a little brother. We wrote episodes about the economy, racism, and climate change, and we filmed a trailer about a certain billionaire going to the moon on a dick while wearing a cowboy hat, months before that exact billionaire actually walked down the Jetway, got in a dick-shaped shuttle and took his ass to space (in a cowboy hat), and also, unfortunately, came back. I pitched and cast and wrote on my dream episode of television, which covered the one subject I had always wanted to write but never thought I'd get the chance: an episode about how 90 percent of gun-violence perpetrators have a history of domestic violence.

The week of the episode taping, I texted Ashley that I knew I was going to cry, and as the head writer and one of the bosses, I was worried it would make me appear weak. She sent me blocks of text every hour on the hour, reminding me that feeling so deeply did not make me weak, instead it just proved how much the content mattered. As the writers and I rewrote the script, I suffered two intense panic attacks and had to hide under my desk. I talked myself through breathing exercises and shoved ice inside my armpits and tried to quell memories of ███████████. As soon as I made it through each mental attack I would crawl out from under my desk, reapply lipstick, and then throw my shoulders back and attempt to walk calmly back into the rewrite. The night of the episode taping we were wearing masks on set, for COVID protocol, and mine filled up with a steady stream of tears for an hour straight.

After we filmed that episode, I told Jon why it had been so important to me, but what had come to matter even more was that Jon had eagerly taken on the episode topic without ever knowing what had happened to me personally—because he already knew how much it mattered.

When I walked back into the Emmys for the second time, it was because I had been nominated for two Emmys for Head Writing *The Problem with Jon Stewart*. I sent nineteen photos to Ashley checking to see if there was too much cleavage showing in my light blue velvet dress, and attempted to hand-stitch some of the fabric together to cover it up. Ashley texted back *Yes, a little much* nineteen separate times until I had run out of fabric to stitch. The writers I'd hired showed up in outfits that would make Dolly Parton blush, and I took in their style choices as if it was my first win of the night.

We were seated at a table close to the front, which I felt sure meant that we were going to win. RuPaul took to the stage to accept their award, and of course, his speech was brave. He boomed into the audience, "How lucky, how lucky are we to be here. We are all a part of television. Never let that be lost on you. Rise to the occasion, children! Live in the moment!"

When our categories were announced, we lost both awards to a show that was about pasta. Sure wish there had been a section in *Us Weekly* preparing me for that when I was younger—you know, just a helpful little paragraph below Halle Berry's gown would have been nice.

This time, back at the Emmys, Ashley was not sitting beside me because she was onstage as one of the presenters. She was a part of the show, a woman in an iconic gown who I would have worshipped as a kid.

Ashley and I have been through so many phases of life when one of us was twirling from the top of the mountain, while the other had tumbled down to basecamp, but every time one of us was about to topple off and quit forever, the other was on a high-enough ledge to reach out her hand and pull a bitch back to safety. Our circumstances and paycheck brackets might have gone up over the years, but the intensity of the emotions have always been the same—from when Ashley was the lead of a show I was kicked out of to when I was on my seventh Second City job while she was just getting her first. Every time we hit a high and a low, Ashley had taught me that boundaries, space, and respect in a relationship must be your lifejacket so that, should it be necessary, you can reach out and save your drowning friend without sinking yourself. Our friendship taught me the secret to true, steady, everlasting love: taking care of you first. Cue Oprah! Cue the free cars! Somebody make a long-winded bumper sticker!

When I watched Ashley up on that stage, just like everyone else in the audience, I was enamored with her talent and her heart, but I also was a selfish li'l ho. I looked up at her and thought, Holy shit, that person—that radiant beaming light of a human—I get to know her and love her, and she loves me, too. How fucking lucky am I that I walked out of the bathroom stall at just the right moment, a backpack full of lip gloss.

BRIDESMAIDS

Less a label, more a temperament

When I was a child, I used to wrap my arms around my knees and promise myself over and over again that I would never get married. *I would never, I would never, I would never…*

And this would be the wonderful baggage I'd bring with me more than two decades later as I went to pick out my bridal bouquet! As I gazed upon different shades of blush peonies, I thought to myself, what floral arrangement says *I'm a spunky, yet modern maximalist, who's blown most of the budget on emergency therapy sessions to cry about the tradition of fathers walking a bride down the aisle?*

Throughout my engagement to my now-husband, Yassir, I absolutely loved being a bride-to-be, while concurrently not believing the role was mine to play. I imagined I'd walk into our wedding aghast and stroll up to the altar with a shocked grin on my face, pointing at it, like, "Who put this thing here!?" And of course I'd have to make a dorky face every second I'd be holding my bouquet, so that we would all know how weird this was. *Me? Married? Eye roll!* All the while knowing that when the photographer arrived, they'd find me draped in heaven's purest shade of virgin-saint-Crest-whitening strips and donning the iconic bridal expression, a soft gaze on the ground, as if one is intently searching for quarters on a dirty beach.

I was not a changed, perfect human when I met my husband. In fact, I was still very much the kind of woman who would yell at men with equal fervor if they had ghosted me or if I got back to their apartment and discovered they owned a record player. I deeply wanted a committed, healthy relationship, but I was terrible at choosing partners—and I was quite terrible at being one, too. I imagine that there are a few men who, if they are ever asked *What's your worst dating story?* will tell a tale that involves me.

Throughout my twenties, I often felt that dating was obliterating my emotional operating system. Every casual hangout triggered insecurities that caused me to tailspin and flail about internally for weeks. Underneath my outgoing, cackling laugh was still the wreckage of ███████████████.

███████████. Each time I went on a date, I would clutch my phone afterward, waiting for the validation of being liked by some random guy as if it could heal my old wounds. I'd anxiously stare at my phone for hours till I finally heard it buzz and look down to see a text from a man whose best offering was *I'm spinning at midnight. $10 at the door. Can't get you on the list.*

When I was thirty, I did all the annoying, cloying clichés they tell you to do when looking for your person: I focused on myself and my own happiness, I accepted invites to every event just to get myself out of the house, I got on every dating app and swiped *yes* on anyone who seemed like they showered semiregularly. I even made a detailed list of qualities I wanted in my future partner—not things like *has a sense of humor* or *likes to have fun* but qualities like *is currently in therapy* or *has at least one close male friend who he seeks advice and support from.* Then I did some self-analyzing and asked myself if *I* had a list of qualities that someone else would be hoping for, too. I took a good hard look in the mirror, applied a bold lip, and thought, Fuck it—worse people have certainly found love!

I have always believed that the most aggravating phrase you can hear when you are dating is that when you find the right person *you'll just know.* And yet, the moment I met my husband, Yassir, *I knew.* Ugh, I know, gross! But it's true.

Yassir and I were set up by Robby, his best friend and my coworker at the time at the first Jon Stewart show. I was living in New York City and Yassir was in Los Angeles, so for a while we chatted online and through texts. On the third day of messaging him I ran into work and told Robby I had never laughed so hard in my life and I was head over heels. I leaned over his desk, aggressive, almost angry: "Tell me he's a good guy. *Tell me he's a good guy!*"

A week later I picked up the phone and heard Yassir's voice for the first time, and I watched goose bumps run up and down my arm. I was so deeply drawn to Yassir I began making plans for a fake work trip to get out to LA so I could meet him in person. I needed to make sure he wasn't a catfish, and if he was, I wanted to see if that catfish was at least somewhat stable. Luckily Yassir was already scrounging up a reason of his own to fly to New York City. We met on the corner of First Street and Avenue A. He was facing away from me as I walked up. I called his name and he turned around, lit only by the streetlamp. There was probably trash blowing, a rat puking, and a knife fight on the corner, but in that moment all I saw was his handsome, smiling face. We hugged and walked to a hookah bar, because I had a rule against dinner on a first date. (It's a trap! You'll be there for hours even if the guy sucks!) We spent the whole night talking. Then I asked him back to my place. In the morning (hell yeah, that's right), he called his mom and told her he just met the girl he was going to marry, while I was gushing the same thing at the same time to my younger brother Jesse.

The decision to be married was quite easy because one day I

looked up and I already was. Label or not, I had monogamously committed to Yassir, and I never wanted that to go away. After four years of being together we had already lived in three different apartments, a dozen Airbnbs, and moved from Los Angeles to New York City and back four separate times for our various jobs. We'd seen each other through all kinds of different phases, like the one where Yassir banned me from the kitchen because I put dishes in the dishwasher wrong, and the banning actually felt more like a personal victory than a punishment. And a more permanent phase where I discovered that Yassir collected comic books, and I vowed then to not notice for the rest of our lives.

We adopted a dog who I nicknamed Needy-Quarantine-Dog, because he spent the entire pandemic in our laps. We became those people who call each other Mom and Dad when they get a pet. I knew we'd gone so beyond overboard obsessing over our dog-son when an article popped up online about it. The "article" was on one of those gutter sludge sites called something like FamousPeopleInfoFacts.com where it's written by bots, pulling haphazardly from Wikipedia and online bios, purporting to dish on what certain people in Hollywood were up to. Right in the middle of the internet splooge that spelled my name *Cheleasea*, there was a section that said *Yassir and his wife have not yet conceived a child. The husband and wife, however, consider their dog as their baby.* Even the blog algorithm had seen our Instagram feeds and said *Too much, baby girl, too much.*

I fell so deeply in love with Yassir that I became someone who picked up the mass-produced romantic cards in the holiday aisle to hide in his office with adoring messages, not for our anniversary or his birthday but for the ooey-gooey-makes-others-vomit reason: *just because.* The glittery pink embossed cursive fonts that said things like *You are the only note I want to play in the sweet symphony of time, your love is an everlasting harmony,* and I'd swallow a little sob in my throat as I thought, So true, grocery-store card, so true.

After Yassir proposed, we began to look at the price of a wedding, aka 24-hour shrine to ourselves. I began to feel guilty that we would spend our money on something that felt so superficial or wasteful, and he had the same worry. We each sought out advice from our inner circles and therapists and came back with the same conclusion—that it would be worth it to not only celebrate our union but to celebrate with the community who had helped us come so far and led us to become the people we are, the types of people who could even find each other to begin with.

It was time to plan a motherfucking wedding.

Yassir and I had made a deal that I would take the lead on our wedding and that when we buy a house one day, he would take the lead on all the paperwork and procuring. We each walked away thinking we got the easier end of the deal. And despite knowing almost nothing about weddings, I loved every moment of planning it. It is by far the stupidest thing I have ever done, in the stupidest industry I have ever been a part of, and yet nothing this goddamn stupid has ever been this much fun. Wedding planning was such a joyful break from the actual stakes of my real life that to this day, whenever I get really stressed out, I instantly start looking up the latest bridal couture and let it transport me back to the easy-breezy land of calligraphy pens, leafy archways, and bespoke champagne glasses that say *Feelin' Bubbly*.

In many ways, I had been preparing to run a wedding my entire life. I can run a schedule like it's an Olympic event, and I'm obsessed with dressing up. I have two modes: pajamas and Met Gala, and I never pass up an opportunity to turn up the volume on either. Now, I don't want to talk my producing skills up too much, but if I'm being fair and reasonable, I would say I'm like the van Gogh of producing, or a Picasso on my bad days. And as I surveyed our culture's preset bridal color options, my entrance into the wedding world was like telling van Gogh it was time to create his masterpiece, but his only supplies would be tea lights and some dried bird jizz.

Neither Yassir nor myself had come from a norm-core Americana background, nor had I approached any past relationship dreaming of the day I'd post a staged picture of us laughing under a waterfall with the caption *I did a thing*. In fact, Yassir and I kept our engagement to ourselves for a year, celebrating privately with friends and family. Over the course of that time, we planned our way into a wedding that I eventually started calling "a marital concert," because our vendors were so confused by our requests that I thought it would be best they stopped thinking of it as a wedding at all. I ended up trying on over one hundred and twenty dresses from seventeen different stores and five different websites. I loved every second of it and disliked almost every single dress. I spent most of my brain cells that year on questions like *What goes in the center of the tables?* but with the stakes of WHAT GOES IN THE CENTER OF THE TABLES!?!?!

Now, I didn't see this coming, though I absolutely should have: my bridesmaids were one of the most deeply meaningful parts of the wedding process.

At first, when Yassir proposed, I didn't even want them. I thought bridesmaids were a label meant to describe the burden placed upon the women you love most as you force them to buy matching platform sandals that say #Bitchelorette! I didn't want bridesmaids, I wanted a Skull and Bones society, a brigade of Angelina Jolies doing international charity work, or a flying legion of flaming massage chairs filled with gals in sweat suits. I had never had the finances or type of job that allowed me to participate in people's weddings, and I had only ever been a terrible bridesmaid myself, which is why I was always relegated to standing in the back. Once, when the bridesmaids each held a different type of flower that made up all the variety of flowers in the bride's bouquet, I was handed the leaves. That's who I was at weddings: Foliage Girl.

My female friendships were the foundation of all the good things in my life, and instead of looking forward to their participation in our wedding, I was worried that having bridesmaids would turn my friendships into trite displays of matching sparkly robes meant to drain their bank accounts while "bringing out my eyes." I refused to use the label at first, calling my friends "the women in my life who mean a lot to me and are helping me with the wedding." Finally I caved, because at least *bridesmaids* is easier to say, and thank God I did. I was so wrong about all of it. These bridal-party traditions created such phenomenally life-changing memories that I ended up not caring that the pictures of us at every event looked like a group date on *The Bachelor* when all of the women gather on a balcony and scream, "Brad! We're ready for love!"

For my bachelorette party, we descended upon Santa Fe, New Mexico, where my family has lived for the past twenty years. My mom met us at our rented house with custom New Mexican martini glasses just for the occasion, plus packets of hangover cure, because she's always looking out. That first night we showed up at The Cowgirl and partied like it was Bungalow 8, which is the name of an elite club I read about in *Vanity Fair*, so I hope that reference means something to someone. The band turned up the volume, the over-fifty crowd (which is the only crowd in Santa Fe) joined us on the patio, and we all began to rage as women in modest, long-flowing skirts twirled me around and men in cargo shorts asked my bridesmaids to buy *them* a shot. When The Cowgirl closed, we called the one cab service in town, and he began making multiple trips to get us all home. On his last drive up the mountain, I piled onto my bridesmaids' laps and stuck my head out the window because there was simply no room inside for my hair. I watched Santa Fe fly by as the wind chilled my gums and I was whiplashed with wet drops of either my tears or my saliva. I had spent the happiest years of my youth in New Mexico, feeling healed by the calm of the desert, but I had spent much of that time alone. Aside from a coworker or two, I had wandered the city solo. Now I was back, in my favorite place on earth, and this time I'd brought the friendship with me.

I had eleven official bridesmaids, but over those two years of wedding planning, I found myself gathering more and more along the way. I've found that *bridesmaid* is not so much a designated label as it is a temperament.

I found a bridesmaid in a boutique as I tried on one particularly expensive wedding dress, and the mom of another bride whispered, "Don't bother. Same gown is on sale across town." I found a bridesmaid at The Cowgirl when a silver-haired woman in a blue velvet dress cleared a circle around me and made everyone chant *La Reina! (The Queen!)*. Our flight attendant on the way to New Mexico became a bridesmaid when she slipped me an extra drink while whispering, "Thanks for not 'woo'-ing while we're in the air."

My incredible mother-in-law, Vicki, became a bridesmaid when I saw a picture of gorgeous designer shoes that were $1200 and she flatly said, "I can make those with one trip to Michaels and a glue gun." Then she did. A comedian named Pam became a bridesmaid when she sent me a message that said, *You don't need a dress, you need a couture costume...and I can sew.* The salesman at Sephora became a bridesmaid when he leaned over and said, "Nude lipsticks are a scam. What you need is Pencil Eraser Pink."

At one bridal store, I was struggling to get a sample dress over my ass, and the saleswoman grabbed the bodice and we began jumping up and down together to pull it up. With each jump I squealed, "I'm so sorry," as she whispered back, "Never apologize!" The dress stopped midway up my hips, cutting my ass into a shelf of flesh sitting over the zipper. We were both breathing hard at this point. "Thank you for trying," I wheezed. I don't remember her name, but she was also a bridesmaid.

I began posting jokes about wedding planning online, and strangers would reply with tips and tricks and opinions. I ran dress polls, I shared prices, and more than once I received a message that said *Please, I must know if you chose a dress. I am worried for you!* My DMs filled up with bridesmaids who'd been brides themselves, encouraging me to blow the lid on weddings, take it all to the max, enjoy every ounce of it. With each all-caps message I felt the spirit of their foreboding mothers haunting them as they typed YOU DO YOU! CAVE FOR NO ONE!

As each detail came into place, it felt as if all my bridesmaids and I had run a coup on the bridal industry, casting out gold-embossed-calligraphy Martha Stewart, and exchanging her for lawn-mower-riding-slash-stock-trading Martha Stewart, as I stood atop the wreckage screaming, "IT'S MY SPECIAL DAY!"

The night before the wedding, I celebrated in a hotel suite full of my official bridesmaids. I sat in the center wearing a full-on wedding dress that I'd purchased from a preowned gown website because I was desperate to wear a '90s Celine Dion unhinged-castle-lady dress at least once in my life. I was surrounded by the momentous women from every phase of my existence, who had seen me through every eon of growth.

I had often felt like my sense of self was fractured between all the worlds and phases of life I had lived, from being a high-school dropout to going to a fancy boarding school, from awkward comedian to working comedian, from the trauma-filled friend to...trauma-filled friend with an Amex. Now, looking around the room at each bridesmaid, I could finally feel the full puzzle click into place.

There they all were, the women who loved me, raised me, and carried me to this magical moment in my life. How could I have ever not wanted bridesmaids, when bridesmaids were how I'd survived?

At the end of the night, I jumped into the hotel pool in the wedding dress I was wearing. As soon as I popped my head above the water, I turned to see my mom jump in behind me, also fully clothed. My two brothers and my childhood friend Noe came out of the hotel restaurant where they were eating dinner and dove in the water next. We all laughed as we treaded water in a circle and I felt as if I might break into pieces from bliss. My family had grown up somewhat fractured, never spending more than a few years together all under the same roof, and all that physical distance had worked to make me believe there was some emotional distance in our family unit. There in the pool, that falsehood was shattered as I got to feel the depth of our bond—a family who will cross the hotel room floor as if it's an emergency so they can jump in a pool fully clothed to be with their sister. The wedding hadn't even started and I thought to myself, damn, I can't believe I almost skipped this part!

Then security showed up to let us know that the pool was very much closed and escorted us out in our sopping-wet clothes. I turned to the party and yelled, "Like that's gonna stop me! Where to next?" My bridesmaids rushed forward, grabbing my drenched body and escorted me up the stairs. "To bed! The bride is going to bed!"

The next morning, Yassir and I remained separate before we saw each other at the altar, but we texted back and forth in shock. It was happening. We were getting married.

The dress code was Try and Outdo Us, and two hundred and sixty of our loved ones arrived in capes, feathers, headpieces, and jewels. Outside the venue, we'd covered a giant billboard on the street with a huge picture of our moms. A choir and live band sang "Amazing Grace" to begin the wedding. My mom, my godmother Grace, and my aunt Sharon paraded down the aisle with my stepdad Edward throwing flowers from behind them. A gaggle of my nieces, nephews, and my brothers trailed behind throwing confetti. Then my official bridesmaids all marched out: Ashley, Kenzie, Ali, Jo, Akilah, Kate, Brigitte, Taylor, Annarose, Joanna, and Alex, clutching handfuls of gold confetti and releasing them as the trumpets blared. I had told my bridesmaids to turn the hell up, and they arrived in sparkly jumpsuits, iconic gowns, and body jewelry.

As the music crescendoed, all the lights turned off and the room became pitch-black and filled with fog. A spotlight fell upon me in the back, and as the drummer began to play, I walked myself down the aisle, then ran the last ten feet because I just couldn't wait. When I got to the altar, Yassir and I clasped hands and began a dance break. Everyone we loved was on their feet screaming and cheering. We exchanged our own vows and then kissed as husband and wife while the choir sang "Oh Happy Day."

That night I wore three different dresses, and my ceremony dress was gold and created by Rey Ortiz, who also designs for drag queens. Every time I changed, I did it with the help of one of my bridesmaids. Earrings were fastened and shoe straps were buckled, and I took the moment to tell each of them how much I loved them. There was no sit-down dinner, but food trucks full of pizza, green chili empanadas, tacos, fried chicken and waffles. A coffee cart made our guests custom lattes with our dog's face drawn in the foam, you know, just to make sure everyone knew we were truly out of our minds. The speeches that night felt like the best stand-up comedy show I'd ever seen, because all our loved ones also happened to be performers, since Yassir has one quality that I definitely hadn't put on my list... He, too, is a comedian.

Yassir and I asked all the guests to join us on the dance floor for the bouquet toss. We surprised the crowd by throwing hundreds of flowers from the balcony as the DJ, Yassir's cousin who used to spin for a strip club, began the dance party. We had a room called The Museum of Us filled with pedestals and plaques of special moments, and the outfits we wore on our

first date together on mannequins. In another room there was
a small basketball court for people to shoot hoops over a graphic
on the floor that said *The Court-ship of Yassir and Chelsea*. The
tables had stacks of books with library cards that said *Before we
ever met in person, we sent each other books*, which was true (fucking AWWW, right?). We cut a grocery-store sheet cake back
and forth with a double handsaw that had our names engraved
on it. We invited everyone to find us in the back room and take
a selfie and then hired stand-ins who vaguely looked like us to
pose with our guests for "Pictures with the Bride and Groom."
At the end of the night, we opened up a room filled with three
hundred tacos from Taco Bell. Our registry was a fundraiser
for two organizations, one in New Mexico and one in Georgia, that helped single moms and domestic-violence survivors,
and we donated every gift.

Twice that night, two bridesmaids screeched with laughter
as they gestured around at the epic joy, and whispered, "I hate
to bring up your exes...but can you imagine if you hadn't held
out for Yassir?!?"

When the final song came on, all our loved ones swarmed
around us: the bridesmaids, our moms, the groomsmen, all our
friends. And then, one final guest arrived: our needy quarantine dog ran into our arms and joined us for the last dance. He
was also a bridesmaid.

MOM

(I love you, I'm sorry, please forgive me, and thank you)

Days before my fourteenth birthday, my mom, myself, and my younger brother Jesse were moving across the country in a U-Haul that was so chaotically packed, plants and a few dishes fell out when we lifted the back door. We had just escaped Bubba in Utah and driven through the night to meet my godmother in Colorado. On my birthday my mom handed me a card. Inside she had written how she was proud of me and how she knew we had been through a lot together, but things were finally going to be turning around. She signed it, *This is our year.*

I had a strong feeling that she was right—this really was going to be our year. Bubba was out of our lives for good and my mom already had a lead on a job at the post office. I'd applied for a job at the local coffee shop as soon as we arrived, and I'd already had my first shift and experienced the euphoria of turning the tip jar upside down. I felt sure we were on the brink of prosperity, and that birthday card was flush with reassurances, even though at the very moment I held it in my hands, we were homeless.

Without anywhere to live, we had parked the U-Haul in an alley and took up residence in a small two-room office building in town that my godmother had rented out for her new holistic-health clinic, while Grace continued to live in her off-the-grid cabin in the middle of nowhere. My mom had surveyed our options and determined that squatting in the office building was a better choice than all of us sleeping in one bed with Grace in the wilderness and using a bucket every time we had to pee.

I read the card my mom had given me while sitting on one of the massage tables that we slept on at night as makeshift beds. During the day we ate peanut butter and jelly sandwiches, and at night my mom made us warm dinners on a hot plate. We showered at the community bathrooms down by the river where tourists rinsed off after a hike, and we did our laundry every couple weeks at a new friend's house—a man who was just desperate to date my mom, despite the fact that he had a girlfriend.

After a couple months of living in the office building, my mom found a house for rent outside of town. We moved in with another one of my godmother's friends, Amy, who was going to live with us to split the rent and provide a second set of parental eyes when my mom had to work. It was just your regular ol' two-parent household of traumatized gal pals who were trying to get their midlife grooves back!

Most of that year was spent hiding-while-crying. My mom, because of the divorce and the stress of keeping our family afloat, and me, because of all the bullying at school. At night my mom would sneak out into the yard, crying as she sat in the grass, while I would hide out in my room behind a journal, crying into the pages, then we'd meet in the kitchen for dinner, with big, strong smiles on our faces. It was not our year. It would have been the worst year of our lives, except worse years had already come before it, and worse years would come after it.

I have twelve of those cards from my mom. Some have cartoon drawings of precocious dogs in sunglasses, others feature naughty old ladies photographed in black-and-white but with shiny Photoshopped red lips. Every card has the same inscription inside, in my mom's beautiful cursive: *This is our year.* She gave me one on my thirteenth birthday, and on my twelfth birthday, and some birthdays before that. I got them for Christmases, and Easters, and sometimes just because it'd been a hard week. The pile had slowly stacked up over time, creating an accidental abacus, a tally of all the years that it was most certainly Not Our Year.

My mom kept giving me these cards because she always believed that lottery days were just around the corner. The fight never left her, no matter how often we got knocked down—sometimes quite literally by husbands, other times emotionally by debt and bills. My mom got herself and us kids to the finish line by waving an it's-all-okay victory flag long before we'd earned it—and then one day, finally, everything *was* okay, and eventually our year did arrive.

But the unfortunate thing about being okay is that once you're there, you're at risk of losing touch with those you survived with. Once you're out of the fight, you can start to get hit with the reverberations of all the times you lived the lie of okay, but it really wasn't, and it can be hard to face each other after that because you're a mirror of all the things you both want to forget.

When we reached the land of okay, my mom was triumphant, enjoying our newfound serenity, while I became unmoored as I looked back at what we'd come through.

In my mom's generation, resilience had an important requirement: that you would hide your pain, take the high road, and never speak of the struggle. Resilience meant you were to show up and keep working with the bad man who is always bad to you, and you do it smiling, because good women kept their mouths shut. After learning how to survive by keeping her head down, my mom was hesitant to acknowledge everything we had been through, because not acknowledging it was how you showed strength. Hiding had helped her survive, and that need to hide was passed down to me.

I was cautious about sharing who we were and what we'd

been through for a long time, but over the years, I've found that I quite like where we came from. Every time I'm at work in fancy Hollywood writers' rooms and I hear a coworker say something like "My old private school helped fund that pervert fascist's political campaign, but I'm still giving them money so my daughter can get in there one day!" or "Our new house is under construction, and I'm so jealous of the roofers. Imagine how simple of a job that is, no stress at all…" or "My toddler's favorite food is sashimi," I think to myself, Thank fucking God I grew up on mac and cheese and libraries.

My mom taught me resilience and how to fight back and showed me how, through it all, to protect your gentleness. I refused this for so long, relying on anger and pain to push me forward when I felt weak, but one day I woke up and there it was, a small kernel of gentleness had remained. My mom had planted it there long ago and nurtured it through each phone call and text and trip to see me, urging me not to wall off my heart.

I was given so many gifts by my mom, so if there is one thing I'd like to give back to her, it's to tell the story she's never been able to share and to tell that story how I see it: with immense pride.

Before my mom and I were surviving together, she was surviving alone. She grew up in small houses and trailers with a beach cooler in the corner that acted as their fridge. When the power shut off, the ice would melt, everything would spoil, and then they'd have nothing. She had many hungry days. She spent the babysitting money she earned to buy an SOS sponge to clean the floor so she wouldn't be so embarrassed of their home. This would be futile, because her mom, Debbie, habitually took stray animals into their home, and when they peed on the floor, she simply laid newspaper over it. After enough time had passed, the flooring was just layers and layers of compressed wet newspaper.

At fourteen years old, I had my mom's love and a beautiful birthday card. When my mom was fourteen years old, she ran away from home and married a twenty-one-year-old Navy veteran. Her home life was so bad that running away to marry this man—and lying about her age in the process—was a better option than staying put another moment. Her mom didn't even stand in her way, and in fact, she might have encouraged it.

Now, if that sentence didn't hit you the first time, let me say it again: a fully adult man helped a literal child run away from home and then married that child. That man was my dad, aka Limoncello.

Here's my favorite part of that story: Limoncello is a short man, maybe 5'5" or, in his cowboy boots, 5'7". And he's not a secure short man; he's a short man who is very upset about it, and you know what that means—he owns a motorcycle.

Now, when Limoncello met my mom, they were the same height. But the funny thing about kids is that they're not done growing. By the time my mom was eighteen, she had hit a statuesque 5'10". Limoncello spent his life very upset about it, being a short man with a wife five full inches taller than him, but hey—maybe don't marry children.

They moved to Hawaii, held a wedding on a hill with some hippie friends, and later took jobs running a health food store. After years of operating the store, they got wind of a gig where you could make tons of cash to mine for gold in Alaska, and so they moved first to the Yentna River and then the Kahiltna and tried their luck. When their nets didn't pull up anything larger than shiny golden flakes, they returned to Nevada and took out a loan to buy a small used tractor and started a business together plowing snow, building homes, and clearing out septic tanks. My mom knows how to lay the foundation for a house, regrout a bathroom, shingle a roof, rewire your electrical, and renovate your entire home from studs to curtains, should you need it.

They divorced when I was four, and Limoncello kept their

business and gave my mom nothing, and she didn't dare ask for more—she was just happy to finally be free from him. She had been parented by her husband and had emerged from it all a stunning, tall thirty-four-year-old woman. Once again she sought out the only route to security she'd ever known and quickly married my stepdad, Bubba, hopscotching her way out of abuse and into it again, one dud at a time.

After nine tough years with Bubba, my mom emerged again, freshly divorced, having never been single a day in her life. I was just entering puberty at this time, and in an odd way we went through a sort of prepubescent phase together, learning together what crushes and dating were like. But I also knew for sure that I never wanted my mom to get married again. As she started to date men more seriously, I would beg her to dump them and just remain single until I graduated high school. When that didn't work, I took matters into my own hands and began to sabotage prospective candidates. Edward, the man who would eventually become my future stepdad, came to our house for the first time when I was fifteen. I opened the door, called him Daddy, and told him I needed braces. Somehow *that* didn't work, so every time he came into town, I would send my mom flowers from other fake boyfriends I'd made up, hoping he'd think she was cheating. One time I called the home phone when I knew she and Edward would be there and pretended to be a bill collector letting her know she was hundreds of thousands of dollars in debt.

My mom and Edward were off and on, and just before they were on for good we moved to New Orleans. That summer we were incredibly strapped for cash, so much so that I remember scrambling for change to buy the $1 burger at McDonald's. There was a night I woke up to find my mom sobbing and throwing up from stress, and she confessed to me that she had only $100 left to her name. The next morning when I found my mom in the kitchen, she'd put on a cheerful face and showed me a flyer she saw at the coffee shop for a big gala that night. Tickets were $50 each. She exclaimed that we should put on our finest dresses and buy the tickets with her last $100 and go have the time of our lives because being depressed was no way to live. We might have gone to the gala and made that once-in-a-lifetime memory, but I was intent on being the fixer, and I angrily left the house in search of a second job.

My mom was trying to teach me something they never tell you about suffering—how to have some fun during it—which is perhaps one of the most important aspects of enduring. Like many daughters, my personality was created in opposition to my mom's. My mom is whimsical and adventurous, always down to go with the flow; I am a stubborn overachiever who gets caught up in the details. And of course, her personality was formed in opposition to her mom, as goes the electric slide of generational trauma.

My mom's mom, my grandma Debbie, stayed in her same trailer all those years while my mom traveled across the country in search of better. My mom was often so close, no more than a few states away, and yet we never saw my grandma when I was growing up. Later in life, after my mom was settled into her happy ending with Edward (who valiantly endured all of my hazing to eventually win my approval), she began to reach out to her mom and tried to form a relationship again.

Through my mom's stories, I began to hear the tale of the rose ring, the only family heirloom that exists in our blood-line. After one of Debbie's divorces, she took all of her wedding bands and engagement rings and had them melted down to cre-ate this massive gold ring in the shape of a giant rose and took the one tiny diamond from the last ex-husband and placed it in the middle. This ring was hers and hers alone, and it symbol-ized power and autonomy, and all my mom's cousins and the wives of brothers and uncles looked upon it, wondering who in our family would be gifted the heirloom one day. But Debbie was often in financial trouble, so every time she was in a tight spot she would pawn the ring for cash, and when she was back on her feet she'd go and buy it back.

When I was twenty-seven, Debbie's health deteriorated, and my mom devoted herself to fully patching things up between them before she passed. My mom cleaned her trailer for weeks, emptying decades of newspaper from the flooring, and spent hours by her side in the hospital.

I was sitting backstage at The Second City in Chicago, where I worked as a comedian performing a show every night. As I put on my makeup, an intense energy entered my body. I stared into the mirror, overtaken by a voice in my head that asked me a flurry of questions about myself and my life. It was gone just as soon as it arrived, and I caught my eyes in the mirror and shook it off, the mascara wand still dangling from my fingertips. I turned to my best friend, Rebecca, and whispered, "I think my grandma just died." And while I seem to be describing my grandmother's spirit passing through my body, just so we're all clear, that had never happened before and has never happened since. I had only met Debbie once as an adult and a few times that I can't really recall when I was a kid. I was surprised that she would visit me as she departed this plane, or even that I would hallucinate that she had. My most recent memory of Debbie was that she had written on my Facebook wall telling me she was so proud that I was on *SNL* but kept falling asleep before she saw me on-screen. I have never been on *SNL*.

A few minutes after I felt that intense energy wash through me, my cell phone rang, and my mom told me the news of her death.

I flew to the funeral to be with my mom, as she said goodbye to hers. When we got to the church I recognized the little accoutrements as the Church of Latter-Day Saints. I guess at some point, Debbie had become a Mormon. I thought of her up there in the muumuu she loved to wear and whispered, "Don't take the doughnuts, Grandma!"

The service began and a little woman dressed in pastels used a remote to power the podium up and down for each person who spoke. The machine was loud and rambling, and the rising and falling took minutes at a time. As the Mormon minister running the funeral spoke about Debbie, he kept calling her Sister Anderson. This was perplexing at first, because *Anderson* wasn't her last name, it was her sister's last name. On the tenth time he called her Sister Anderson, Debbie's *actual* sister, Laurel, called out from the pews, "That's not her last name, that's *my* last name!"

Which is how we found out that later in life, Debbie had married her sister's ex-husband behind her back, also taking his last name. They had lived just two hours away from each other, so I guess Debbie employed some sort of different-zip-codes-now-he's-my-ho type of rule.

Every single speaker at her funeral mentioned my grandma's cats. My mom's cousin's son gave this really sweet speech about how Debbie had the kindest heart in the world and took in every stray soul and animal and then gave a long description about the time she attempted to return an empty can of cat food to Walmart. The badass thing about my grandma is that she succeeded.

The podium rambled up, the podium rambled down. Laurel was slowly processing that her sister had married her own ex-husband, someone onstage was naming all five of her cats, and the minister had fallen asleep. Edward, who had only met Debbie once, started laughing uncontrollably at the madness of it all, and once he started he couldn't stop, and I began laughing at *him* laughing.

And then I saw my mom say goodbye, and nothing was funny anymore.

Watching my mom up at the podium, her eyes swollen shut

from crying, I saw the girl who deserved so much better than she'd gotten but never stopped trying to do better for me and my brothers.

Throughout my adult life, my mom has often come to me in the worst of our fights, defeated, as she asks, "Do you not remember anything good about your childhood?"

As I sat there in the wooden pew, I realized what I should have said during all of those times.

I remember *you*.

I remember you, Mom. I remember your kindness that only grew stronger, no matter how cruel your situation was, and how you'd stand up for us when pushed too far. I remember being nine years old, watching you throw a drink on that woman who accused us of not being members of the pool club we were swimming in (which was true, but what a bitch). I remember you making us apple crisp and lasagna every time I came home and attempting to teach me how to cook, over and over, despite how many times I burned the dish or added too much salt. I remember you volunteering to be the school-lunch chaperone just to spend more time with me. I remember you marching into the history fair and yelling at my mortal enemy, Chelsea A., for copying my middle-school presentation about the first American female astronaut and the events of the *Challenger* explosion. I remember you sewing me the most elaborate Halloween costumes and custom birthday dresses, which I would turn into daily-occasion wear as I climbed trees and pedaled around on my tricycle. I remember you getting a job at the local casino as a seamstress, making costumes for the showgirls and helping them dress every night. I remember you putting me in a carrier on your back and taking me backstage with you as you worked, which I think explains my entire personality.

I remember you whispering instructions about how to protect myself with good energy and how to say an affirmation when I was scared. I remember you teaching me the New Age prayer you learned yourself as a teenager and telling me to repeat these four phrases whenever I felt stuck: *I love you, I'm sorry, Please forgive me, and…* You hesitated at the fourth and final one, adding your own twist on the final line of the prayer: "The last line is either *Fuck you* or *Thank you*. They're interchangeable depending on the moment." It became my rallying cry when I couldn't fathom how to keep going. I always chose *Fuck you* because in my lowest moments, I needed the backbone.

I love you, I'm sorry, Please forgive me, and *Fuck you.*

I will always remember you, Mom, making me laugh even as it all went to hell.

Once, when I asked you how you remained so strong to overcome all the obstacles you dryly replied, "I kept going, and here I am."

It is the women who crack a joke when the ship has been set on fire who have my undying allegiance.

Before Grandma Debbie died, my mom had been waiting to hear who would get the rose ring, hoping if Debbie left it to her instead of one of the female cousins who lived nearby, it would be a sign Debbie still loved my mom, and forgave her, even though she never came back home again once she'd left.

After a couple dire weeks in the hospital, the moment to determine the ring's future arrived. My grandma was lying in the hospital bed, my mom sitting on a chair beside her. Debbie reached out her hand and beckoned my mom close. It was time. My mom leaned in, and as Debbie whispered who she'd deemed to be the next keeper of the ring, my mom heard a name that wasn't hers. She grimly nodded and asked Debbie where the ring was so she could deliver it to its new owner. Debbie gave her the address of a pawn shop.

My mom faithfully went and purchased the ring back. At the funeral, she slipped it into my hand.

Maybe my grandma knew that I, too, love gaudy rings. Maybe

she gave it to me to make up for all the time we never spent together. Maybe she thought I was on *SNL*.

I think my grandma gave me the ring as a gift, hoping that I could love her through it, that we could spend time together in this life, and that maybe I could forgive her for not being the best mom to my mom, and she could forgive me for not trying harder to know her. I often think she was too afraid to give it to my mom, unwilling to ask her for the forgiveness she'd never earned. But that's all my mom wanted, too: forgiveness from her for never coming back home. I think all we want, in the end, is for our moms and our daughters to forgive us.

Now I wear the ring for momentous occasions so that my grandma can experience them by my side. When I sold a TV show about my adventures with my mom in the Southwest, my grandma helped me hold the pen, the rose ring clanking against the metal as I wrote my first big Hollywood check out to my mom and told her to turn the fuck up at the local mall. In the byline of the check I wrote *This is our year*.

CHELSEA DEVANTEZ

Onward

Remember Earl?

████████████

███

███

███

███

███

███

███

███

███████████████████████████████████████

██ years after The Big Scary Domestic Violence Thing, I was onstage performing a show. As I sauntered across the stage, a sheriff walked into the building, took the escalator upstairs to the production offices, and with the foreboding command of a badge and uniform, asked my bosses where he could find me.

███

███

███████████████████████████████████████

██
█████████████████████████████████
██
██
██
██
██
██
██
██
██████████████

The cop handed me a folder. I began to read through its contents. The first page was a letter ████████████ had written, along with some paperwork ████████████████████ ████████████████████████.

I sifted through the papers and found the instructions the sheriff had followed. The police had tracked me through my social security number, which led them to my job at the theater.

On the top of the instructions page, they had listed my name. My new name: Chelsea Devantez.

I began to panic and asked the cop how this was possible, if it was their office that had written that name down, or if ████████ ██ ██ ██ ██ ██ ██ ██████████████.

So, here the offender returns. I tried waving around that 8½" x 11" saying, *Not this time, boys!* It turns out Earl wanted to ██████████████████████████████████████, which meant ██████████████████████████████.

I felt overwhelmed. I felt helpless. I felt nothing. ██████████.

███
███
███
███
██████████████████████████████ I was urged by everyone
around me to ███████████████████████ and move on.
So I ██
████████████████████.

At the time, I had no proper help or even awareness that I might be suffering from past trauma that was affecting my current state of being. I spent that winter vacillating constantly between panic and a numbness so potent it stained every moment of my life. It seemed like any conversation I had about ████████████████ was happening a mile away as I watched from behind plexiglass. I led every choice with fear, and when the veracity of that fear exhausted all my resources, I mentally checked out.

I had never told people about ████████████████████████, but my rage at any patriarchal injustice had been slowly eking out of me ever since. In one of my shows I would walk out onto the stage and ask, "Is anyone here from Wyoming? Let's hear it!" People would whoop and holler as I'd call out more states: Minnesota, Texas, Michigan, Kentucky, and so on…and then, at the height of cheering, I'd say, "Those are states where it's legal for a rapist to sue for joint custody of a child!"

As the audience took this slap in the face, a Jock Jams song would blast through the speakers, and the rest of the cast would join me onstage to dance and ride the wave of horrified laughter.

But after The Big Scary Domestic Violence Thing resurfaced, ████████████████████████████████████ ████████████████████████████ the case ████████████████████████ my world onstage began to look and sound different. The applause every night felt ominous and untrustworthy. *Clap. Clap. Clap.* Then the clapping became gunshots. Slapping. Hitting.

Clap! Clap! Clap! Every night onstage I spent the first two minutes scanning the audience as I crisply delivered each punch line. I lived equally in two realities, one where my past stayed the past and everyone had moved on, and another one where ██████████████████████████████████████ and could easily buy tickets to my shows. *Clap! Clap! Clap!*

The events came back to me louder than ever before, and they've hovered close ever since. Sometimes the memories are quiet, hanging in the distance, absent for weeks, and other times they drone in my ears at night. When the hauntings get worse and my dreams began to stretch and blur the events, I tiptoe into my office. I push aside the stacks of books I keep on top of a trunk, then I unlock the lid and lift it open. I pull out the ████████████ and hold it in my hands, looking at the directions provided on how to find me. I read over the letter and assure my wandering, broken brain that I'm not making it all up.

Even after The Big Scary Domestic Violence Thing surfaced again, it was still many years before I could fully accept the fuckery I had endured. Then slowly, finally, with enough hard-earned resources and therapy, I had the privilege to get angry. Really angry. I began to thrash back against the demons, even though it was many years too late.

I became so livid at the past that the momentum of my rage empowered me to feel as if I might be able to get justice. Not real justice, of course, ha ha, oh no, that would be ridiculous! No, I was aiming for that sweet, sweet *poetic justice.* I thought that surely there would be some comeuppance for him somewhere.

After ██ years, I finally spoke The Big Scary Domestic Violence Thing out loud.

Eventually, I arrived at this moment here, where I began to write the memoir you're holding in your hands. I dragged out all my hoarder boxes, running my hands across a lifetime's worth of journals, the court paperwork, and all the other little haunted knickknacks.

Memories in hand, I tapped away at my keyboard, drinking little sips of whiskey to be like all the Big Boys who wrote our dustiest books, thinking, *Look at me*, tappity-tappity-tappity, *I'm writing my story!* Tappity-tappity-tappity, *I'm sharing my truth!* The process to publish the book began.

And then, one day, a meeting was called ███████████

· That's why there are black bars in this book.

I had thought that savings, friends, connections, healing, time, and likability could anoint me some power. But none of those things are power. Only power is power.

I had gathered so many achievements that had allowed me the privilege to reach back and reclaim some dignity—I had money, lawyers, a great job, an impressive résumé. There were even some famous people in my phone who I could text, and every now and then they write back! To the outside eye you would never have known I was having breakdowns. I barely even want you to know now! I only put them in the book because the fight to remain perfect is over.

I suppose I had fallen for all the girl-boss merch and was living in my own Hear Me Roar fantasy out here in my She-Shed, thinking I could earn my way into some deserved justice. What-ever shall I do now with my *The Future Is Female* shirt? Add a handwritten addendum to the bottom in Sharpie? *Yeah, maybe the future is female, because it sure as fuck isn't the present!*

Because at the end of the day, I got all the things, and it still wasn't enough. Now, just think of any victim of domestic violence out there who has even an ounce less.

When I first began to write The Big Scary Domestic Violence Thing, I worried that I couldn't trust my traumatized brain, that maybe it felt worse than it actually was, that maybe it wasn't really that bad. But when I went back to the ███████, documents and my diary entries, and placed shaky phone calls to those who watched it happen, I found that it was actually worse.

One night, deep into my fact-finding mission, I discovered the journal where I said I was going to write the whole story down, from start to finish, just once, and then I was never coming back to it. I wrote in timid cursive that I was leaving that part of my life in the pages inside the Purple Striped Floral Diary and not a shred of it was going to follow me in the forthcoming literal and metaphorical chapters of my life. At the very end of the journal, I wrote a section titled Lessons for My Future Daughter, hoping that she could avoid the fate I had found myself in.

The advice section has pieces of wisdom like *Know you're more than this* next to things like *If you start dating someone, hack into their email as quickly as possible to find out if they are a liar.* When I reread these sentences in my thirties, it instantly transported me back to all the fights I had with boyfriends as I yelled, "Show me your phone, fuckhead!"

Whoops. Sorry, boys.

I had written all those lessons supposedly for a future daughter of mine, but after going back and reading them as an adult, it was clear who those lessons were really for: me. Grown-ass, adult me. I was the one who needed to hear her cries for strength and resurgence because lately I have felt like I'd touched my breaking point. After making it through unfathomable obstacles, I am somehow lacking that earlier fortitude. I have spent hours mulling over a mean anonymous comment, months struggling with a passive-aggressive boss, years wondering if I should even exist. I've handed my dignity, my resilience, and my worth over to strangers, begging them to validate me as a person. To tell me I'm okay. That I should keep going.

Young me would never.

Young me would not falter, and she would never consider backing down. She got in a car with two broken windows from ██████████████████████████████████████.

Young me had a fucking go-to-court outfit.

Young me had an unshakable will that I find myself longing for, the version of me who got back up instantly, who changed her name for the final time while wearing her mom's sweater and a wrap skirt that was too small, then held a party with her new friends to celebrate.

Back then, I had been elated at the prospect of a new last name and that with it I could phoenix myself out of the ashes like a tattoo on Ben Affleck's divorced back. But when it came time to choose a surname, I was lost. I couldn't just use my mom's last name because ████████████████████ ████████████████████████. Even if I could have used her name, I'm not sure I would have. At the time, I was really angry at her for not being around enough when I was ████████████ ████████████████████████, I was angry at her for the husbands she'd picked, and I was angry that she had already started dating so shortly after her divorce, and I worried that one day she'd get married again and change her name, which she did, and I was mad at that, too. I already knew that I was donor-conceived and that I would never have an actual father. I decided that I didn't want to follow anyone else's path anymore. I wanted to belong to myself.

If I could go back in time I would tell myself to have fun with it, not to take myself so seriously, maybe choose something flashy like *Sparkletits* or *Cupcakez*. I would tell myself to change my first name, too, because I do believe my personality is serving closer to an *Emerald* or a *Kiki*.

But I so desperately wanted to be seen as normal, and that guided a lot of the decision for me. For a while I was set on choosing Chelsea Zeta, the romanized spelling of the Greek letter *z*, which I tried on for size by passionately signing my journal entries with it. Yet I had no deeper reason for choosing *Zeta*, other than thinking the name sounded nice and *z*'s were cool, so thankfully, instead of picking out my legal name with about as much effort as playing a game of MASH, I kept searching.

I was in the library, strolling my finger down the page in a book of baby names and their meanings when I saw *Devante*—it's a Spanish boy's name, and it means righter of wrongs. I immediately knew this was what I wanted to imbue my life with. We've all been taught that last names come from dads, so it felt a bit beautiful that my name could be a nod to what I'd been told about mine, while still being completely my own. I added a *z* to the end because, like I said, very cool, and it made it so that it was no longer a boy's first name but a surname I would be the only person in the world to have. I like that the *z* made it visually resemble *cherchez*, which is a French verb that means *look for*. I had read the word in the lyrics book to Gloria Estefan's cover of "Cherchez la Femme" and its translation felt searingly potent.

I adored my glamorous new name: Devantez was emblematic of all the hopes I had for myself, yet entirely made up, which, as a donor kid, felt like a dab of fate. The judge stamped the documents, and it was done. Baptism by damage, renewed all the same.

I can still go back to that moment in the library, sitting at a table and searching for inspiration. I can smell the pages from the stack of baby-name books by my side and hear the comforting thump of hardcovers being lifted and replaced on shelves. I remember sinking into the chair with resolve, promising myself that I would never ever give my power over to anyone, and I would never change my last name again, no matter what.

In many ways I have always had Young Me in the back of my head, whispering, pushing, reprimanding, sometimes screaming at me to get back up, to not let her years be in vain, to not become one of those people we hated when we were younger, someone who didn't know how good they had it. Young Me made promises: that if I ever found money in life, I would never forget what it felt like to be in need, that if I ever got rid of my eating disorder, I would never hate on my body or anyone else's, and that if I ever got the chance to make my own art, I would give it everything I had.

Everything I've attempted and achieved has always had her momentum behind it. I've had the gift of walking through life with Young Me in my ear.

But she had to go through life without *me*.

Young Me combed through books and lived in the libraries and poured over celebrity memoirs looking for glimmers of an answer, hoping for something to make that day okay, to escape the sadness, to explain how to climb to a dream, to hand over the keys to the dauntingly difficult entertainment world that would offer some creative emotional reprieve. But *me*? Older Me? I now know those answers.

And so, if another Young Me is out there, searching, I hope she found a gift or two in these pages that help her to continue onward.

I hope she learned something about forgiveness, but only for those who earn it.

I want her to know that one day I looked down to see a text from Rebecca. Our contact began slowly, a gentle text here and there, until finally it built to a flood of apologies. I found myself emailing Rebecca the chapter I had written about us and asked her to meet me at a Stevie Nicks concert three days later. I was not entirely sure she would show, but of course she got there early and I was the late one.

We sat in the arena as distant strangers who knew everything about each other, and though I know she must have felt some things had happened differently, Rebecca only gave me one note on the essay: "Don't call yourself dowdy, bitch." I drank wine straight from the bottle and stood and swayed to the music, vibrating in the presence of a once-was soulmate, listening to Stevie sing about heartbreak, fucking up, and how there's some people in life you'll just love forever, no matter what.

I want Young Me to know that when she can't find a way to forgive, with enough time she might forget, and that feels pretty fucking great, too. After I saw Limoncello on the wedding boat, the intensity of the wound dissipated, and with time, so did he. Nowadays I only think of him when an older gentleman on a Harley passes me on the highway. If he's wearing cowboy boots and a bandana, I scream and wave out the window calling, "Dad? Dad???" just for fun.

Young Me will be enraged to hear that when Bubba introduced her to the concept of suicide, it stuck in her brain and it will be a demon she must continuously fight off, but she'll have lots of help from the people who love her. I feel sad to let her know that suicide is ultimately the route Bubba chose to leave this world, this time using pills and alcohol. He didn't even bother telling his son goodbye or that he'd been diagnosed with cancer a month before. I have since found forgiveness for Bubba because he helped to give me one of the most precious and wonderful humans in my life, my little brother Jesse.

I hope she understands that trauma may push her and her siblings apart at times, but it can all be overcome. She will cry when she hears that Lucas held her hands and helped her down the stairs in her gown on her wedding day, and it wiped away the pain of all those years they spent apart.

I want her to know that opening up changed everything, and writing this book brought her and her mom closer, not further apart.

I know that was her biggest fear.

If there is another Young Me reading this, I hope she learned that humiliation has many faces, and no one is actually strong, they are just putting one foot forward, and that alone is enough.

I hope it was clear that it's the community she builds around herself that matters more than anything she'll ever do.

I hope she always carries extra lip gloss in her bag, just in case.

If nothing else, I hope she knows that normal is a vicious prank, and likability is a slow poison, and that she should forever be too much and never make herself less.

I hope she continues to live for Young Me and shouts her own story wherever she goes, since in the end, I could not.

★ ★ ★ ★ ★

ENDNOTES

A note about the book

Writing a memoir when you have c-PTSD is a wild ride. Traumatic events can be hard on the brain, but thankfully I have twenty-one very moody journals from childhood, which held the details of the events described in these pages. Hilariously, it does mean this book was, in a sense, fact-checked by a child.

Chelsea, Unidentified Time and Place

"Children who experience domestic violence in the home are also at higher risk of continuing the cycle of abuse as adults, either by becoming abusers or victims themselves. They are also fifteen times more likely to be physically and/or sexually assaulted than the national average." —Abraham Lincoln[1]

---

1   Okay it wasn't Abraham Lincoln who said this. Would have been fun though, right? This an excerpt from: Harrison, Olivia. *The Long-Term Effects of Domestic Violence on Children*. The Children's Legal Rights Journal.

Britney Brody

"This is The Place." —Abraham Lincoln[2]

Shitbitch

"It will soon be illegal in Colorado for men to donate sperm anonymously." —Abraham Lincoln[3]

"Adults conceived through sperm donation are supes fucked up." —Abraham Lincoln[4]

"Compared to kids who grow up knowing their biological parents, donor kids are more than twice as likely to struggle with addiction, depression, anxiety, and criminal activity." —Abraham Lincoln[5]

"He first began to donate sperm while he was in college, receiving $100 a visit from the sperm bank Xytex. His motivation, initially, was to pay his lawyer after he was charged with

---

2   Actually, wait, it was Brigham Young! It's also the title of the Utah State song written in 1996 by Sam and Gary Francis, all about how Brigham Young discovered Salt Lake City.

3   No, wait…wait… That's actually not a quote at all, but you can read about the Colorado bill they passed banning anonymous sperm and egg donation at https://www.denverpost.com/2022/06/01/colorado-donor-conceived-persons-protection-act/.

4   Damn. That wasn't old Abe either. But you can find more information on the harmful effects of donor conception on the humans conceived from it in several studies in the catalog of the Institute for American Values. Or just meet a donor-conceived person and spend time with them! Kidding, kidding.

5   Abraham did not say this. This quote comes from a study I am very thankful for. I cried when I read it because it made me feel so normal, however I have some notes for what they titled the damn thing: "My Daddy's Name is Donor." (Yikes.) The Institute for American Values. Elizabeth Marquardt, Norval D. Glenn, and Karen Clark, Co-Investigators.

underage drinking." —The reasoning of Dylan Stone Miller, the biological father of 96 children, *The Wall Street Journal*[6]

Delta

"In the freezer are frozen grapes…to suck on whenever she gets a sugar craving." —Abraham Lincoln[7]

---

6   This is just a fun quote I read recently that punched me in the fucking gut, because imagine reading this quote about the man who created you, as 96 of his children inevitably will one day.

7   The source of the frozen grape quote that would haunt me (and you) for the rest of time, was Skip Hollandsworth interviewing Kelly Clarkson for *Texas Monthly*.

ACKNOWLEDGMENTS

Yassir, my husband, love of my life—my lunchtime phone call, my laugh in the middle of the night—my absolute everything. I must tell anyone reading this that it was my husband, Yassir, who saved my book. When I couldn't tell the story that was most important to me, I nearly canceled the whole thing, until he said: "Just black it out then." His brain is perfect, his love is everything, he is all the exclamation points in the world shot into a rocket made of cocaine. Meeting him felt like fated soul-mate bullshit. He's also hot. I love that for me.

To my business partner and manager, Jordan Moncada (she's not the one with the Fiat, don't worry), you stood on the lawn and looked into my swollen puffy eyes and said: "You have to tell your story." Jordan, you have helped me fall apart and build something new at the same time. There is no book without you. You elevated my entire purpose in life. You are pure magic.

I am still in shock that I get more than one Amazing Grace in my life. Grace Towery, my editor, thank you for seeing me, and choosing me to have a book. You saved me from myself, you met my fire with fire, and you never said a word about how bad I am at commas. I didn't know you could fall in love with someone in the margins. It couldn't have been anyone but you.

Thank you to the Zoom full of women who changed my

life: Eden Church, your fierce spirit, and your lipstick shade, I'm wearing it now. Lindsey Reeder, your joy, your ferocity, your vulnerability. Laura Gianino, your incredible skills, your eloquence, and also your beautiful personal writing. To Justine Sha, for your passion and hard work on the campaign. Thank you to Vanessa Wells and Bonnie Lo for copyediting; Angela Hill and Sara Watson for production; the incredible marketing by Rachel Haller, Dayna Boyer, the digital marketing from Brianna Wodabek (that mug!). The last-chance-dance hero book cover by Elita Sidiropoulou. The audio and subrights, Carly Katz and Nora Rawn, and proofreading by Elena Gritzan and Judy Brioux. Thank you, Heather Connor. Thank you to all the support staff. Thank you to Peter Joseph.

To my best friend Alex, you stood by me in the hardest, worst years of my life, when it would have been far easier to turn away. Then again, you stood by me in the years following when I tried to push you out because I could no longer bear any reminders. You were supposed to be a chapter title in the book, and it crushes me that you're not in these pages. I treasure your joy, your strength, your free spirit, and I want everyone to know that at my wedding you asked Jordan Peele what he did for a living, and then smoked all our guests out.

To Jon Stewart, I had to delete so many effusive adjectives from that chapter because I could spend paragraphs talking about your character. We all know your talent, how you changed politics, how deeply you made us laugh, and made us all care. But I feel beyond lucky that I also got to experience your character and your friendship. Learning from you was the greatest gift of my life, and having you read my writing and pull me into the career I so desperately wanted to be a part of is a dream I lived, but still doesn't feel real to me. My last night at the show will forever be one of the best nights of my life.

To my aunty Sharon! You were a chapter title, but that changed when I found myself drowning in the story of Bubba.

In real life, outside these pages, you were the hero who saved me from drowning way back when. Thank you for showing me what a hilarious, confident badass looks like so young in life.

My mother-in-law, Miss Queen V, another almost title chapter in the book, and I mourned having to cut the magical purse story. Thank you for loving me and teaching me how to enjoy life. You are truly your title, the queen of all queens.

To Emily H., the first friend I made after The Horrors Had Happened. You were so loving, wise, and caring, when I can only imagine I was a small nightmare of chaos covered in a glitter rollerball. You saved me that day you handed me those little "C" and "D" charms. You made me feel lovable, and worthy of celebration. You found the episode I was too afraid to share. You forgave me for being such a teenage idiot. I cannot think of you without crying. I love you I love you I love you.

To Akilah, who sat in a rocking chair on the porch, steady and sturdy as you swayed, back and forth, muttering that we would find a way. You sat with me and a martini and went through every word, every emotional nook and cranny. You made this book better, you make me better, you are the gift of my thirties.

To Ashley Nicole Black, Brigitte Muñoz Liebowitz, Kenzie Elizabeth, the first readers of my book, and also characters inside it who I've already professed pages of love to. Well here it is again, I love you so much!!!! Jo, thank you for saving my life. You've been my sister since day one, and I wouldn't be here without you. You taught me grace and forgiveness, and then re-taught it to me the next day. Ali, thank you for making my twenties so fun. You are the source of all my epic weekends, and of how I finally healed. How can I ever repay you?? Judi, you had the best outfit at the wedding and I loved being your roommate. Poonie, thank you for coming back. Annarose, you have my whole heart and always will. To Traci Thomas, my new friend and book savant, it is thanks to you this book has a better beginning.

Ms. Z—I later heard that you said my name at graduation and made them all sit in what had happened. Thank you for helping me survive and teaching me about writing.

Mr. A, remember when you called me the dumbest smart person you'd ever met in front of all my classmates? I have a book now, loser. Mr. History Teacher, I don't even remember your name, so that feels like a real win for me. You're not even worth the trip to the garage to find my yearbook and write the correct initial. You witnessed everything. You heard him say it. You did nothing. You're a dinky little fucknut.

To all the dudes I dated who aren't in the book—ya welcome.

To the teachers who made me into the artist I am: Anne Libera, Andy Miara, Mary Scruggs, Karen Finley, Tim Crofton, Hannah Tyson, and Mrs. Torgelson.

To Jenn, Molly, Elizabeth, Sindy, Jeanine, and Lucia, whose names appear in this book as "roommates," but are the anchors of my teens and twenties, and I'll love y'all forever.

Sam Irby, Emily Gordon, Joni Rodgers, and Kate Bowler, you saved my sanity and in one case, my book cover. You are literary gawds!!

To Danielle Robay, damn, you're a literal angel!! You picked me up on my lowest day in the book process and helped me stay strong until the end.

Sierra Teller Ornelas and Marcos Luevanos, the funniest and smartest writers, and my pop culture soulmates? Thank you for helping me find the right title. And thank you for your friendship, it's meant more to me than I've ever been able to express out loud, so I hope putting it on the page forever delivers it with the esteem I mean it with.

To my UWC classmates who I connected with later in life, your friendship helped me understand the years I kinda blacked out. Thank you for your kindness: Taylor, Alice, Maria, Yulia, Krishna, Christina, Divvya, Ale, Gilia, Brais, Jamie, Andres, Kevin, and Lindsay.